Building the KRMx0

The Illustrated Guide to Build Precision CNC Router

KRMx01 Series Book 1

Michael Simpson

Kronos Robotics
June 2012

Building the KRMx01 CNC
KRMx01 Series Book 1
Published by Kronos Robotics
Leesburg, Virginia

All rights reserved.
Copyright © 2012 by Michael G Simpson

No part of this book may be reproduced or transmitted in any form or by any means, electronic or mechanical, including photocopying, recording, or by any information storage and retrieval system, without permission in writing from the publisher.

ISBN 978-1-938687-10-5

Dedicated to my son, Geran.

Forward

The KRMx01 is a CNC router you build yourself using basic tools. Each chapter is a step-by-step project in its self. Each chapter presents you with a listing of tools and components required to complete the chapter. In addition each chapter includes time and cost estimates so you can budget your time as well as your funds.

Table of Contents

Getting Started 1
Stand Assembly 19
Y-beam Assembly 31
Table And Rails 47
Y-carriage Construction 63
X-beam 75
X-carriage 83
Z-carriage 93
Motor Mounts 107
Installing the ACME Screws 135
KRMx01 Electronics 145
Mach 3 155
Installing Stepper Motors 171
Cable Hookup 179
Adjusting the Drive Train 191
Router Hookup 201
Conclusion 207

!! IMPORTANT !!
Please Read

For more information about the KRMx01 CNC and KRMx01 download files visit the following link:

http://www.kronosrobotics.com/krmx01/dz19781_9386_87105/

Chapter 1

Getting Started

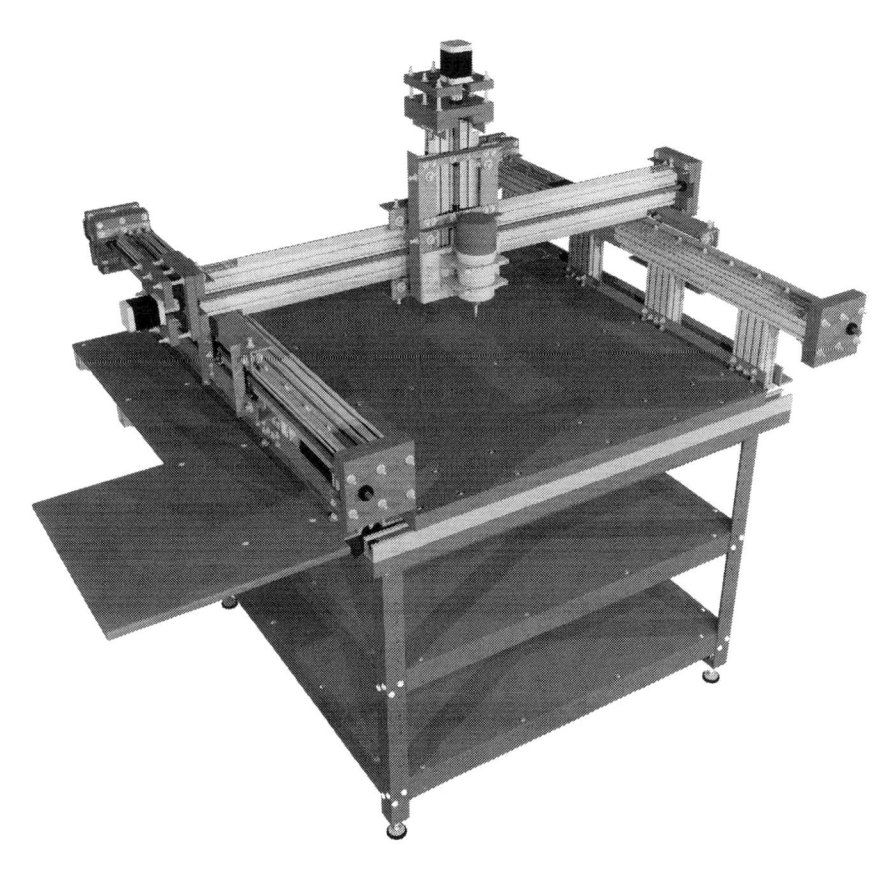

Building your own KRMx1 CNC machine may seem intimidating at first, but this book will help to guide you through the process in simple steps. Each chapter begins with a list of the parts needed and the tools required to assemble them. Any prerequisites required to complete the chapter tasks are also listed. Finally, an estimate of both the cost and time it will take to complete each chapter is included as well.

The KRMx01 CNC was developed for the solitary builder who wants to construct their own CNC machine. As most people want the most value for their buck (and I am no different), I gave equal importance to both operational precision and cost of construction while determining the best design. The KRMx01 CNC you will build here is the 5th generation machine and was achieved through trial and error on four early models, with each version built to completion and thoroughly tested. Lessons learned and refinements made along the way are passed on to you, the reader, in the form of Tip boxes sprinkled throughout the chapters.

Even if you don't plan on building the KRMx01 CNC, the information contained in this book will help you in your own designs.

In this chapter you will learn about the benchmarks for precision, cost, and construction, and also delve briefly into things you should know regarding size and upgrades. You will also learn a bit about basic construction techniques, and how to handle the various materials used.

Precision

Precision on a CNC is a balance between torque and speed. For instance, a lower speed single start ACME screw will yield more torque and precision but less speed than an 5-start ACME screw. A rack and pinion system will yield an even higher speed but less torque and precision (depending on gearing). A compromise was made by settling on an 5-start ACME screw. ACME screws are very simple to implement. The 5-start screw are faster than the single start screw and the loss of torque and precision is minor.

It is important to note that the precision of a CNC is not a constant. Speed is a major deciding factor in the amount of precision achieved and the faster the machine cuts, the less precise it is. There are many things that can affect how fast it cuts. Large bits can cut faster than smaller bits. The amount of material you are removing will also determine the speed. The rigidity of construction and level of tuning will likewise affect cutting speed and precision.

One feature of the KRMx01 that helps with precision is the inclusion of two ACME nuts on each ACME screw. This allows you to dial out any wear on the nuts and helps reduce backlash. Two nuts also reduce by half the load on the nuts, thus reducing the wear.

Cost

All materials and parts are purchased as required to complete each chapter. Purchasing materials this way should bring the cost of building the KRMx01 to less than $2500. Savings can be achieved by purchasing the electronics kit up front, which is the most expensive part of machine. Another possible area of savings would be the stand, which in this case was obtained from Woodcraft. Depending on what you have available you could save more than $200 here. While you can probably build the KRMx01 cheaper you can also spend more. If you purchase your nuts and bolts piece meal from a local hardware store this can add up. For that reason, the nuts and bolts used in this book were obtained from TSC (Tractor Supply Company) which sells them by weight.

The chapters in this book are written with the idea of spreading the cost over time. Read the chapter to find out what you need, then use the components list and prerequisite text to help you source and acquire the materials needed before starting. You aren't going to build the CNC in one or two weeks so there is no reason to purchase every single component at once. The most expensive purchase will be the chapter dealing with electronics, and will cost approximately $450. No other chapter requires more than $250 in parts/materials and most require less than $100.

One final thing on cost. Most of the components used in this design are reusable if you decide to build another CNC. The electronics used here are also used on many other CNC's. The ACME screws and nuts are reusable, as are the bearings, shaft collars, shaft couplers and even the 80/20 extruded aluminum. All are reusable.

The tools needed for completing the chapter are also listed. Keep in mind the tools list is only a suggestion as your skills may dictate something different.

Construction

The KRMx01 is mostly a steel and aluminum design. The two aluminum Y-beams are attached to 1/4" Steel angle which in turn are connected to steel cross struts. Riding on the Y-beams are two Y-carriages made from 3/16" steel. The aluminum X-beam sits on the two Y-carriages to form a very low center of gravity gantry. The X-carriage is made from 3/16" steel with an extruded 3" x 2" piece of 80/20 aluminum that forms the Z-beam. The Z-carriage is made from 1/8" steel angle and rides the 80/20 Z-beam.

The bearing blocks can be made from any material you wish – MDF, particle board, Melamine, even plastic. The blocks are attached to the beams with 1/8" steel angle. Since the ACME screws ride on the bearings inserted into the blocks, there is no wear on the blocks and they hold up very well. The blocks originally were originally designed in aluminum, but this added undue cost and complexity, and provided no advantages.

The cutting table on the KRMx01 is four sheets of 3/4" particle board sandwiched on either side of the steel struts, forming a massive energy absorbing surface. The clamp table is made from MDF and mounts on the main table surface with recessed screws.

Upgrades

The KRMx01 CNC was designed with upgrades in mind as time and expense permits. Using 80/20 beams makes it easy to add or change the original design. The very first upgrade you will add to the machine is the Dragon Cable. This upgrade as well as others can be found in our second book in the KRMx01 series, "Upgrading and Operating the KRMx01 CNC"

Size

The KRMx01 has a 43" x 32" x 6" cutting surface. It will hold larger material and will allow you to slide a much larger piece through the machine. The cutting surface was originally planned at 48" x 48" but tests showed that the ACME screws tended to whip, which reduced operational accuracy and speed. Those test also showed that a 43" x 32" surface worked best for 5 start ACME screws.

Something to keep in mind about CNC sizes: for any particular size you will need quite a bit of overhead space at each axis. For instance, the Y axis has a cutting size of 43" and needs a CNC with a front to back size of 65". In addition to the actual foot print of the machine, you need access space to load and unload stock. The final foot print of the KRMx01 CNC is 65" x 75" x 69". If you decide not to add the side table you can cut it down to 65" x 65" x 69"

Measurement and layout tools

One of the most important tasks you will perform during this project, is marking and layout. With the correct tools these tasks can be done efficiently and accurately.

There are certainly all sorts of straight edges you can use to make marks. Most of what you need can be accomplished by the use of a 12' tape measure and a set of squares like the ones shown in Figure 1.1. Not only will you need the squares for marking holes, but you will also need them for making adjustments.

Figure 1.1

In addition to a set of squares you will need a digital caliper. The model shown in Figure 1.2 can be purchased at most home centers. It has an extra feature of being able to display fractions and decimals, and the ability to easily convert from one to the other.

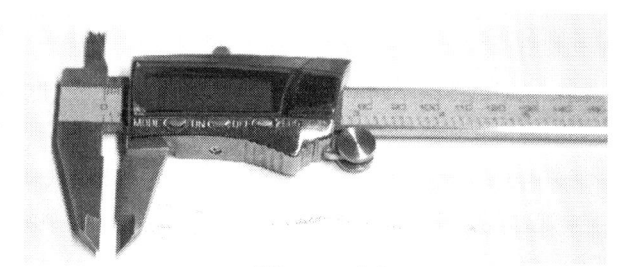

Figure 1.2

Make a Guide Block

If you don't own a drill press, one alternative is to make a drill guide. Even if you own a drill press there are times that using a guide block is more practical.

Make the guide by taking a scrap piece of MDF and creating a block 1" x 3" in size. Place a mark dead center on both sides of the block. Next, drill a hole all the way through the block with a 1/8" drill bit as shown in Figure 1.3.

Try to keep the drill as straight as possible when drilling the hole. If the hole is straight when you flip over the block it will be dead center on the mark. If it isn't dead center, then you will have to try again.

Figure 1.3

To use the guide, first mark the part to be drilled with a punch as shown in Figure 1.4.

Figure 1.4

Chuck a 1/8" bit into the drill, then add the guide block to the bit and place the tip of the bit in the dent made by the punch as shown in Figure 1.5.

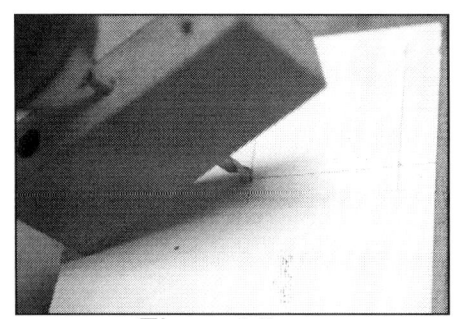

Figure 1.5

Swing the block and drill around until the block is flat against the surface as shown in Figure 1.6.

Figure 1.6

After your hole is drilled, you can safely enlarge it. The pilot hole will keep it nice and straight.

Once you have an accurate guide block, use it to make a couple of extras as the hole will eventually get larger with use.

You can also create a guide block with multiple holes.

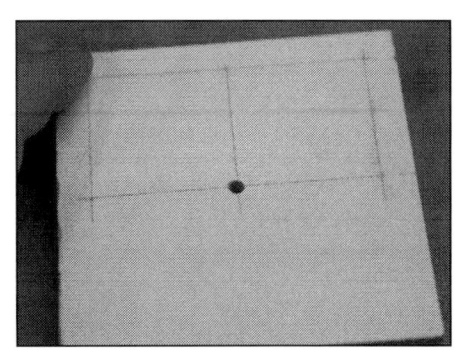

Figure 1.7

Building the KRMx01 CNC 5

Working with steel

The KRMx01 CNC utilizes steel angle for the carriage construction. Steel is also used as part of the table construction. Steel angle is available in various thicknesses and lengths at your local home center. It has various names:

- Steel angle
- Weldable angle
- Angle iron

Generally it is sold in 12, 24, 36, 48 and 72" lengths, and in thicknesses of 1/8", 3/16", and 1/4". All the pieces worked in this book are 12" or shorter, with a few exceptions where noted. Note that you may have to purchase larger lengths and cut them to size if these short lengths are not available.

Cutting Steel

While there are a few ways to cut steel, for this project you will be using a reciprocating saw. A reciprocating saw can be purchased for as little as $39 from your local home center. You won't need anything fancy; a battery operated model will work just fine. If you opt for a battery operated model, purchase one that is at least 18 volts.

You will need a metal cutting blade, possibly two for this project.

To cut the steel, it must be clamped securely in a vise or to a table. Place a mark on both sides of the angle using a square as shown in Figure 1.8.

Clamp a piece of scrap to the angle adjacent to the line as shown in Figure 1.9. This will become your guide and is the best way to insure a straight cut.

Figure 1.8

Figure 1.9

Place your saw blade up against the guide as you cut, as shown in Figure 1.10. Once one side has been cut, move the guide and cut the other portion of the angle.

Figure 1.10

After each cut be sure to clean the edges with a rotary grinder like the one shown in Figure 1.11. You can use a metal file, but a grinder will make short work of the task. Be prepared to go through a couple of grinding wheels.

Figure 1.11

Important!

Be sure to use eye protection when cutting or grinding metal. Getting a chip in your eye is extremely painful and will require a trip to the emergency room.

Drilling Steel

The main problem when drilling steel is that the drill bit tends to wander. To solve this problem, a steel punch is used to dent the steel.

Start by marking where you want the hole, as shown in Figure 1.12.

Figure 1.12

Place the point in the middle of the mark and hit it lightly with a hammer as shown in Figure 1.13.

Figure 1.13

In most cases you will need a piece of scrap under the angle if you are drilling on the outside of the part (Figure 1.14). This scrap is optional when drilling on the inside of the angle, but it may provide additional support to the piece. This is especially true when cutting softer or thinner metals, as they can warp under the pressure of the drill press.

When cutting larger diameter holes it's best to first drill a 1/8" pilot hole.

Figure 1.14

8 *Chapter 1* Getting Started

When drilling steel, be sure to use lower speeds on your drill press. Even at low speeds the chips can get very hot. Use work gloves as shown in Figure 1.15 to keep from getting burned by a flying chip.

Do not touch the rotating bit with the glove or you could risk injury.

Figure 1.15

Drill Press Fence

Throughout this project you will use a drill press for drilling most of your holes. The drill press literally guarantees a straight hole. If you use a fence with your drill press like the one shown in Figure 1.16, you can keep your holes lined up, which is important when cutting holes in your rails.

If you don't have a fence for your drill press, you can make one by clamping a piece of scrap MDF to your drill press table.

Figure 1.16

Extruded Aluminum

The KRMx01 CNC utilizes T-slotted aluminum extrusions for the beams that make up each axis. You will be using four 2" x 4" x 72" beams manufactured by a company called 80/20". These extrusions have T-slots that enable you to insert T-nuts or 1/4" carriage bolts, which gives you the ability to make the adjustments needed for base functionality as well as future upgrades.

The extrusion can be purchased from 80/20 through Amazon or one of their distributors. The actual part number is 2040. This extrusion is part of the 10 series and is sold in various lengths. If you order from one of the distributors they will cut it for you.

Figure 1.17 shows four 72" extrusions that must be cut into three sections each of the following lengths:

Extrusion 1 – 56", 7", 7"

Extrusion 2 – 56", 7", 7"

Extrusion 3 – 56", 7", 7"

Extrusion 4 – 17", 7", 7"

This will yield a sizable piece of scrap that can be used for a future upgrade or as a replacement part.

Important !!

You should have all these sections cut before starting the construction process.

80/20 has placed a complete kit of the 80/20 parts up on eBay. They are all new parts and cut to lengths shown above. Use the following link.

http://www.ebay.com/itm/221031363037

Cost: $273 (80/20 eBay, not including shipping)

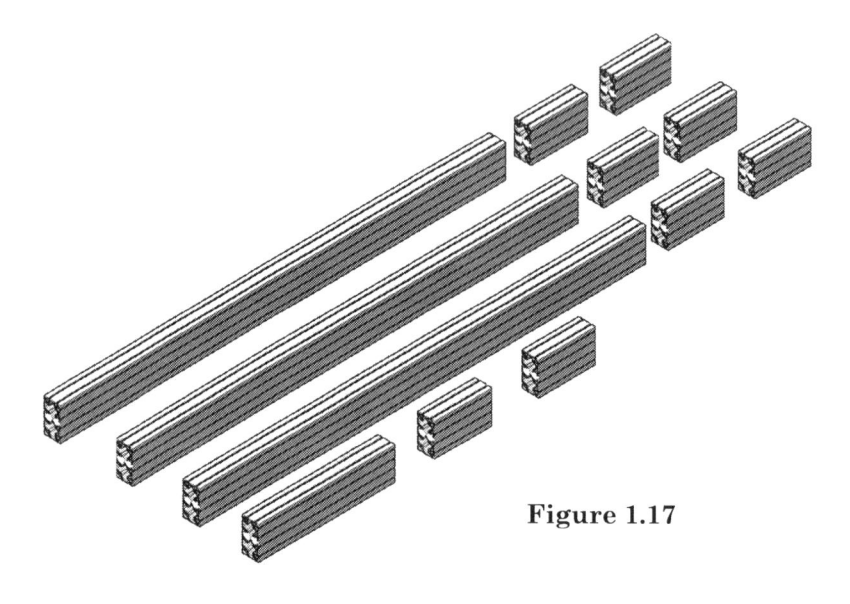

Figure 1.17

Cutting Extruded Aluminum

If you don't purchase the 80/20 kit, you will need to cut the pieces yourself. The best way to cut extruded aluminum is with a power chop saw or miter saw with a blade meant for cutting aluminum like the one shown in Figure 1.18. If you don't have a chop saw, you can use a crosscut sled and a table saw. Again, you need to use the proper blade.

All cuts must be perfectly square. If the cuts are the slightest amount off, it could affect the performance of your CNC.

Figure 1.18

WARNING

Make sure you use eye protection while cutting aluminum. Even the best dust collection system will fail to catch all of the tiny aluminum chips.

Bolt Conditioning For T-slots

One of the advantages of using 80/20 T-slot aluminum extrusion is the ability to simply slide a carriage bolt into one the slots, as shown in Figure 1.19. This makes it extremely flexible. You can purchase T-slot bolts from 80/20 but I found they are both expensive and the sizes needed can be hard to find. For this reason, normal 1/4-20 carriage bolts were used. Note, however, that in many cases the head of the bolt is just a little too tight to slide freely into the T-slot.

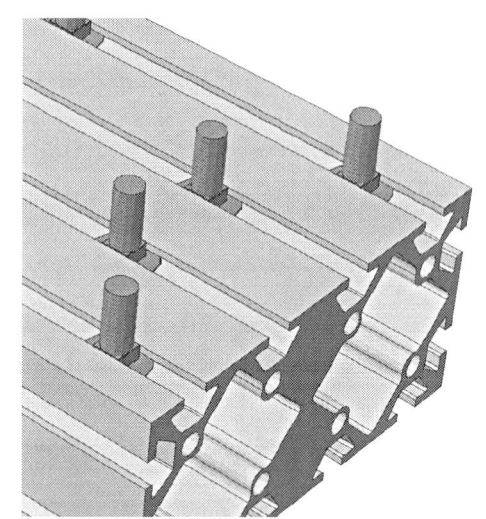

Figure 1.19

You can adjust the bolt head by using a bench grinder like the one shown in Figure 1.20 to slightly grind down the two opposing sides of a bolt.

It doesn't take much, just a touch is all that is needed. Use a small scrap piece of 80/20 T-slot material to test the adjusted bolt. It should slide freely and not bind.

Figure 1.20

The finished bolt should look like the bolt shown in Figure 1.21.

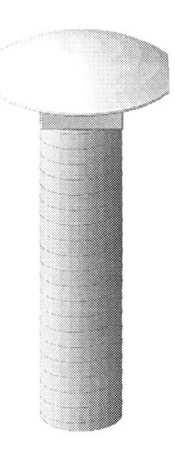

Figure 1.21

12   *Chapter 1*   Getting Started

Matching Bearing Hardware

Referring to Figure 1.22, when mounting the V-bearings onto the various carriages, you will called upon to use washers, hex nuts, and lock washers. Unfortunately, the hardware available at most home centers is not very consistent in thickness.

It is important that the hardware that is between the bearing and the carriage be matched so that each bearing is the same distance from the carriage.

The easiest way to do this is to match four nuts to within 1/64", then match four lock washers to within 1/64" and attach them to the bearing. Then match the four pairs of washers to within 1/64".

The closer you can get the bearings to match, the easier your CNC will be to align.

Figure 1.22

Conditioning Aluminum Rails

Aluminum is a fairly soft material and as such the V-bearings will shape the edges of the rails, forcing them into a V shape. This will cause the bearings to become loose. In order to remedy this problem, you will need to pre-shape the rails.

Do this by making a conditioning board like the one shown in Figure 1.23. All of the holes in the face of the board are 3/8" in diameter, as are the slots, with the exception of the two holes marked 1/2". The two holes on the end of the board are 5/16" in diameter and extrude from the edge all the way into the slot.

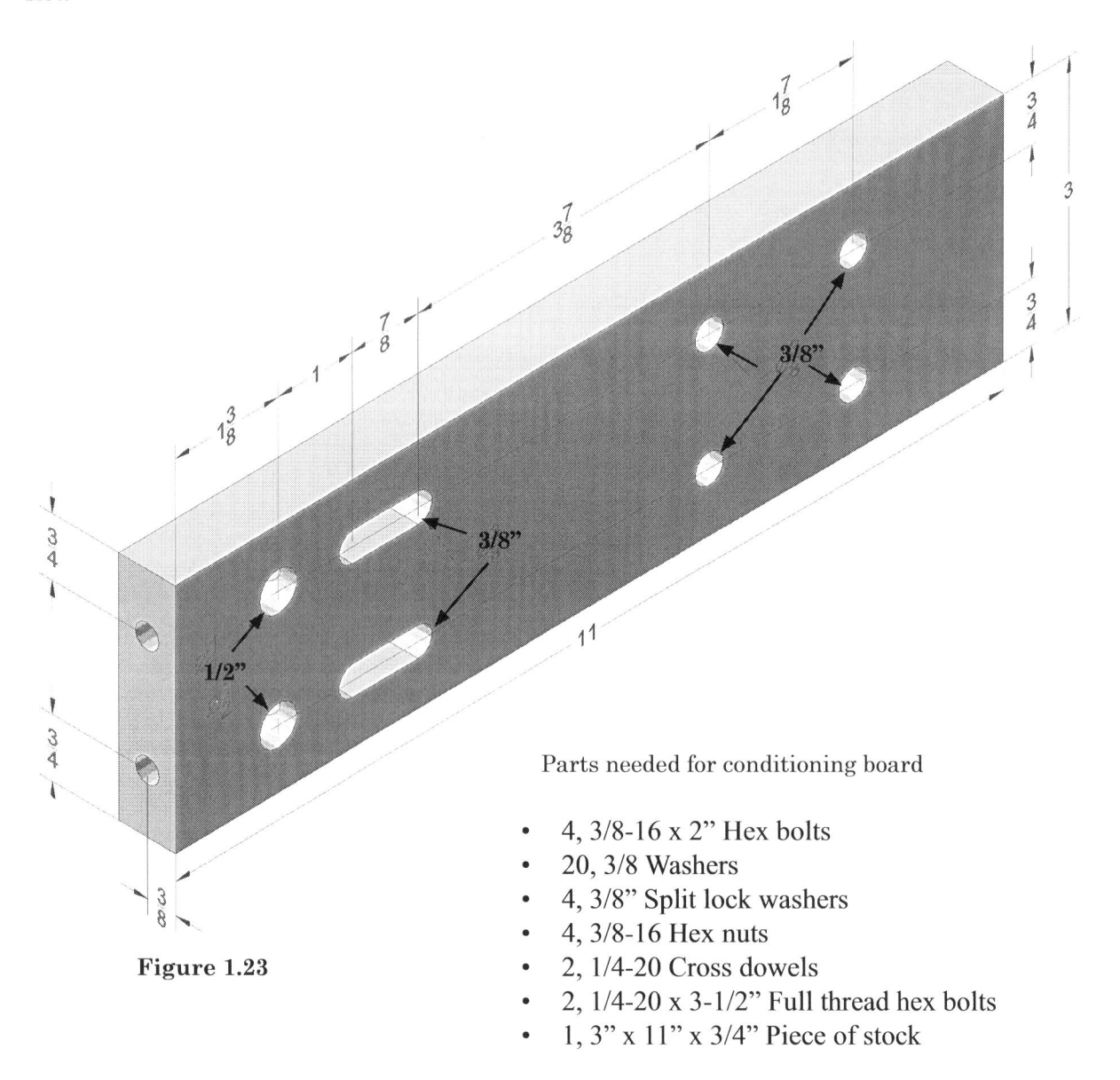

Figure 1.23

Parts needed for conditioning board

- 4, 3/8-16 x 2" Hex bolts
- 20, 3/8 Washers
- 4, 3/8" Split lock washers
- 4, 3/8-16 Hex nuts
- 2, 1/4-20 Cross dowels
- 2, 1/4-20 x 3-1/2" Full thread hex bolts
- 1, 3" x 11" x 3/4" Piece of stock

For this step, you can use the four V-bearings meant for the CNC that are currently not in use.

Step 1 - Install the V-bearings

Using a 3/8-16 x 2" hex bolt, add a V-bearing, lock washer, and four 3/8 washers. Slip the assembly through the holes indicated in Figure 1.24. The bolts that are inserted into the slots should be as close to the left as possible. For the other bolts, use the holes shown for the Y-rails. Use the right hand holes for the X and Z-rails.

Add a 3/8" washer and hex bolt and tighten them.

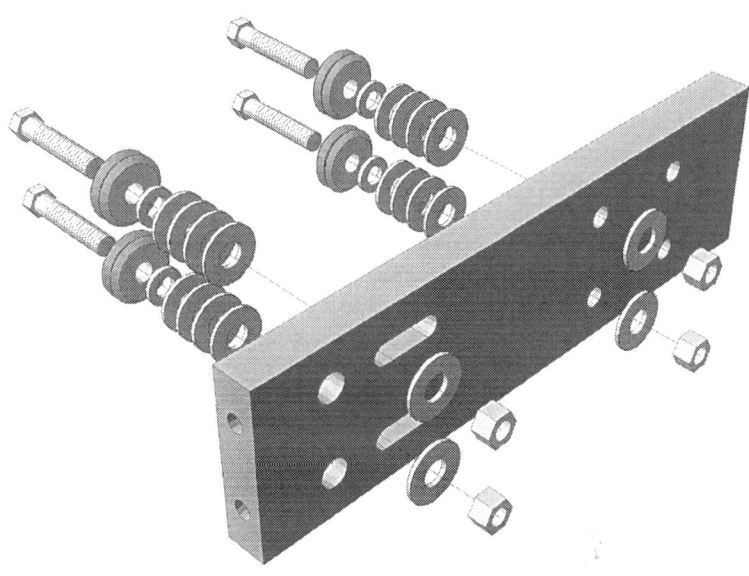

Figure 1.24

Step 2 - Add the Adjustment Bolt

Insert two cross dowels into the two 1/2" holes on the left hand side of the board, as shown in Figure 1.25. Then thread the two 1/4-20 x 3-1/2" bolts through the end of the board and into the cross dowel, as shown in Figure 1.26. Tightening the 1/4" bolts will close the gap between the two V-bearings.

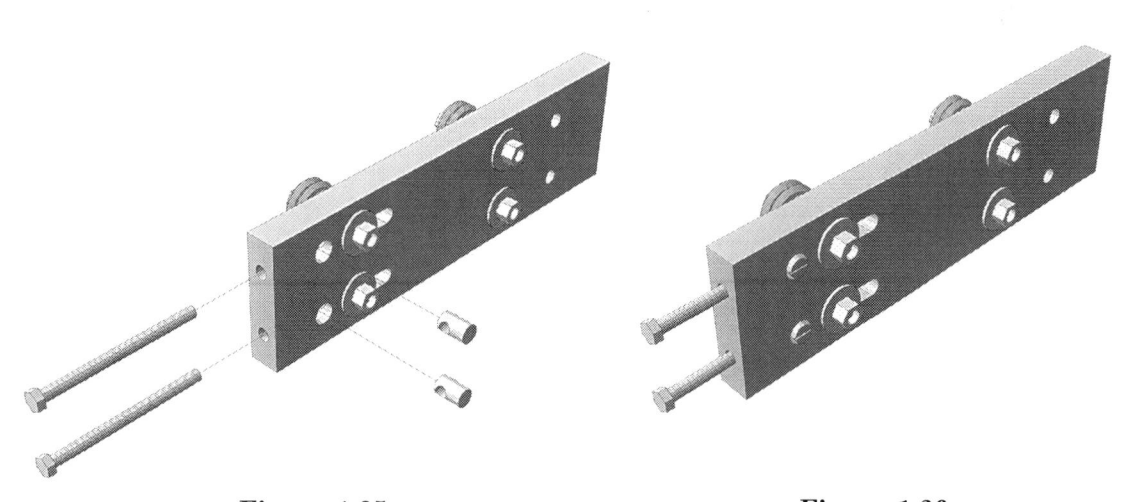

Figure 1.25

Figure 1.26

Building the KRMx01 CNC

Step 3 - Place the Conditioning Board on Rail

Start by adjusting the upper V-bearings so that is up against the top of slots in the conditioning board.

Position the top V-bearings over the top rail, as shown in Figure 1.27.

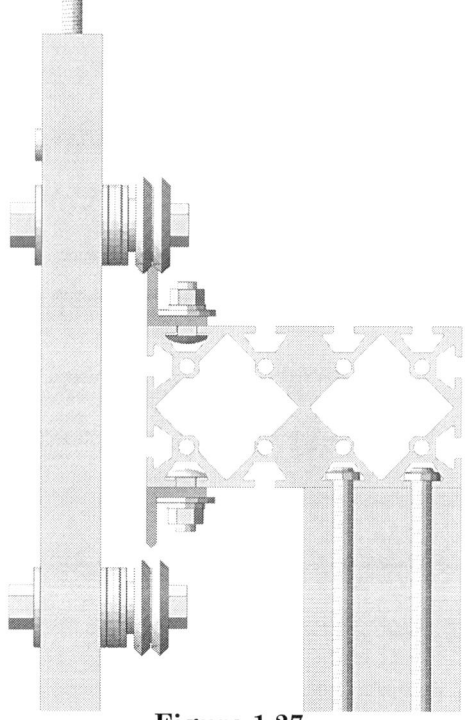

Figure 1.27

By tightening the two 1/4" bolts, you can pull the lower V-bearing up against the bottom rail, as shown in Figure 1.28.

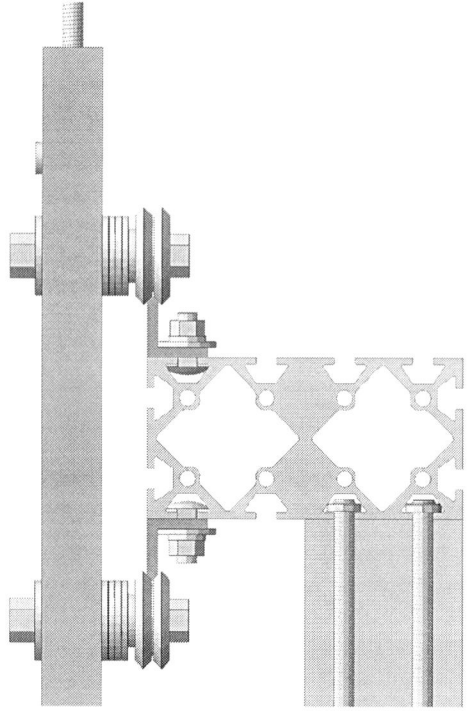

Figure 1.28

16   *Chapter 1*   Getting Started

Step 4 - Condition the Rail

Tighten the 1/4" bolts until the V-bearings are nice and snug against the two rails. Use your hand and run the conditioning board back and forth along the rail, as shown in Figure 1.29. Run it the full length from one edge of the rail to the other. After four or five runs, tighten the 1/4" bolts a little to snug them up again.

Continue the cycle until the rails have a V shape with a 1/16 or 1/32" flat on the top of the V.

Note that you will never get a perfect V, as the bearings have a dead space in the center. This is normal.

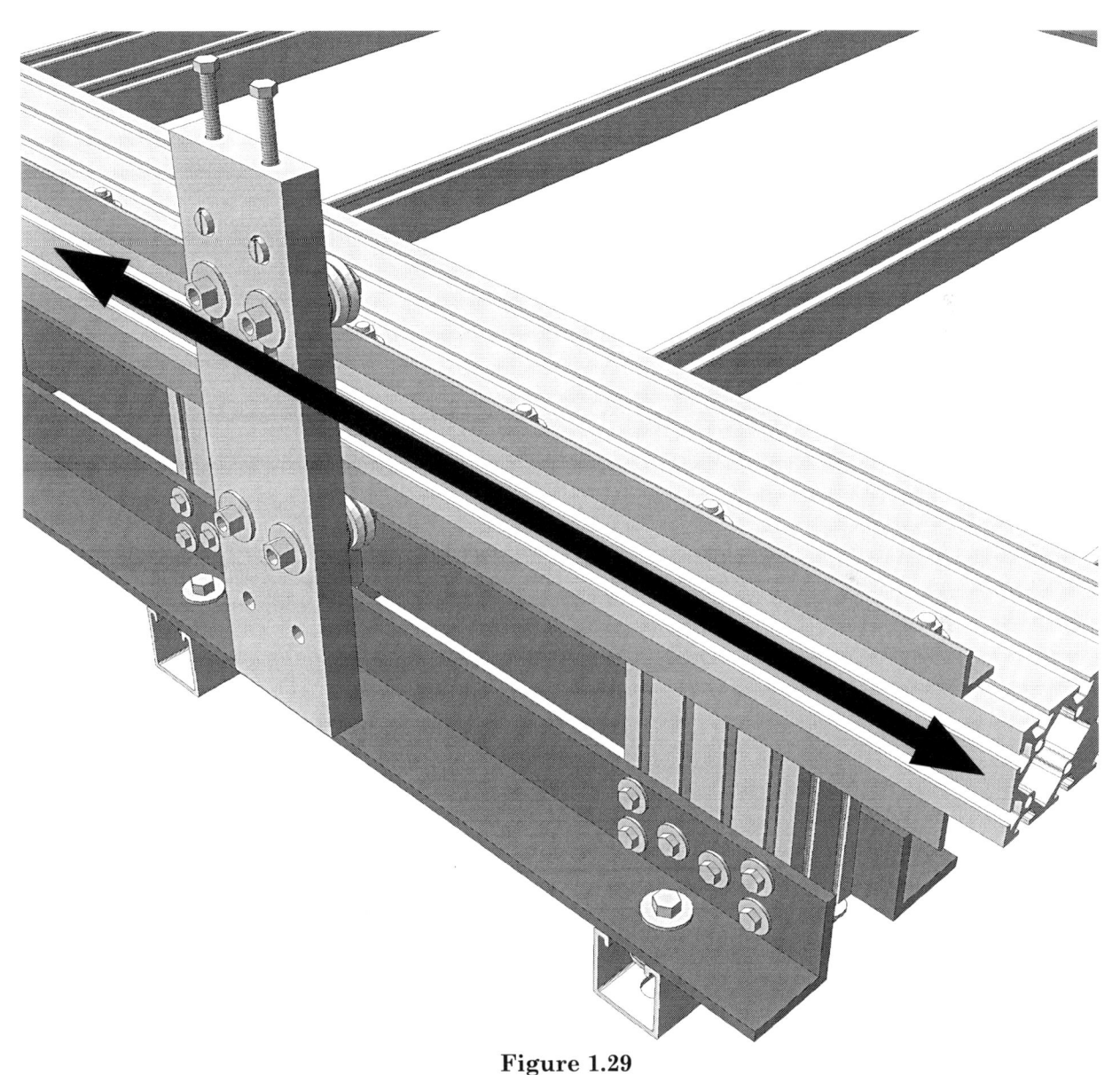

Figure 1.29

Conclusion

Before starting the construction chapters you should have your 8020 aluminum in hand and cut to size. You should also have your rail conditioner built. You will be reminded at the start of the carriage chapters to condition your rails.

One last bit of advice before you start construction: take your time, and visit the Kronos Robotics web site for a complete "Bill of Materials". The bill of materials list will also have links for purchasing your steel cut to size.

Kronos Robotics download site:

http://www.kronosrobotics.com/krmx01/dz19781_9386_87105/

Chapter 2

Stand Assembly

A sturdy stand is an absolute necessity for a precise CNC. If the stand is not sturdy it will vibrate, shake and shimmy as your X and Y axes move. This unwanted movement will manifest in decreased precision and quality.

Whether you build a stand from scratch, or purchase a kit, it will need to be 44" x 44" in order to support the completed CNC. The stand recommended for the KRMx01 CNC is the "Rousseau Workbench System". It is modular in design. You select the legs, and two sets of extenders. The extenders are available in various sizes. The extender size needed to support the KRMx01 is the 40" set.

If you decide to use a workbench other than the one described here. There is a set of metal struts sandwiched between the stand top and the CNC base. The attachment of the two surfaces to the struts may be more difficult if you use a stand that does not have access to the under side in order to drill the mounting holes.

Tools Needed For This Chapter

- 7/16" Wrench (used to tighten the shelve nuts)
- 3/4" Wrench (used to adjust and tighten the feet)
- Power drill
- 1/4" Drill bit
- 3/4" Forstner bit
- Phillips screw driver
- 4' Level

Note that you may find a 7/16" socket and socket wrench works better for tightening the shelf bolts. The power drill is used to drill 1/4" holes through the steel supports and through the shelving material; a close quarters drill may work better for you. (See Step 3)

Components Needed For This Chapter

- 2 sets of 44" Rousseau base extenders, Woodcraft # 148376
- 1 set of 32" Rousseau legs, Woodcraft # 148371
- 2, 43-3/4" x 43-3/4 x 3/4" Particle board shelves
- 2, 48" x 48 x 3/4" Particle board shelves
- 32, 1/4-20 x 2" Carriage bolts (used to attach lower shelves to stand)
- 16, 1/4-20 x 2-1/2" Carriage bolts (used to attach top shelves to stand)
- 48, 1/4-20 Hex nuts (used to attach shelves to stand)
- 48, 1/4" Washers (used to attach shelves to stand) 28, 1/4-20 hex nuts (used to attach shelves to stand)
- 48, 1/4" Split lock washers (used to attach shelves to stand)

Purchasing large quantities of hardware like carriage bolts, washers and hex nuts can result in huge savings if purchased by weight. Check your local "Tractor Supply Company". They offer most common hardware sizes by the pound.

Chapter Estimate

Cost: $198

Time: Weekend

Prerequisites

You should have cut the following shelves

- 2, 48" x 48" shelves out of 3/4" particle board. You can also use MDF if you like. These two shelves are used for the top of the stand.
- 2, 43-3/4" x 43-3/4" shelves out of 3/4" particle board. Again MDF will work for the shelves.

It is best to cut one 48" x 48" shelf and one 43-3/4" x 43-3/4" shelf out of a single sheet of particle board. If you try to cut both of the 48" x 48" shelves out of a single sheet of particle board, one shelf will end up about 1/8" short. While this wont affect your CNC machine, it's easier to align the top shelves if they are the same size.

If you plan on cutting the shelves yourself, a table saw works best. Another option is to use a circular saw and guide system. However, the easiest method may be to have your local home center cut them for you.

Tip

If you are going to paint the shelves, it is easier to do so before they are attached to the stand. Paint all your shelves except the very top. This way you can use the stand as a work bench as you build your KRMx01 CNC. Later you can paint the entire top or a portion as you see fit. As an alternative, you can paint the top and touch it up later if needed.

Building the KRMx01 CNC

Step 1 - Build the Frame

Start by opening the three Rousseau boxes and laying out the components. The leg set will contain a set of hardware and instructions for building the stand.

Using the included instructions, build the stand as it is shown in Figure 2.1. You will be leaving out the two upper shelving supports shown in order to install the bottom shelf. Finger tighten the bolts.

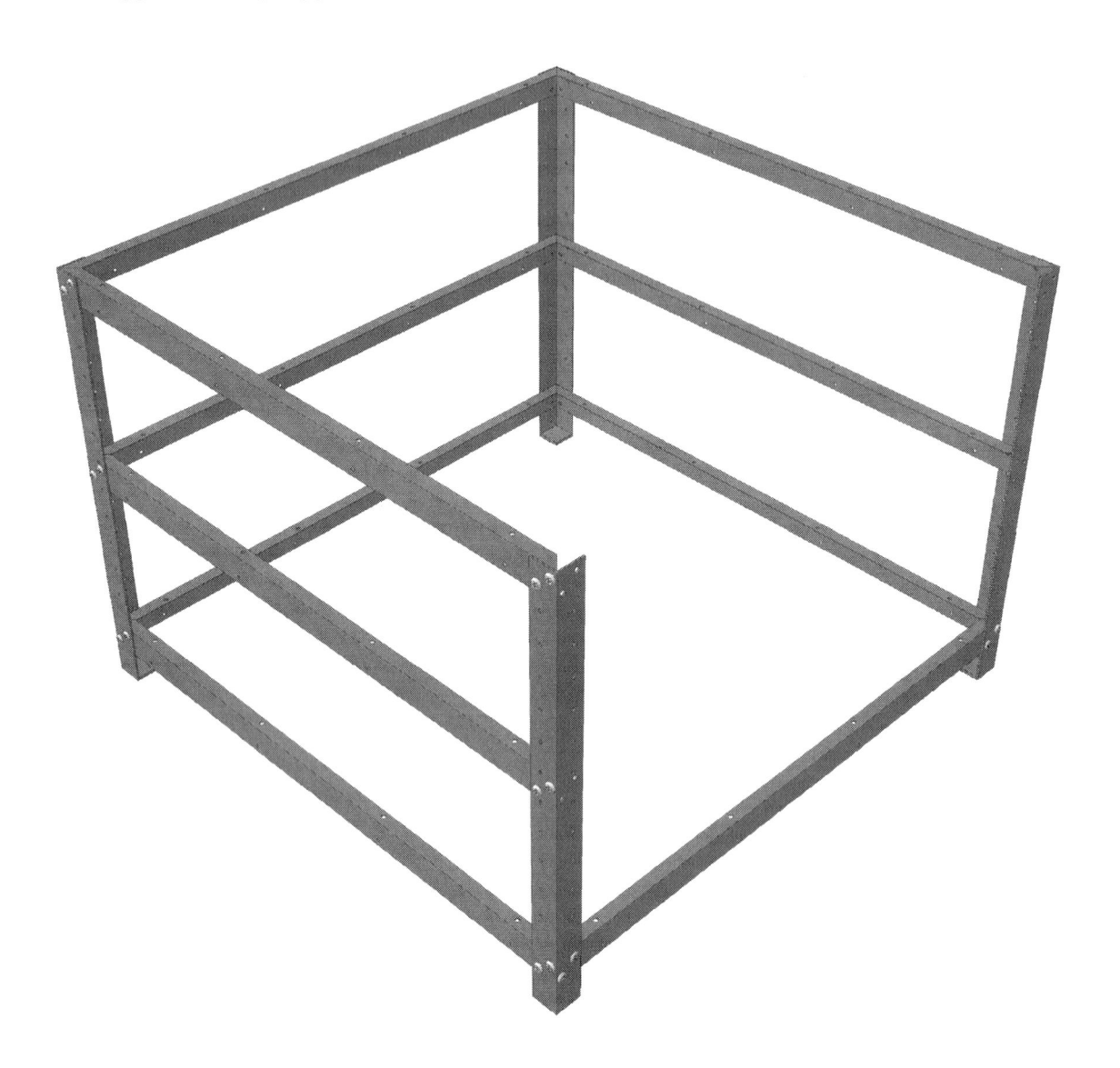

Figure 2.1

Step 2 - Lower Shelf

Insert one of the 43-1/2" x 43-1/2" shelves onto the lower platform, as shown in Figure 2.2.

Using a power drill and a 1/4" drill bit, from the underside of the stand drill a hole through each of the holes in the shelf support, as shown in Figure 2.3.

The easiest way to do this is to use a clamp to hold the shelf in place. Then using a helper, tilt the stand to access the underside.

While the stand is tilted, insert your 2" carriage bolts and slip on a 1/4" washer, lock washer, and nut. Tighten the 16 nuts.

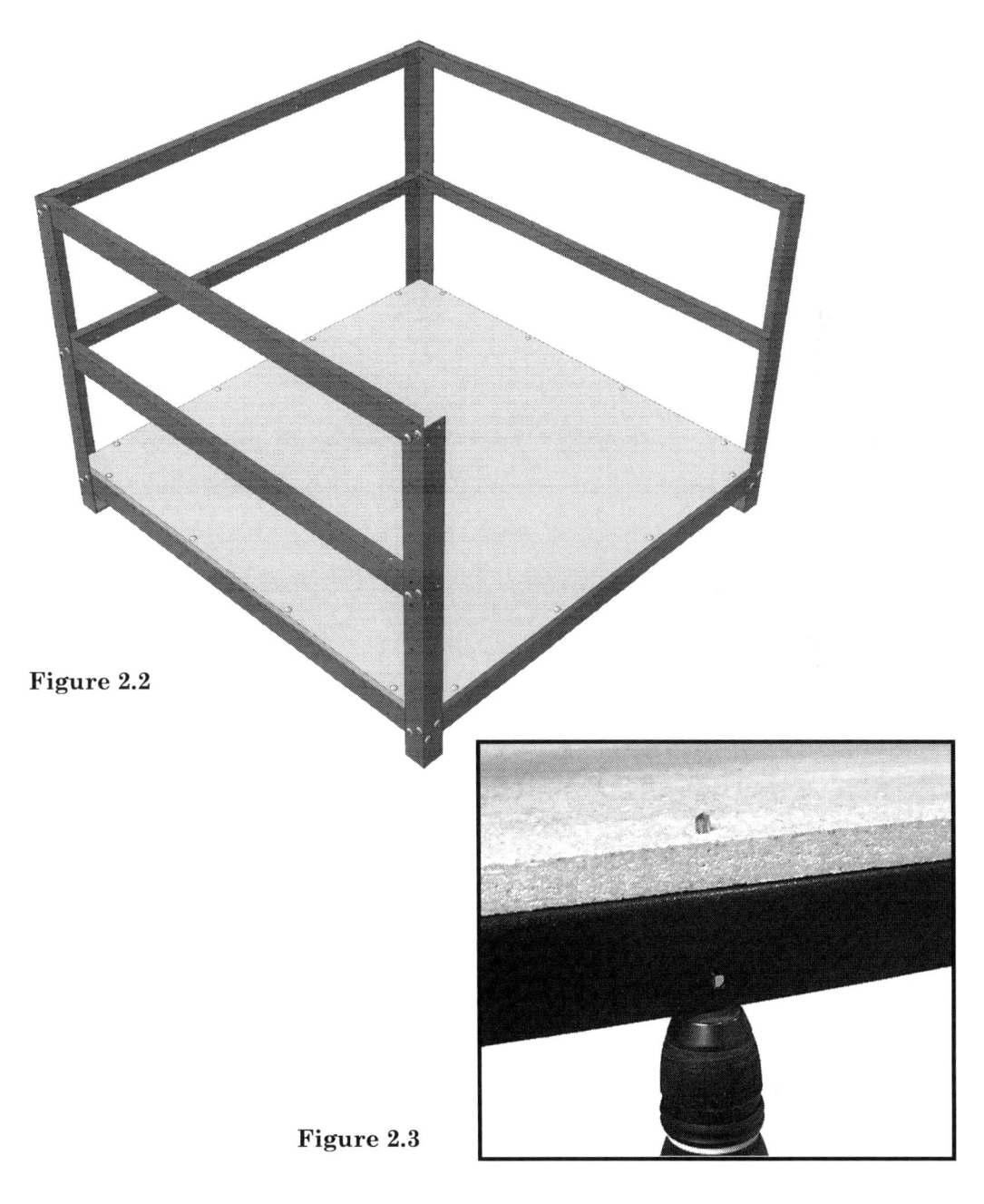

Figure 2.2

Figure 2.3

Step 3 - Middle Shelf

Install the middle shelf support and insert the other 43-1/2" x 43-1/2" shelf onto the middle platform, as shown Figure 2.4.

Using a power drill and a 1/4" drill bit, from the underside of the shelf drill a hole through each of the holes in the shelf support.

You won't need to tilt the stand but, depending on the size of your drill and drill bit, it may be difficult to fit the drill between the two shelves.

You have three options if your drill will not fit. All should be available at your local home center.

- Right angle attachment for your drill
- Close quarters drill
- Flex shaft

Insert your 2" carriage bolts and slip on a 1/4" washer, lock washer and nut. Tighten the 16 nuts.

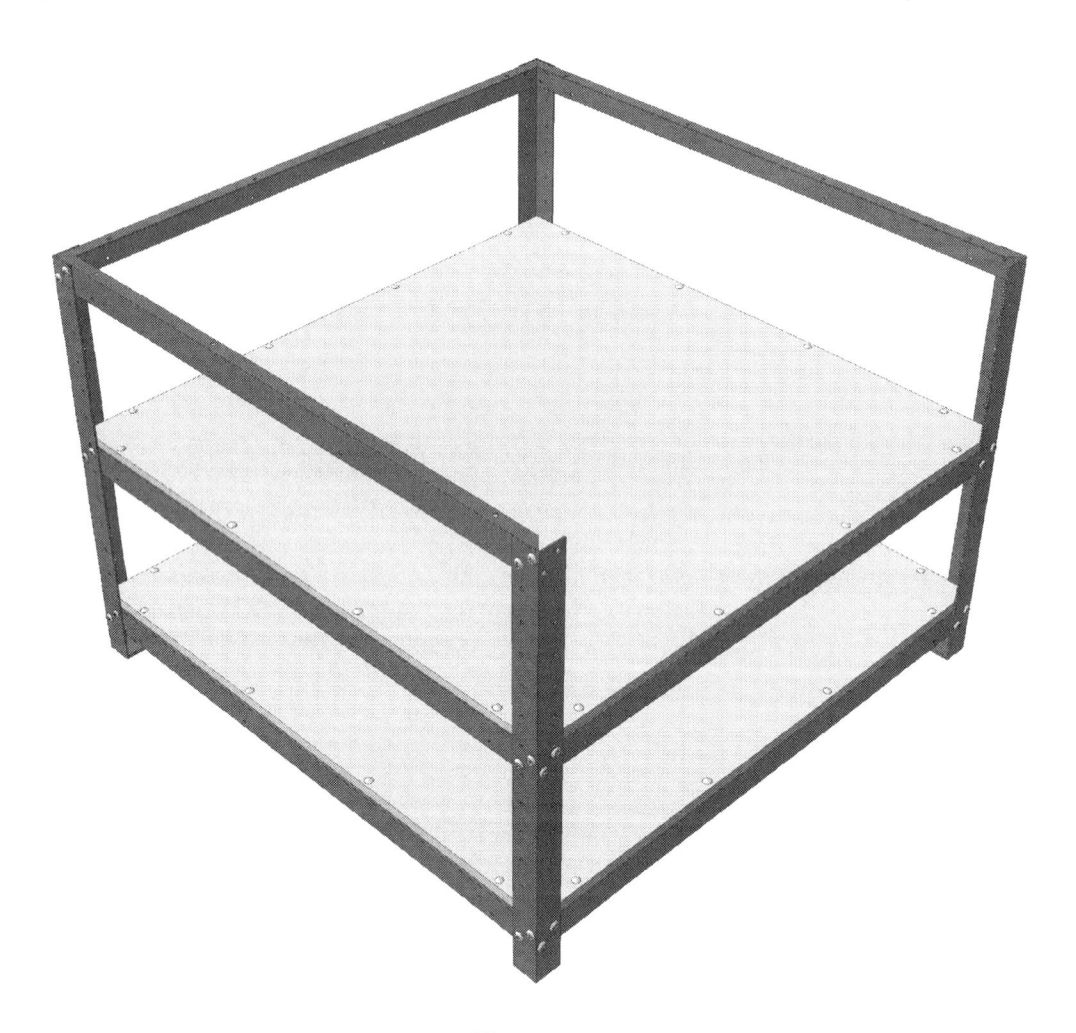

Figure 2.4

Step 4 - Top Shelf Support

Attach the top shelf support, as shown in Figure 2.5.

Figure 2.5

Step 5 - Feet

Take each of the 4 adjustable feet and thread a nut onto the shaft about 1" from the base of the foot.

Insert the threaded rod into the hole in the bottom of the leg and thread the other nut onto the rod, as shown in Figure 2.6.

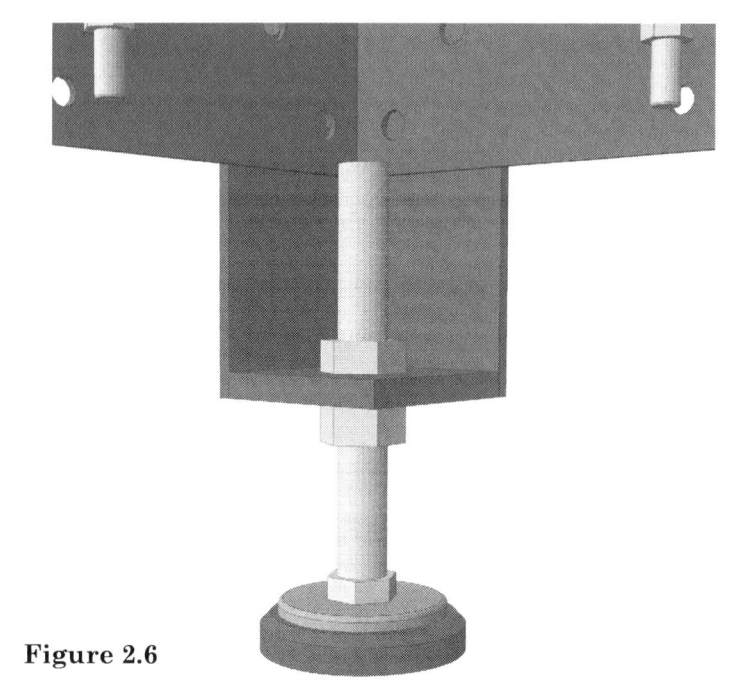

Figure 2.6

Note

You may also use a caster with a 1/2" threaded rod like the one shown in Figure 2.7. This will give your CNC machine some mobility which may be a necessity in a small shop. The down side is that you would loose the ability to level the stand.

Another downside for casters is that they allow you stand to shake. For this reason it is not recommended to use casters unless you build a very small CNC machine.

Figure 2.7

Step 6 - Level the Stand

Place a 4' level across the left side, as shown in Figure 2.8. Raise or lower the feet on each end of the level as needed to make the left side level. Mark the two corners on each side of the level with a pencil to indicate it has been adjusted.

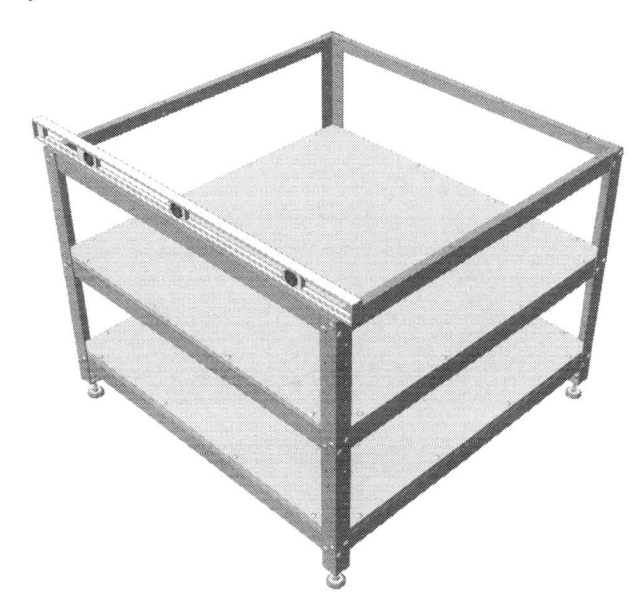

Figure 2.8

Move the level across the rear side of the stand, as shown in Figure 2.9. Raise or lower the foot that has not been marked until the rear side has been leveled. Once leveled, mark that corner.

Figure 2.9

Move the level to the right side of the stand, as shown in Figure 2.10. Raise or lower the unmarked foot as need to level the right side. Once leveled, mark that corner.

Figure 2.10

Move the level to the front side of the stand, as shown in Figure 2.11. This should be level. If it's not, you need to adjust the front left corner and make the rounds all over again. This process may need to be repeated several times.

Once the stand has been leveled, check that the sides are reasonably square. I say reasonably because you need only get the stand within 1/16" or so.

With the stand leveled and square, use a 7/16" wrench and Phillips screwdriver to tighten all the bolts.

Figure 2.11

Step 7 - Stand Table Top

Take the two sheets of 48" x 48" particle board and place them both on top of the stand. Try to keep the edges as flush the as possible, as shown in Figure 2.12, then clamp them together. Note that if these two pieces are cut from the same sheet, one may be slightly less than 48". This is not a big deal. Just make sure the uneven edges are toward the rear of the stand. Move the two sheets until you have the same overlap on all four sides. The overlap should be close to 2", but the exact distance is not important.

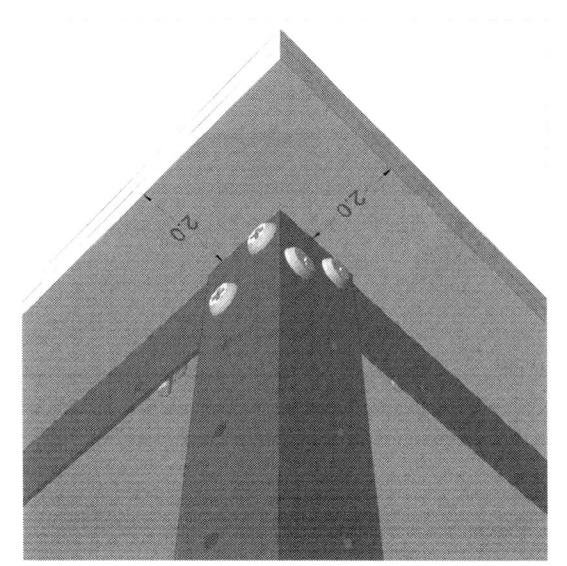

Figure 2.12

Once in place, clamp the table to the stand. From the underside of the shelf, drill the 16 holes through the shelf supports. Note that four of the holes need to have a 3/4" diameter pocket 1/4" deep added to the top as shown by the four arrows. These are needed to keep the carriage bolt heads from interfering with the struts used on the CNC

It is important from this point on that you keep the front of your CNC oriented as shown in Figure 2.13.

Figure 2.13

Building the KRMx01 CNC

Conclusion

Your CNC stand is now complete. It was mentioned at the beginning of this chapter that you should paint the shelf pieces before assembly. It's possible that when you drilled the holes for the bolts that you may have chipped out some of the particle board. If the bolt does not cover any chip-out, now is the time to touch up the paint.

If you have not already painted your shelves, you can do it now. Use masking tape to keep paint from getting on the metal portion of the stand.

Feel free to make any final adjustments to the table components. Loosen the support bolts and re-adjust. The shelving, if cut square, will go a long way in assuring the overall table is square and only the legs to shelving will have to be adjusted.

Note that if you move the stand, it should be checked again to make sure it is level.

Figure 2.14

Tip

Once you start building your CNC, the stand will become very difficult to move due to the weight of the CNC. Be sure the stand is position in place before continuing. The finished CNC machine will need access from all sides but you will mostly be accessing the CNC from the front, or possibly the rear to load stock. Keep this in mind when positioning the CNC. You should give the CNC at least 18" clearance on the sides, 24" from the rear, and enough room in the front to load a 40" piece of stock.

Chapter 3

Y-beam Assembly

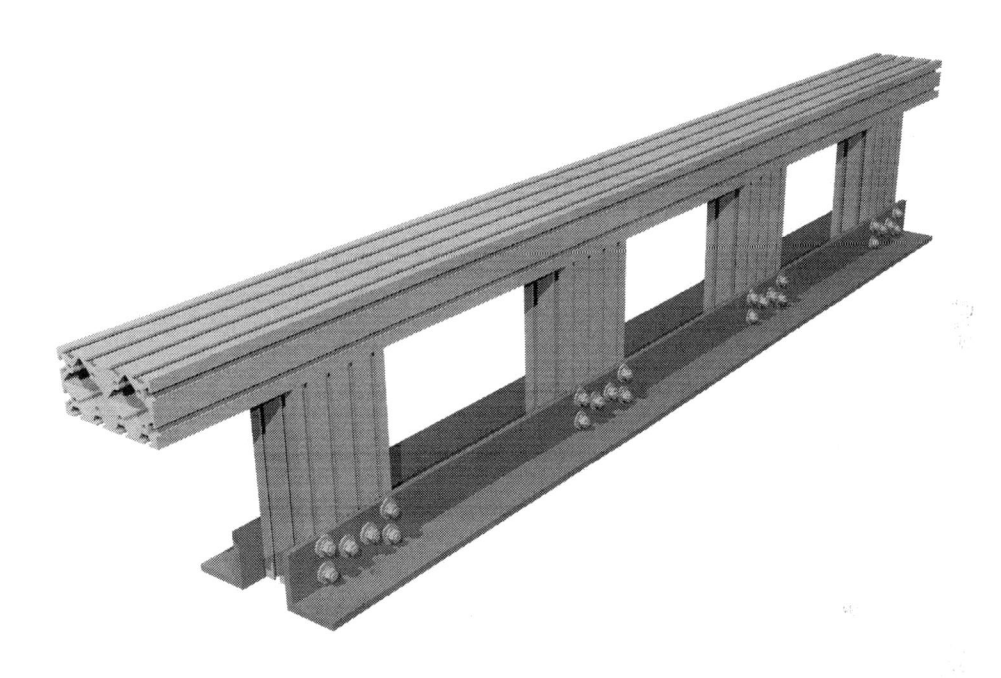

The Y-beam supports more weight than any other portion of the KRMx01 CNC, and for this reason it's the beefiest component. The KRMx01 CNC has a raised Y-beam. This is designed so we don't have to raise the gantry. The lower gantry gives the KRMx01 CNC a very stable and rigid design.

Tools Needed For This Chapter

- 2, 7/16" Wrenches
- Reciprocating saw (used to cut threaded rod)
- Drill press
- 1/8" Drill bit
- 3/8" Drill bit

Components Needed For This Chapter

- 2 Pieces of 80/20 extrusion cut to 56" (purchased and prepped in chapter 1)
- 8 Pieces of 80/20 extrusion cut to 7" (purchased and prepped in chapter 1)
- 4, 2" x 2" x 48", 1/4" Steel angle
- 3, 1/4"-20 x 10' Threaded rods (see text)
- 48, 1/4"-20 x 3" Hex bolts
- 80, 1/4"-20 Hex nuts
- 80, 1/4"-20 Split lock washers
- 128, 1/4" Washers
- 32, T-track oval nuts, Woodcraft #147922 (10 Pack)

As stated in the last chapter, when purchasing large quantities of hardware like hex bolts, hex nuts, and washers, you should shop around and look for companies that offer this type of hardware for sale by weight.

The T-track nuts are also available from Rockler, # 37732. Woodcraft also sells other sizes of T-track nuts, so make sure you select the 1/4"-20 nuts.

Chapter Estimate

Cost: $116
Time: Weekend

Prerequisites

While it's not absolutely necessary that you have the stand in the last chapter completed, if you do, it will make a nice workbench for the construction of the Y-beam.

It is assumed that you have all the extruded aluminum cut for this chapter.

Cutting Threaded Rod

You will need to cut the 1/4" threaded rod into 32, 8" sections. The best way to do this is to mark the rod, sandwich it between two pieces of scrap MDF, and clamp. If you place the top piece of MDF with it's edge flush with your mark, as shown in Figure 3.1, you can use it as a guide for your saw.

Figure 3.1

Once the rod is cut, you will need to clean up the edges. The fastest way is with a bench grinder; however a small rotary grinder or even a metal file will work. The goal here is to clean the cut so that you can easily attach the nuts.

> **Tip**
>
> Before cutting the rod, slip on a couple of nuts. This way, after you cut the rod, removing the nut over the cut end may be all you need to cleanup the cut.

Construction

This chapter will be showing you how to build a single Y-beam, but you actually will need two. They are oriented as shown in Figure 3.2. Notice the overhang and the direction of bolts protruding through the steel angle.

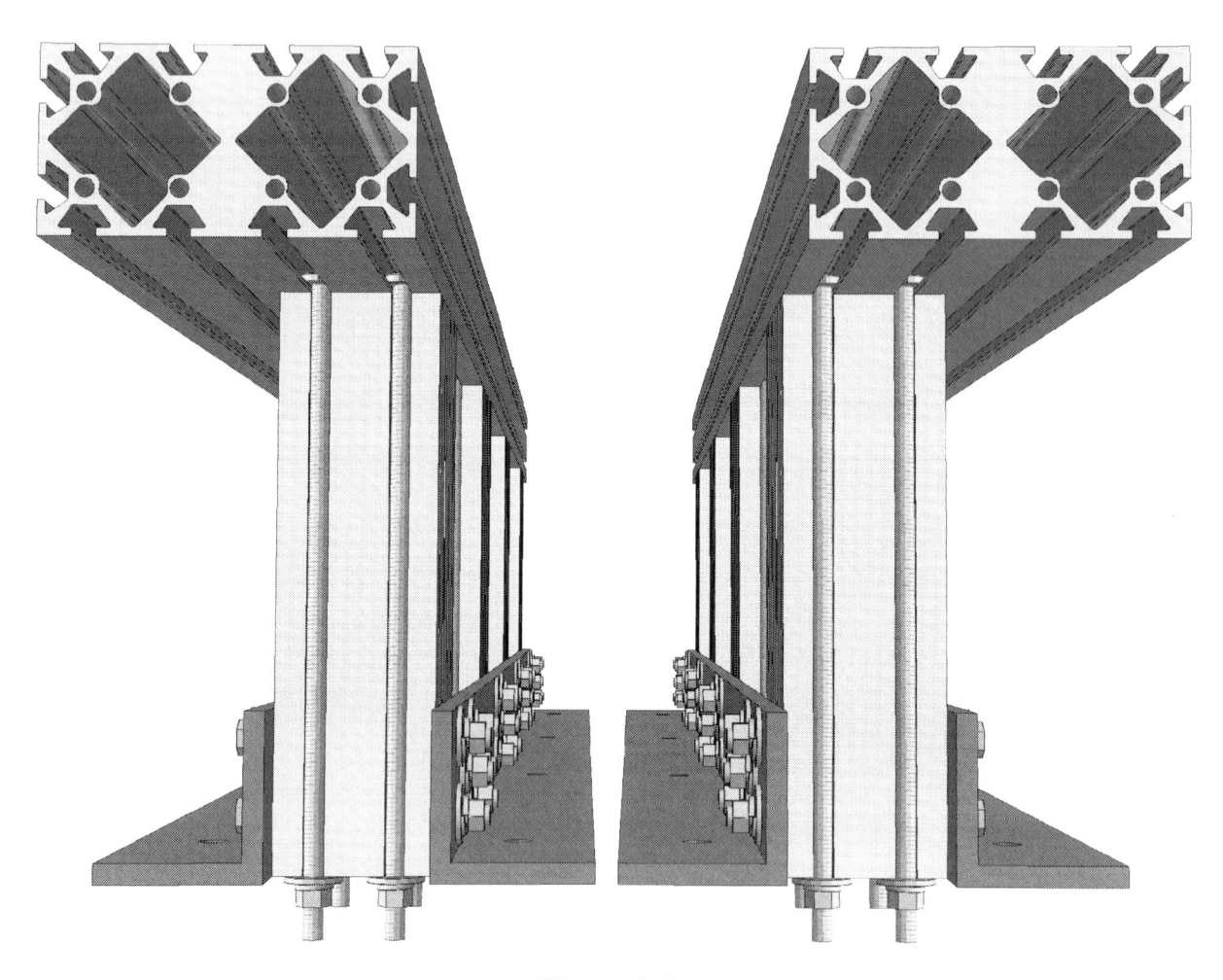

Figure 3.2

Step 1 - Create The Y-beam Angle

The Y-beam angle is used to attach the Y-beam to the table struts in the next chapter. You will need to construct four of these in order to complete both of your Y-beams. They are made from a piece of 2" x 2" x 48" steel angle 1/4" thick.

Use the drawing shown in Figure 3.3 to mark the part. The hole patterns are the same on both ends. Here is one method to layout and drill the parts.

1. Measure and layout the holes with a permanent marker.
2. Using a center punch, dent each mark.
3. Drill a pilot hole with a 1/8" drill bit. The dent will keep the bit from wandering.
4. Use a larger drill bit to create the main hole.

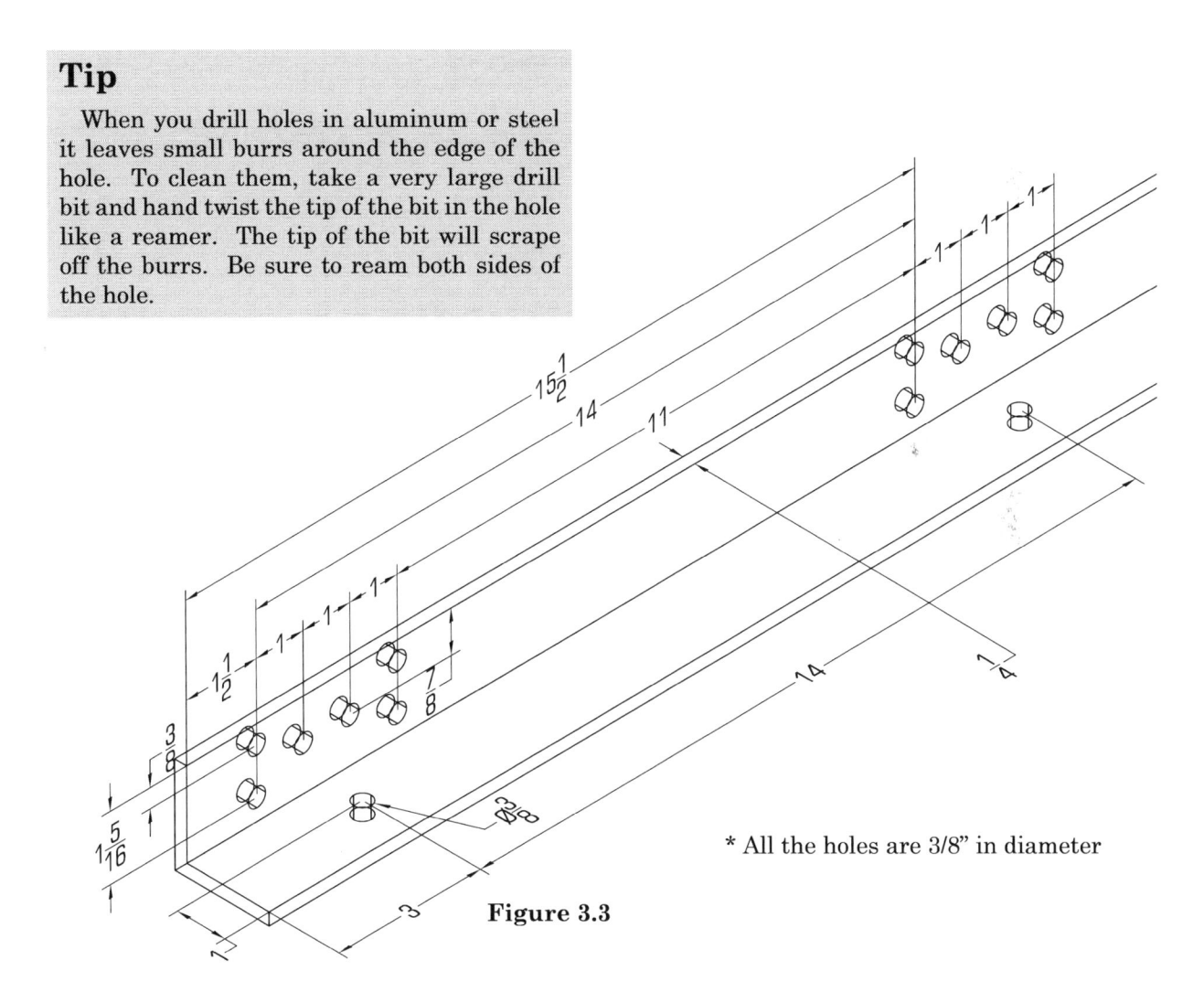

Tip

When you drill holes in aluminum or steel it leaves small burrs around the edge of the hole. To clean them, take a very large drill bit and hand twist the tip of the bit in the hole like a reamer. The tip of the bit will scrape off the burrs. Be sure to ream both sides of the hole.

* All the holes are 3/8" in diameter

Figure 3.3

Use a punch to dent all of the marks, then drill pilot holes in all the dents with a 1/8" drill bit. Next use a 3/8" drill bit to create the final set of holes. It's possible to use a hand held power drill to create all the holes, but a drill press will make the process quicker.

When you have finished drilling all the holes in your angle, it should look like the piece shown in Figure 3.4. Notice the orientation.

The side of the angle with the 24 holes is what is mated to the Y-beam uprights as shown in Figure 3.5. Keep this in mind later in the chapter as we begin assembly of the Y-beam.

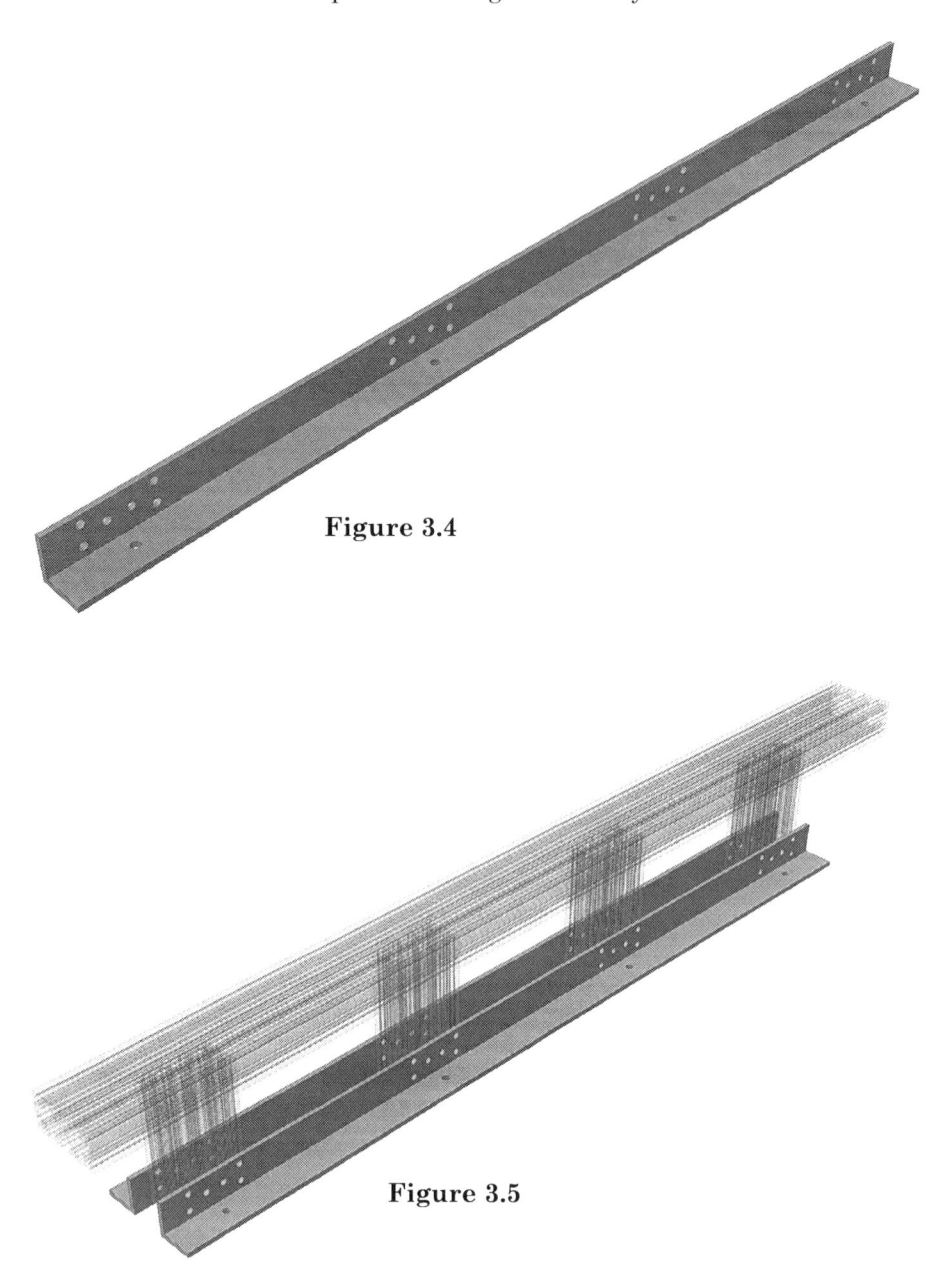

Figure 3.4

Figure 3.5

36   *Chapter 3*   Y-beam Assembly

Step 2 - Create The Y-beam Uprights

The Y-beam uprights are used to attach the angle to the main beams. Each beam needs four uprights so you will need a total of eight to complete both assemblies. You will be using the 7" sections of 80/20 you cut previously.

The holes are all 3/8", which presents a problem as the T-slot openings are only 1/4" wide. This will cause the drill bit to wander as you try to drill the holes in the sections.

The best way to create the holes is to cut a small piece of MDF to 4" x 7" and lay out the holes shown in Figure 3.6. Punch the holes, then drill your pilots and 3/8" holes in the MDF.

Next, clamp the MDF to the upright section and use it as a guide. You can now drill the six holes. A drill press is recommend for accuracy. If you use a fence on your drill press, you can probably get away with not clamping the MDF to the upright.

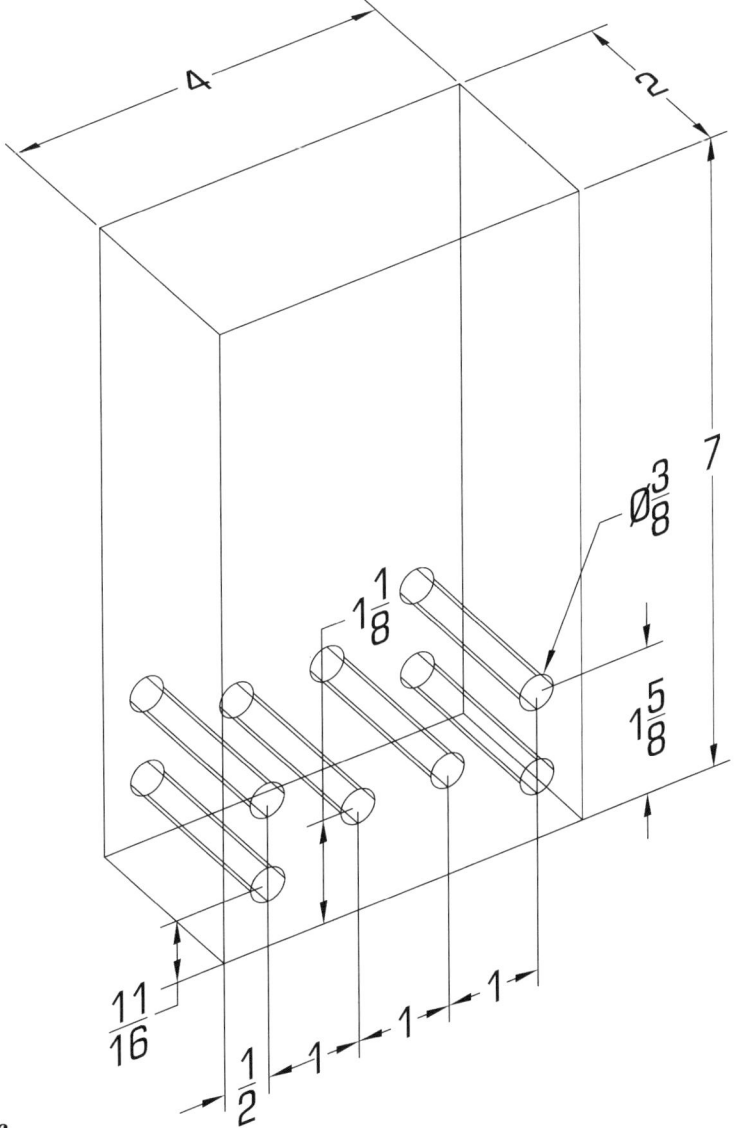

Figure 3.6

Once the holes are drilled into the upright sections, they should look like the ones shown in Figure 3.7. It is important that the holes in the upright mate with the holes in the steel angle you created back in Step 1.

You will be using 1/4" bolts so there is some wiggle room.

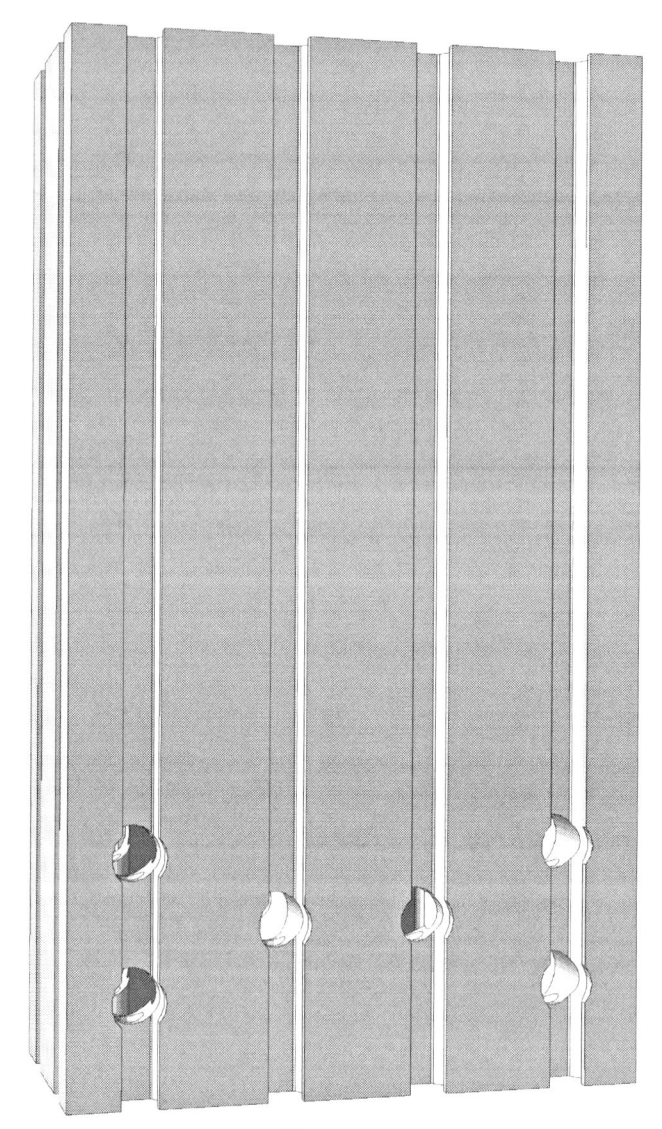

Figure 3.7

Tip

If you clamp a guide block to the 80/20 it will make it difficult to use on a drill press. Use some blue tape wrapped around the guide block and 80/20. This will hold the block in place well enough if you utilize a fence on your drill press.

Figure 3.8 shows how the uprights are integrated with the rest of the Y-beam components.

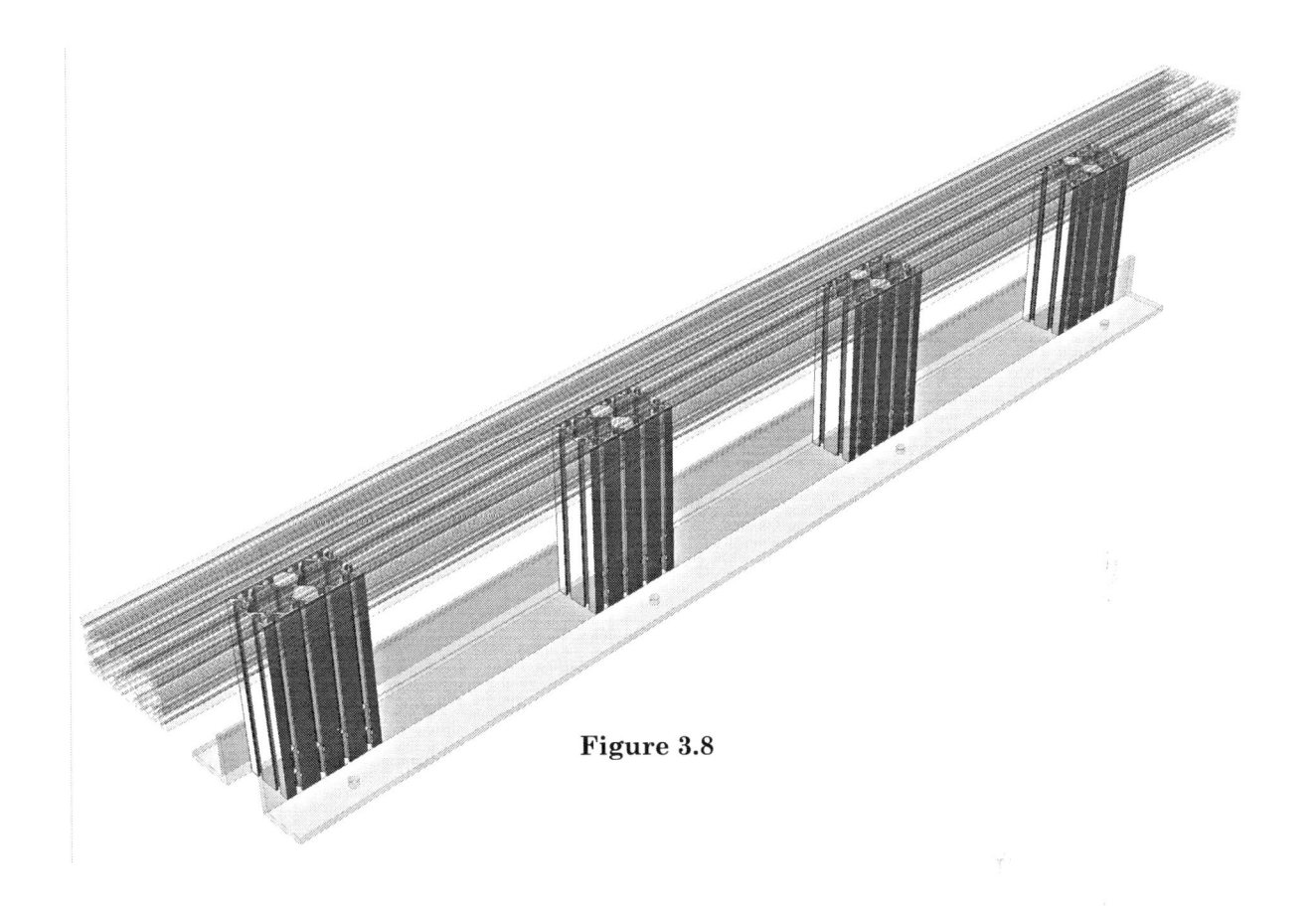

Figure 3.8

Step 3 - Prepare for assembly

Gather all the components needed to complete a single Y-beam.

- 2, Y-beam angles
- 4, Upright supports
- 1, Main beam
- 24, 1/4"-20 x 3" Hex bolts
- 40, 1/4" Hex nuts
- 40, 1/4" Split lock washers
- 64. 1/4" Washers
- 16, 1/4"-20 T-track oval nuts
- 16, 1/4"-20 8" Threaded rods

Pre-assemble the threaded rod by placing a T-track oval nut on the end, as shown in Figure 3.9. Place a washer, lock washer, and nut on the other end as shown. Leave about 1/4" of rod showing on the bottom. Set them aside for now.

Figure 3.9

Step 4 - Attach Uprights to Steel Angle

Place the Y-beam angle on a flat surface and position the four uprights in between them, as shown in Figure 3.10.

Place a washer on a 3" bolt and slip the bolt through a hole in the angle, then through the upright, and finally through the opposite angle.

With the bolt all the way through the three parts mentioned above, add a washer, lock nut, and hex nut, and finger tighten.

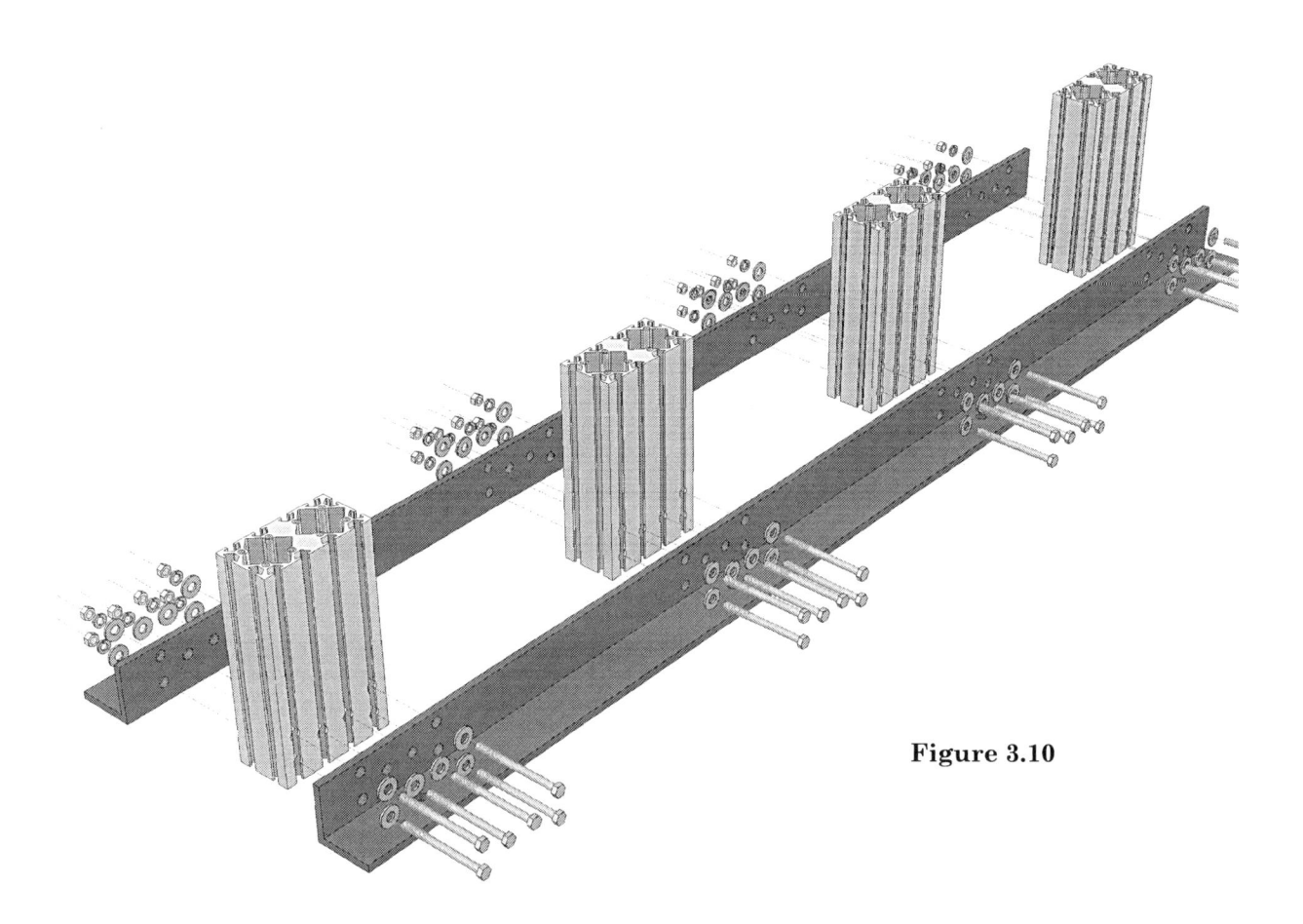

Figure 3.10

Step 5 - Main Beam Assembly

Take the pre-assembled rods and insert them into the main beam, as shown in Figure 3.11. You will need to insert sixteen assemblies into the main beam.

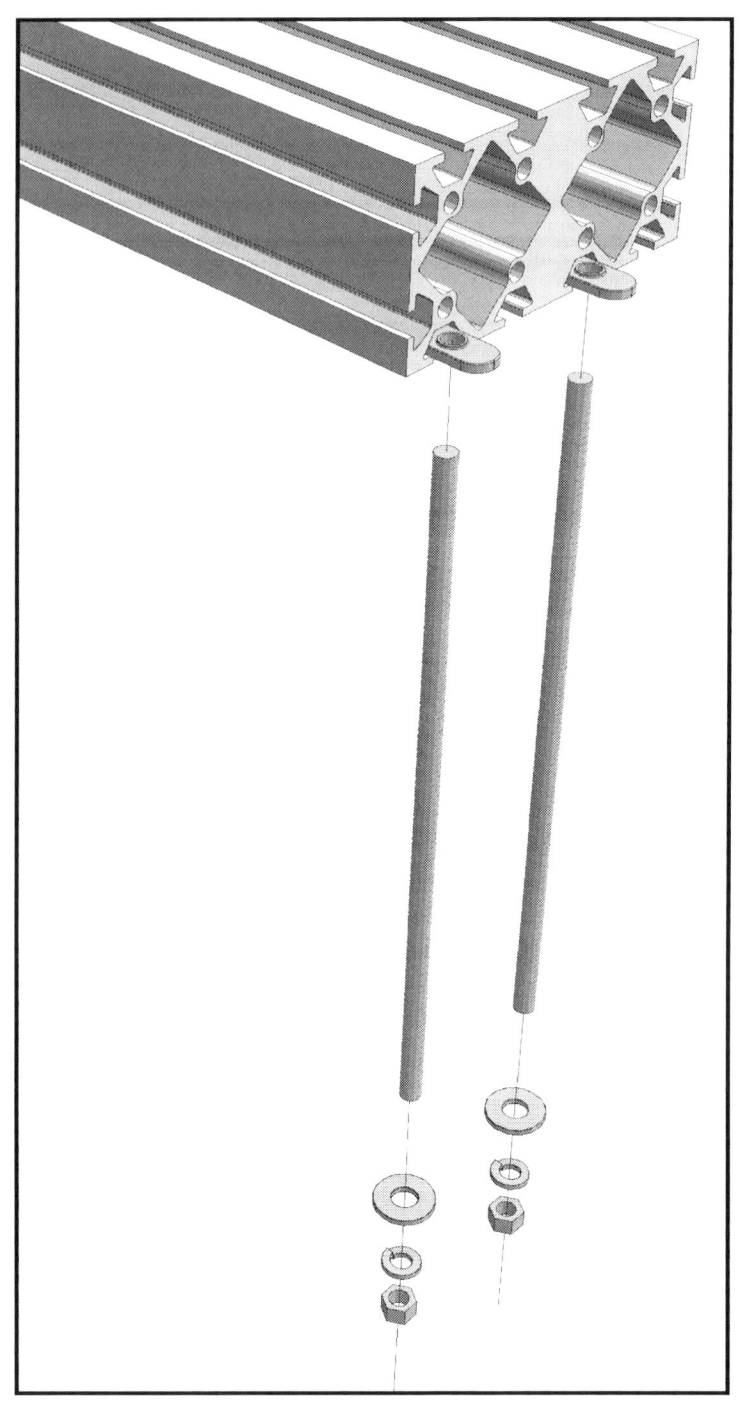

Figure 3.11

The sixteen threaded rod assemblies should be positioned, as shown in Figure 3.12. The goal here is to position the rods so that the beam can be placed on the assembly without the rods touching anything. You will reposition the rods once the main beam is in place.

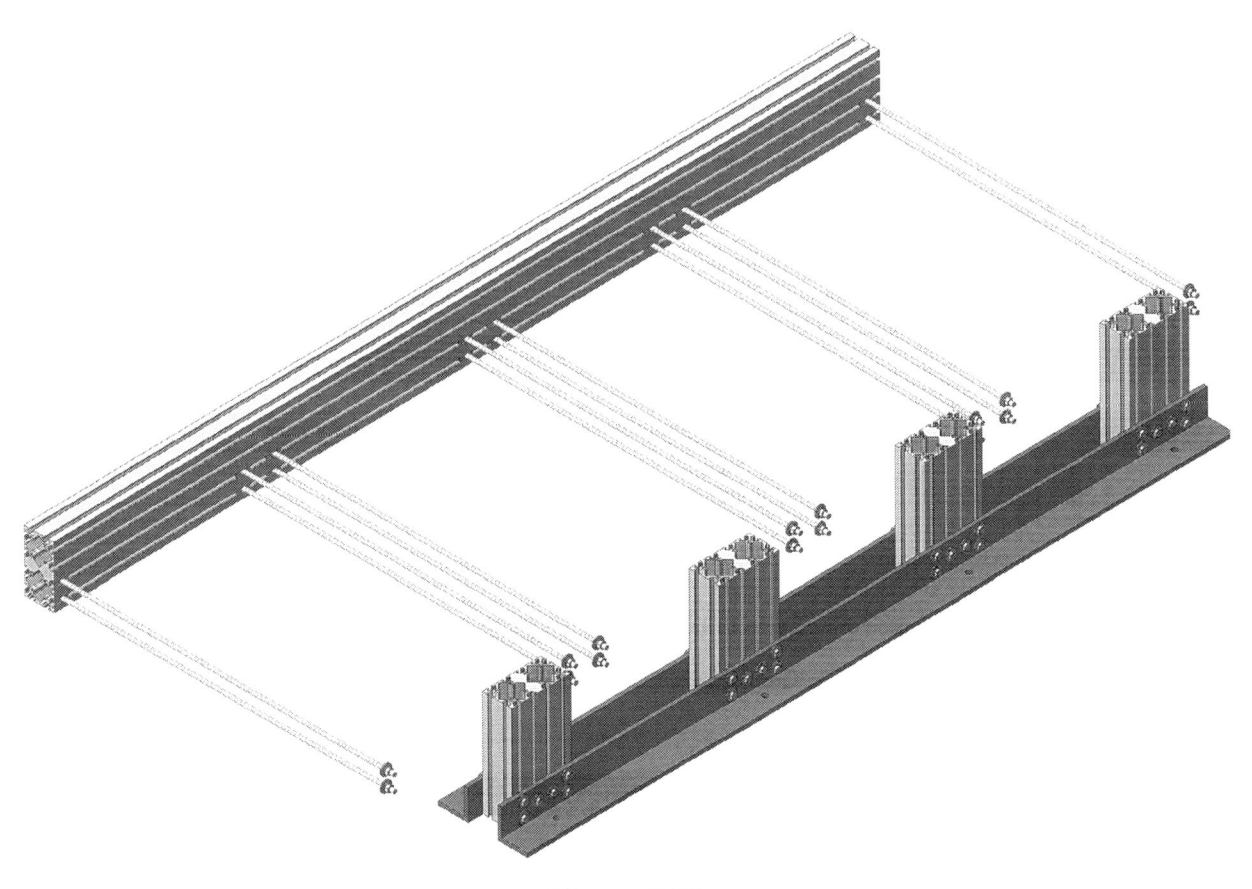

Figure 3.12

Tip

When you insert the rods into the main beam they will have a tendency to slide around. To lock the rods in place you can thread the rod further into the T-track nut, thus locking the rod against the T-slot. Add enough pressure to keep the rod assembly from sliding.

Step 6 - Attach Main Beam To Assembly

Set the main beam on top of the uprights, as shown in Figure 3.13. The end should have a 5" overhang. Loosen one of the end rods just enough for it to slide. Slide the rod into the slot of the upright and finger tighten the nut on the rod to hold it and the beam in place. Repeat on the other end of the beam.

The 5" overhang is very important. While you can use a tape measure, It is recommended that you use a digital caliper for accuracy. The inside of the beam (the side facing away from you in this case) should be flush with the upright. Use a metal straight edge to make sure it is flush.

Once you are satisfied with the position of the beam, loosen and slide the remaining rods so that they engage the slots on the uprights. Tighten all the nuts. You are working with aluminum here, so don't over tighten.

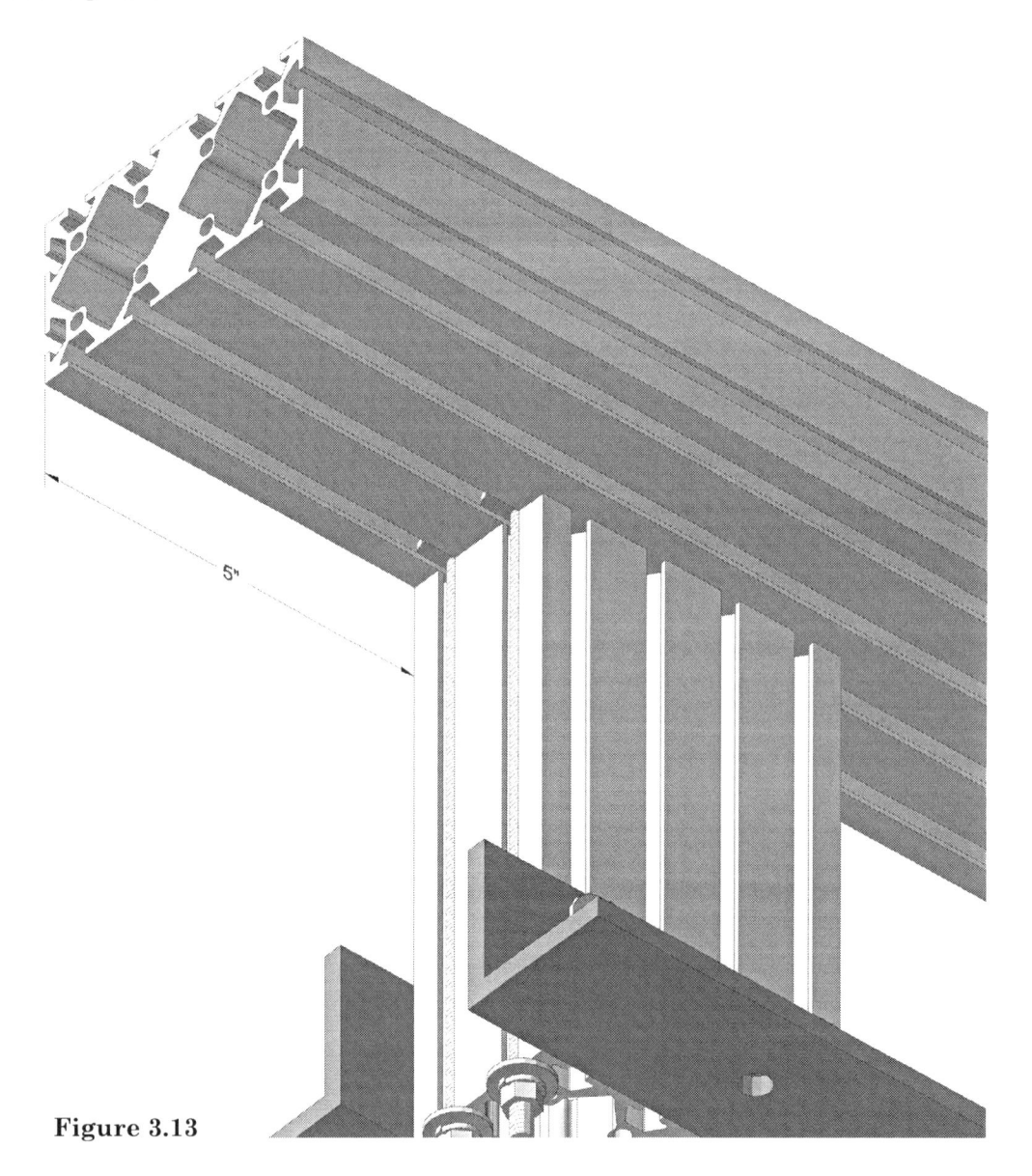

Figure 3.13

Step 7 - Assemble The Other Beam

In Step 6 you were shown how to assemble the right Y-beam. Now you need to assemble the left Y-beam. The only difference between the two is that the main beam overhang is mirrored. You will need to insert the threaded rod into the two slots opposite to the ones you used in step 5, as shown in Figure 3.14. Keep in mind that the main beam overhangs on the outside of the uprights as shown at the beginning of this chapter.

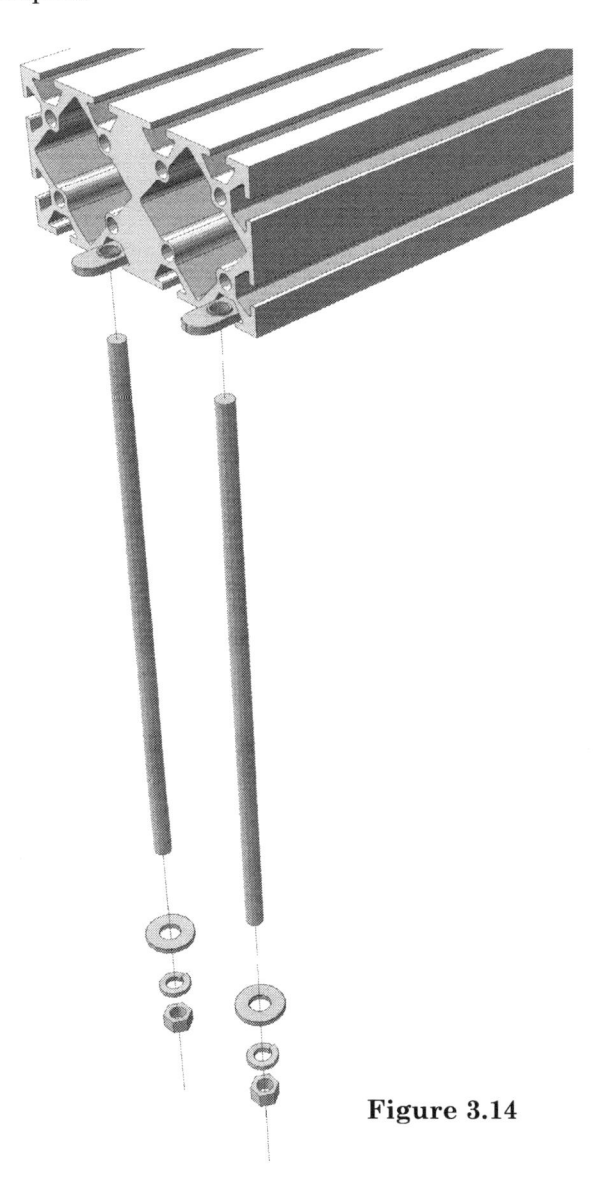

Figure 3.14

Building the KRMx01 CNC **45**

Adjustments

Both Y-beams are now complete. The Y-beams will be positioned like the ones shown in Figure 3.15. The main beams should be overhanging on the outside and on the ends. The overhang on the ends should be 5" in the front. The overhang on the backside is not as important as the front.

The beams as shown here are not necessarily meant to be adjusted. However, it is important that the eight supports be flush with the bottom of the steel angle. If they are not, the beams will not be parallel with the table top.

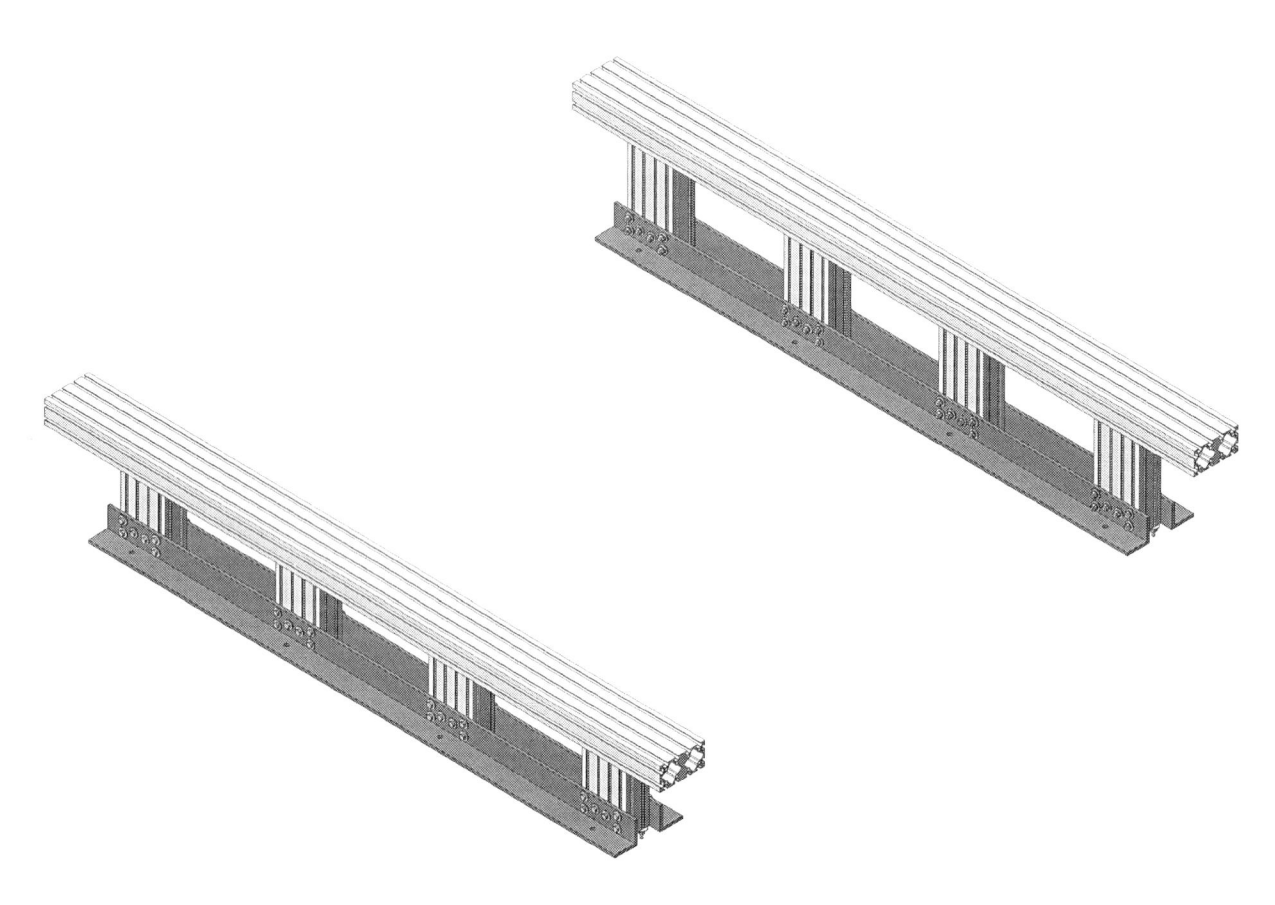

Figure 3.15

Chapter 4

Table And Rails

A solid table is very important on a CNC machine. Its important that the table does not flex and remains flat over time. To form the base for the table you'll use a set of four struts made from 1-5/8" x 5' square conduit. The struts are sandwiched between four pieces of particle board (or MDF) to form the actual top.

You may have noticed what looks like excessive overhang on the left side of the struts. This area will be used to mount an optional shelf for a small LCD monitor, and to hold our cabling system.

Tools Needed For This Chapter

- 7/16" Socket wrench (used to tighten the shelve nuts)
- 2, 9/16' Wrenches (you can substitute a socket wrench)
- Power drill
- Drill press
- 1/4" and 11/32" drill bits
- 1/4" Extended drill bit
- 3/4" Forstner bit
- Reciprocating saw (with metal cutting blade)
- Metal file

Components Needed For This Chapter

- 2, 40" x 48" x 3/4" Particle board or MDF panels
- 4, 3/4" x 3/4" x 72", 1/8" Thick aluminum angle
- 16, 3/8"-16 x 1-1/2" Hex bolts
- 16, 3/8"-16 Hex nuts
- 32, 3/8" Washers
- 16, 3/8" Split lock washers
- 32, 1/2" Washers
- 15, 1/4"-20 x 2-1/2" Carriage bolts
- 106, 1/4"-20 Hex nuts
- 106, 1/4" Washers
- 106, 1/4" Split lock washers
- 35, 1/4"-20 x 5" Carriage bolts
- 56, 1/4"-20 x 3/4" Carriage bolts
- 3, 10' 1-5/8" Metal framing channel (strut) Home Depot SKU # 235918 (MFR # ZA1200HS 10)

If you have problems locating the struts by the part numbers given, go to the Home Depot site and search on the word "strut".

Chapter Estimate

Cost: $111

Time: Weekend

Prerequisites

Top Surface

You should have cut the 40" x 48" shelves already. These shelves are used to form the table top for the KRMx01 CNC, so it is important that you use particle board or MDF. Do not use Plywood.

It is also important that the shelves are cut square and parallel. One of the shelves will be used to align the two Y-beams.

Struts

Mark two of the 10' struts at 5' in order to cut them in half. This will yield you four struts 5' long. Take the remaining 10' strut and cut a 4' section.

The best way to cut the struts is with a reciprocating saw with a metal cutting blade. Clamp the struts to a table along with a scrap piece of MDF as a guide, as shown in Figure 4.1. Use at least two clamps.

Be sure to clean up the cut edges of the strut with a file or rotary tool.

Figure 4.1

Tip

If a bolt does not fit properly into the 80/20 T-slots, 90% of the time the reason is that the head of the bolt is a little too wide. By lightly grinding two opposing sides of head, as shown in Figure 4.2, they will easily fit into the slot. You can use bench grinders, disk sanders, and rotary grinders for this task.

Note that you need to grind two sides parallel to the small square rectangle just under the head. When inserting the bolt into the slot make sure the ground sides of the bolt are against the sides of the groove in the T-slot.

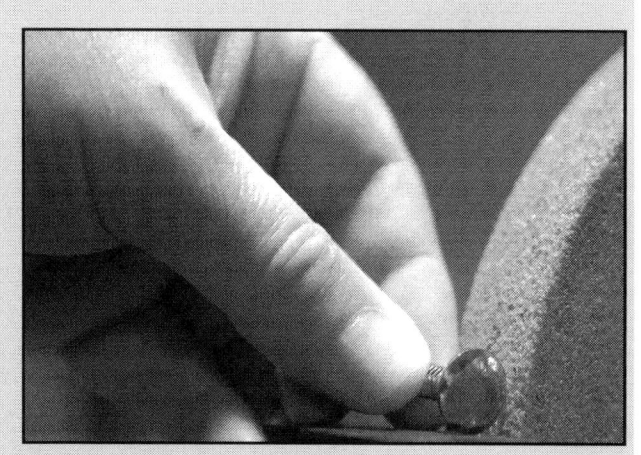

Figure 4.2

Step 1 - Layout The Struts

Start by laying the four 5' struts on the stand as, shown in Figure 4.3. The open side of the strut is pointed up. The rear strut should be flush with the rear of the stand's top. The overhang on the right hand side should be 2", as shown in Figure 4.4. Use the non cut edges of the struts for the 2" overhang.

Use two clamps to hold the rear strut in place.

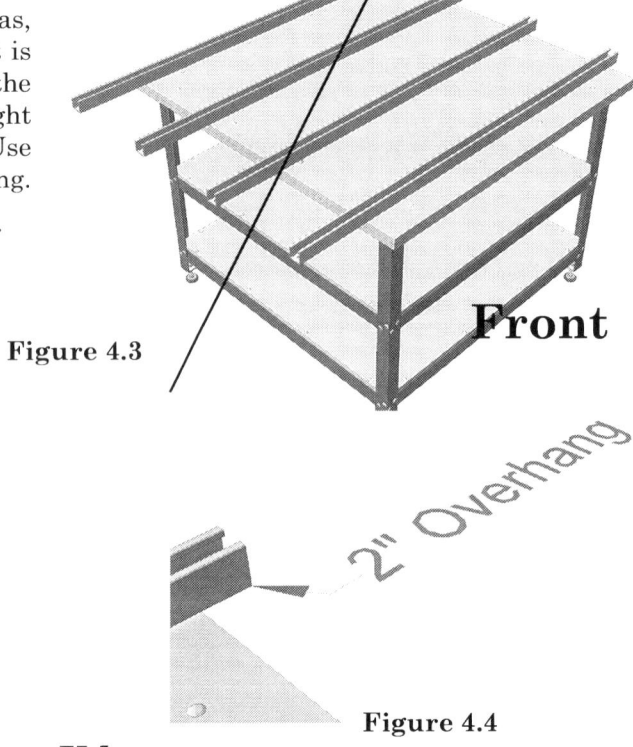

Figure 4.3

Figure 4.4

Step 2 - Attach Mounting Bolts to Y-beam

Place a 3/8" washer on each of the 16 3/8" bolts, as shown in Figure 4.5. Then slip them through the holes in the bottom of the steel angle on the Y-beam assembly, as shown in Figure 4.6. From the underside of the angle slip two of the 1/2" washers, then a 3/8" washer, lock washer, and finally the 3/8" nut, as shown in Figure 4.7. Tighten the nut until the threaded end of the bolt is flush with the nut.

You want the nuts to stay in place but be loose enough to allow the Y-beam assembly to be slipped into the struts.

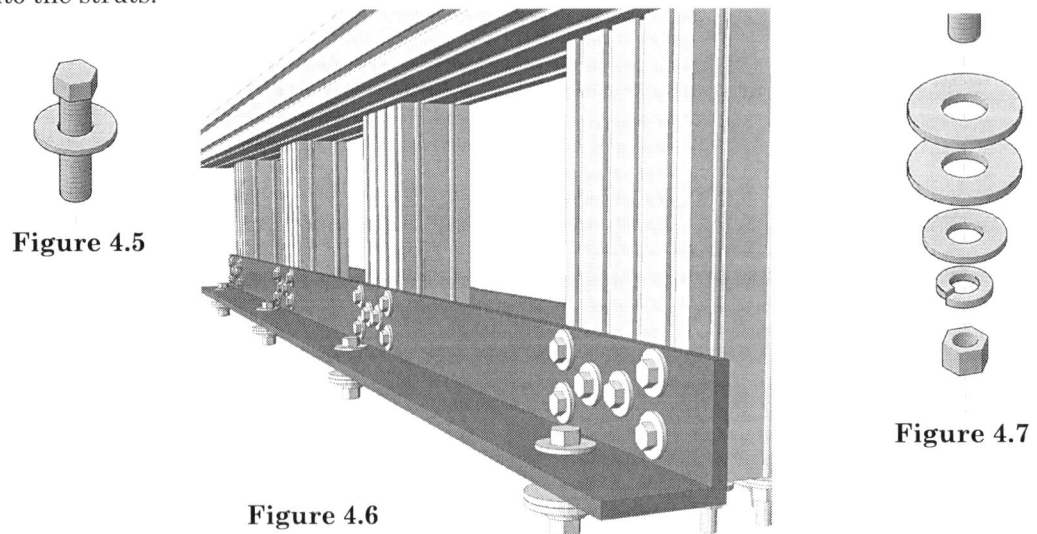

Figure 4.5

Figure 4.6

Figure 4.7

Step 3 - Attach The First Beam

Slide the right side Y-beam into the four struts as, shown in Figure 4.8. As long as the bolts are loose they should slip into the struts. All the strut edges should be flush with the edge of the Y-beam angle.

> **Tip**
>
> Move the two middle struts out of the way. Next slip the rear bolts into the rear struts first. Then insert the front bolts into the front struts. Once the beam is secure in the front and rear struts, slide the two middle struts into place.

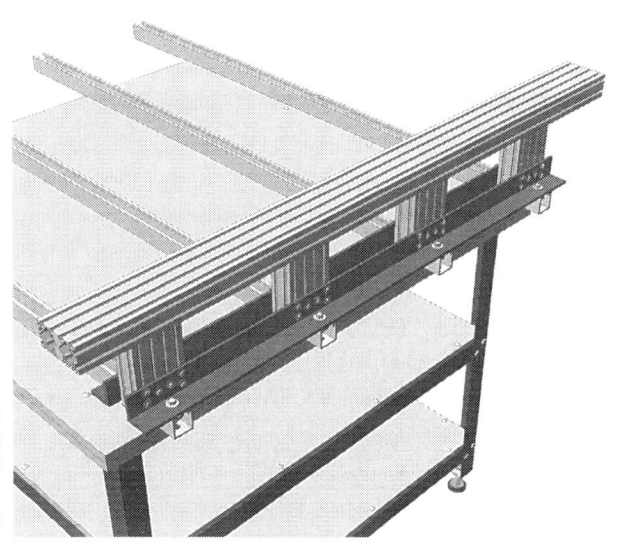

Figure 4.8

At this point you can finger tighten all the nuts and bolts. Shown in Figure 4.9, is how the bolt assemblies fit into the struts.

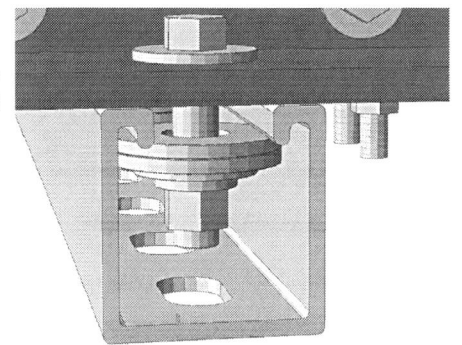

Figure 4.9

Step 4 - Attach The Second Beam

Slide the left side Y-beam into the four struts, as shown in Figure 4.10. You need about 41" between the two angles on the Y-beams. Don't tighten any of the nuts at this time.

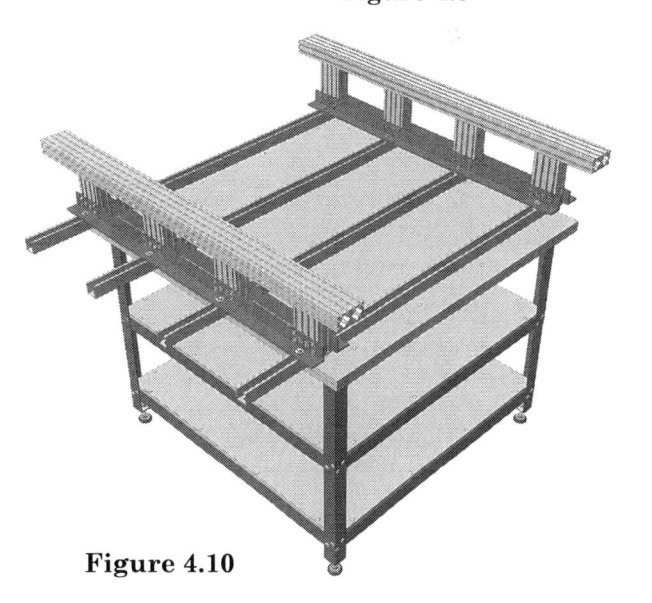

Figure 4.10

Building the KRMx01 CNC **51**

Step 5 - Align the two Y-beams

Take one of the 40" x 48" shelves and slip it between the two Y-beams as shown in Figure 4.11. You want the 40" side of the shelf between the two Y-beams.

The front edge of the shelf should be flush with the Y-beam's angle, as shown in Figure 4.12. By keeping both Y-beams flush with the top, you will insure the Y-beams are properly aligned.

With the right Y-beam flush against the edge of the struts, tighten the front and rear outside bolts. Do this by holding the nut inside the strut with a 9/16" wrench. Use a second wrench to tighten the bolt on the top. Make them snug enough to keep the Y-beam from moving

Next, move the shelf snugly up against the right Y-beam, and the left Y-beam snugly up against the shelf. Tighten the front and rear outside bolts.

Figure 4.11

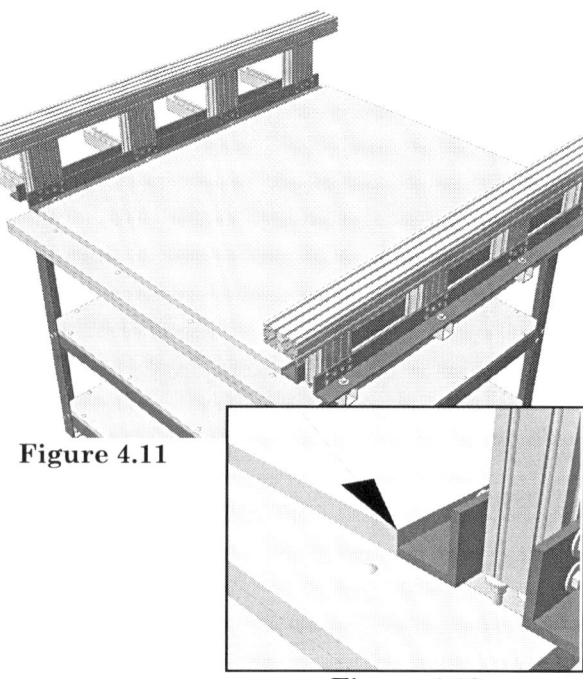

Figure 4.12

Step 6 - Measure the Y-beams

With both Y-beams are locked down, it's time to measure their relation to one another. It's important that they are square and parallel to each other. While we have a little bit of leeway on how square the two beams are, it is a fundamental requirement that the two Y-beams be parallel.

Take a measurement between the two beams at the front and the rear, as indicated by the arrows in Figure 4.13. They should be within 1/64" of an inch. If they are not, either your shelf is not cut accurately or one of your main beams is not mounted flush on the uprights. The easiest way to fix the problem is to make adjustments to the left Y-beam mount by loosening the front or rear bolt and slightly tapping the beam at the base until it has moved into position. If you do have to adjust, retighten the bolts and measure again before proceeding.

Step 7 - Tighten The Remaining Bolts

Remove the shelf to expose the struts. Using a 9/16" wrench to hold the nuts inside the struts, take

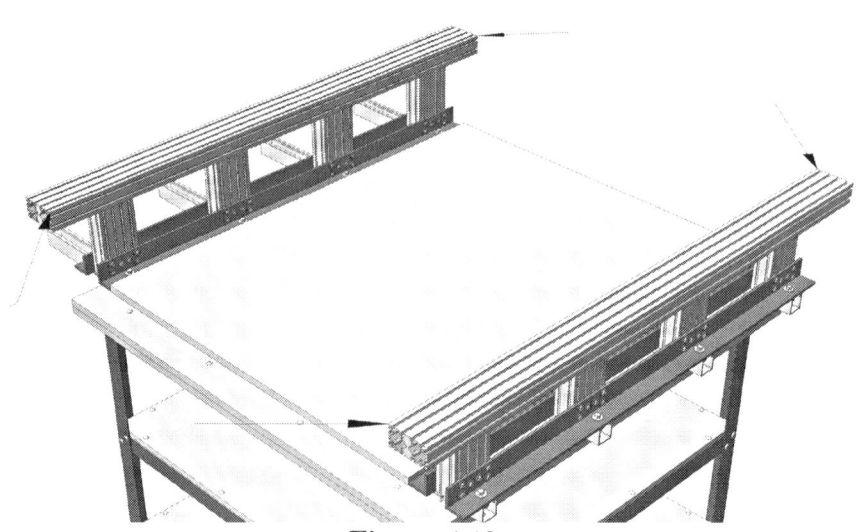

Figure 4.13

a 9/16" socket or wrench and tighten the bolt located on the steel angle. After tightening all bolts, measure one more time to be sure the distance between the beams is equal, indicating the are parallel.

Step 8 - Mount The Y-beam Assembly

Your Y-beams are now assembled into a single, assembly. It's time to attach them to the stand.

Place the complete Y-beam assembly on the stand, as shown in Figure 4.14. The front strut should be 4" from the edge of the panel. There should be a 2" overhang on the right as shown in Figure 4.14. Once aligned, clamp in place. Note that the main beams have been removed from the illustration for clarity

One problem you are faced with when using the struts is that the hole patterns tend to be inconsistent. This makes using direct measurements for drilling mounting holes somewhat problematic. To compensate for this ,you will drill holes for mounting by simply counting the holes in the strut.

Using a power drill, drill a 1/4" hole into each of the slots in the struts at the indicated positions shown by the arrows. The actual placement of the holes is not that important.

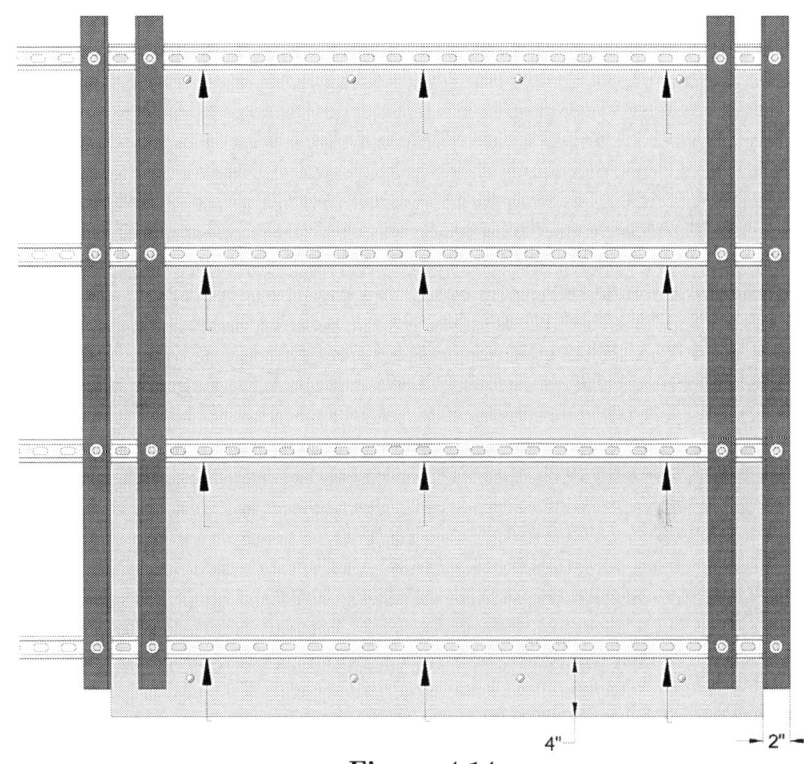

Figure 4.14

Drill all the way through the two layers of particle board that form the stand top.

Once the holes have been drilled, insert a 1/4"-20 x 2-1/2" carriage bolt into one of the holes from the underside of the stand. Place a 14" washer, lock washer, and 1/4"-20 hex nut on the bolt and tighten with a 7/16" socket wrench. Do the same for the remaining 11 holes you just drilled.

You can now remove any clamps that you were using to hold the struts in place.

Step 9 - Attach The Front Support Strut

Take the remaining 48" strut and place it in the stand top flush with the front edge, as shown in Figure 4.15. Clamp in place.

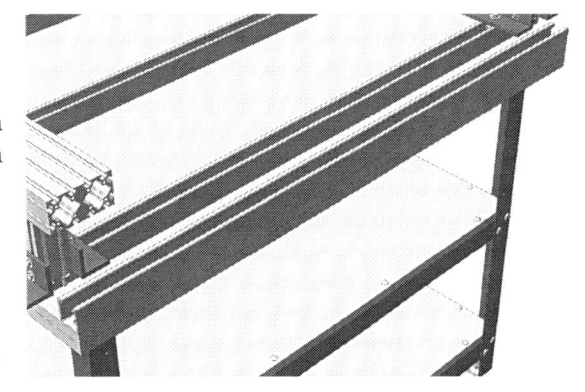

Figure 4.15

Building the KRMx01 CNC

Drill a 1/4" hole into each of the slots in the front support strut at the indicated positions shown by the arrows in Figure 4.16. Drill all the way through the two layers of particle board that form the stand top.

As before, insert a 1/4"-20 x 2-1/2" carriage bolt into one of the holes from the underside of the stand. Place a 14" washer, lock washer, and 1/4"-20 hex nut on the bolt and tighten with a 7/16" socket wrench. Do the same for the remaining two holes you just drilled.

You can now remove any clamps that you were using to hold the strut in place.

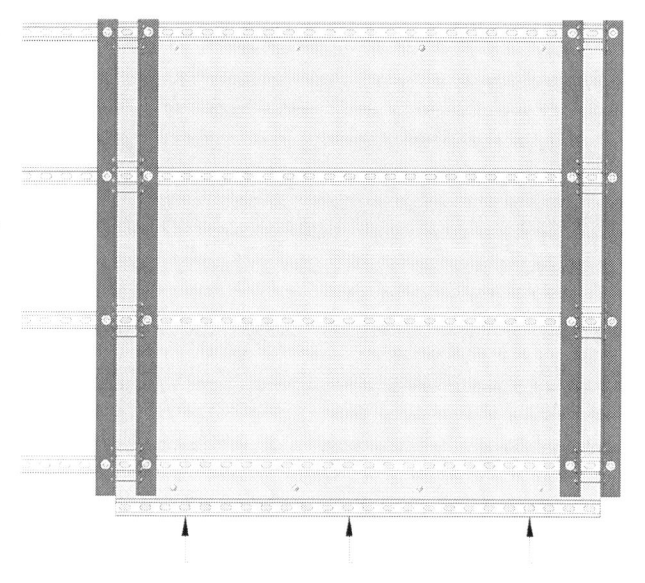

Figure 4.16

Step 10 - Drill Pilot Holes For CNC Table Top

In order to attach the CNC table top to the struts you need to first drill holes through the slots in the struts just like you did in Steps 8 and 9. Using a 1/4" bit, drill 35 holes into the slots, as indicated by the arrows in Figure 4.17.

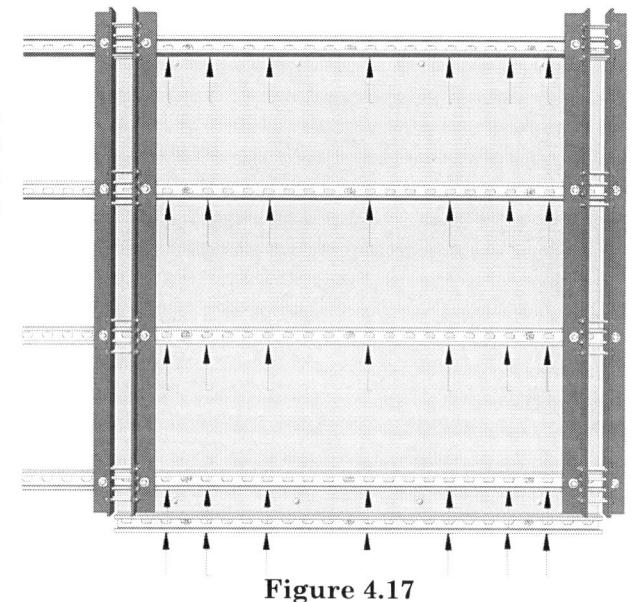

Figure 4.17

54   *Chapter 4*   Table And Rails

Step 11 - Prepare to Drill Table Top

In order to drill accurate holes into the table top we need to use the holes we drilled in Step 10 as pilot holes. Take both 40" x 48" shelves and place them on top of the struts. Make sure the are flush with the front, as shown in Figure 4.18. Clamp in place.

Note that you may need to move the clamps as you drill the outside holes. For this reason be sure to use four clamps; one at each corner.

Figure 4.18

Step 12 - Drill Table Top

You will be drilling from the underside of the table through the pilot holes you drilled in step 10. You will be drilling through almost 5" of material so you will need an extended 1/4" drill bit. The bit should be at least 6" long.

You can purchase extended drill bits at your local home center. Woodworking stores also sell extended drill bits for drilling pen blanks.

You most certainly will need a close quarters drill or an attachment for your drill, as an extended drill bit and standard power drill will likely not fit between the shelves.

Once the 35 holes have been drilled you will need to create a counter sink so that the carriage bolts can be recessed below the surface, as shown in Figure 4.19. You need to recess the carriage bolts so you can mount a clamping table later.

Figure 4.19

Building the KRMx01 CNC

If you place a Forstner bit inside portable power drill it is very difficult to keep the bit in place when you start the hole. The best way to counter this is to create a guide. To make the guide, take a piece of scrap material and drill a 3/4" hole into one end. A piece of scrap 4" x 12" works the best.

To use the guide, place the hole in the guide centered over one of the 1/4" holes in the table. Clamp or hold this guide. Insert the Forstner bit in the hole. Start slowly at first. The counter sink holes need to be 1/4" deep.

Tip

Since part of the hole was drilled back in Step 10, you can place the extended bit into the hole before it is attached to the drill. You can then chuck your bit into th drill. Once the hole has been drilled all the way through, you will need to loosen the chuck and remove the bit, when the hole is finished. While this seems like a timely process, it will gain you a few inches of clearance.

Step 13 - Bolt Table Top to CNC

Take 35 1/4"-20 x 5" carriage bolts and insert them into the 35 holes in the table top shown in Figure 4.19. Attach a 1/4" washer, 1/4" lock washer, and a 1/4"-20 hex nut, as shown in Figure 4.20.

Make sure the front of the two panels are flush with the strut on the front of the CNC, then tighten the nuts with a 7/16" socket or wrench.

Figure 4.19

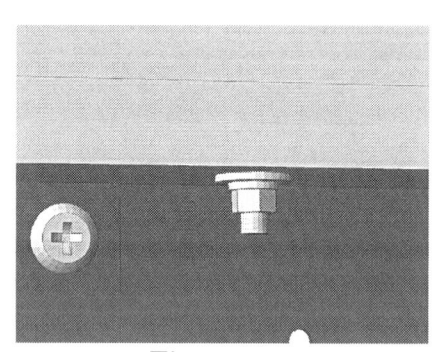

Figure 4.20

56 Chapter 4 Table And Rails

Step 14 - Cut Aluminum Angle

The Aluminum Y-rails can be cut any number of ways.

- Band saw
- Jig saw
- Reciprocating saw
- Miter saw

The easiest way is probably with the reciprocating saw. Place a mark at 54" on the aluminum angle. Clamp it to a workbench and cut, as shown in Figure 4.21. You will need 4, 54" rails.

The cuts are not critical, but be sure to use a metal cutting blade in the saw. Once cut, clean up the cut with a rotary grinder or file.

Figure 4.21

If you are going to use a metal vise to hold the rail, be sure to protect the rail with some scrap wood to keep the vise from damaging the rail.

Note that the scrap cut from the 72" piece of aluminum angle can be used to make your Z-rails. They should be 15-1/2", so you have a little wiggle room.

Tip

If there are any labels on the aluminum railing you will need to remove them before attaching it to the CNC. A heat gun or blow dryer will soften the glue so that you can peel it off, as shown in Figure 4.22. Be sure to remove any adhesive that is left behind.

Figure 4.22

Step 15 - Layout Y-rails

The rail holes are symmetrical. That is to say, the seven holes on the right side of the rail are exactly the same on the left. Mark both sides, as shown in Figure 4.23.

The best way to mark the holes is with a fine tip permanent marker, then to dent with an center punch. The placement along the length is not critical. The distance from the edge is critical and should be as close to 1/4" as possible.

Building the KRMx01 CNC

Figure 4.23

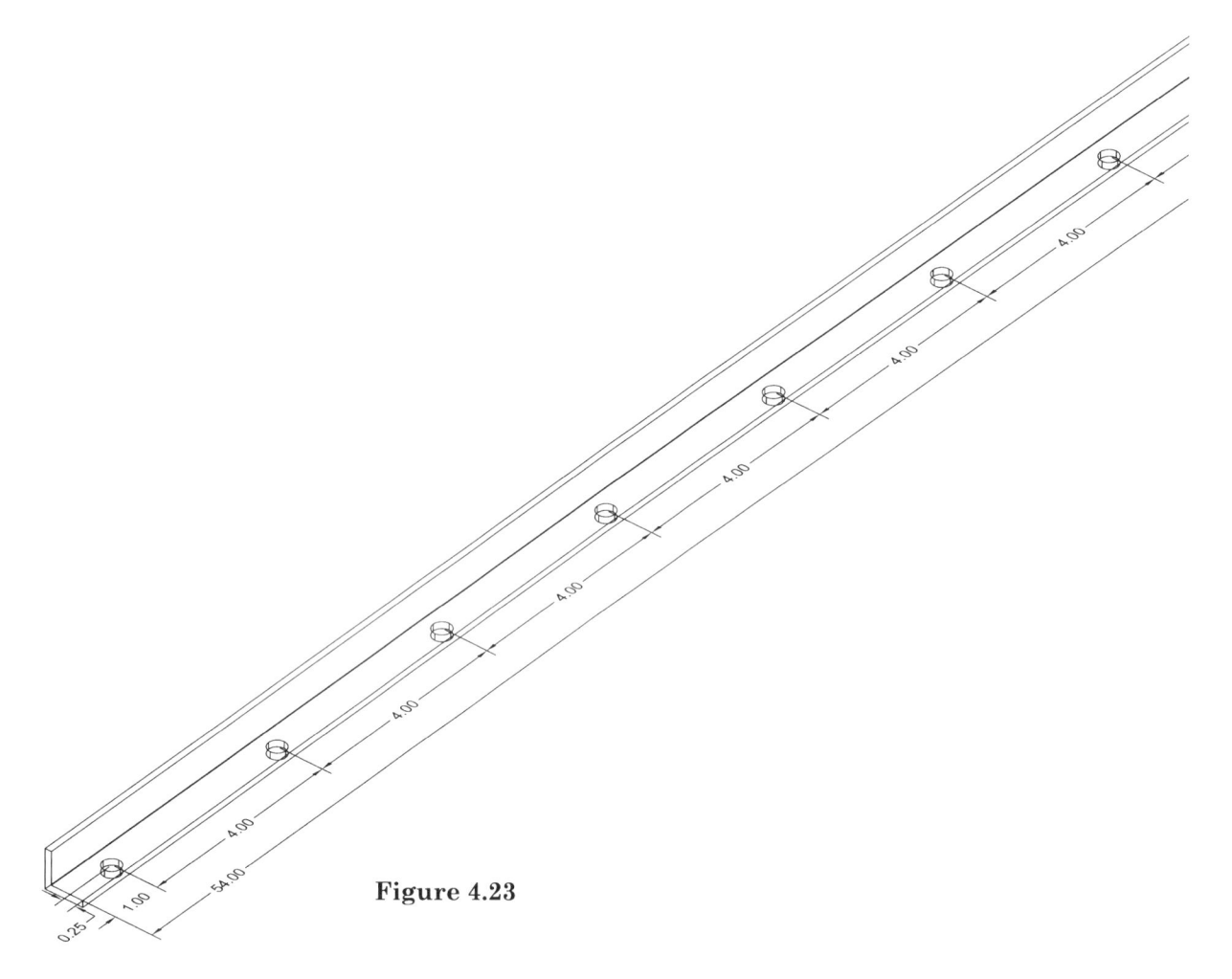

Step 16 - Drill Holes

While it is possible to drill the holes with a portable drill, for the best accuracy use a drill press. A fence like the one shown in Figure 4.24 will ensure that all the holes will be the same distance from the edge, which is the most critical factor when making your rails.

First drill a 1/8" pilot hole at all your marks, then drill the final hole diameters with a 11/32" drill bit.

Figure 4.24

58 Chapter 4 Table And Rails

After drilling all the holes, be sure to clean them up by reaming them with a larger drill bit, like the one shown in Figure 4.25. A 1/2" drill bit works well for this. While it is recommended that you do this by hand, you can also use a portable drill at a very slow speed. Be careful when using a drill; if the bit catches it can ruin the hole.

Figure 4.25

Step 17 - Layout Mounting Bolts

Lay a drilled Y-rail on top of one of the Y-beams. Place it 1" from the edge, as shown in Figure 4.26. You will be using the Y-rail as a guide for placing the bolts. Keep in mind that the Y-beam shown here is on the left size. You will need to flip the rail when doing the right side.

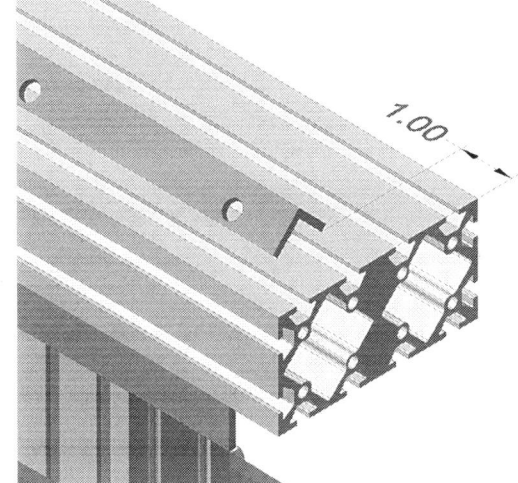

Figure 4.26

Slip 14 of the 1/4-20 x 3/4" bolts into the slot on the Y-beam, as shown in Figure 4.27. You can slip them in from either side of the beam. If a bolt is too tight to slide in the slot, don't force it. Try twisting the bolt 90 degrees and inserting it. If it still does not fit, you may need to grind the bolt as outlined in Chapter 1.

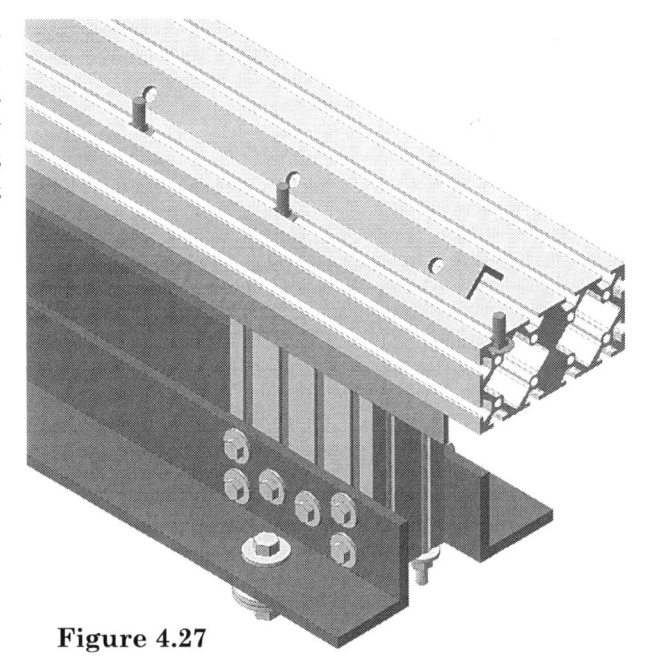

Figure 4.27

Building the KRMx01 CNC **59**

Step 18 - Attach Rails

Position the rail over the bolts on the right beam, as shown in Figure 4.28. Be sure the rail is 1" from the front edges of the beam.

Note that the beam is being shown at a different angle so you can see the bolts.

Once you have the bolts positioned for the top rail, proceed with positioning bolts for the bottom rail. This step can be a little tricky, but you have a couple of options. The first is to have a friend hold the rail in place while you slide in the nuts. The second is to use a rail to place small marks near the slot. Use these marks to align the bolts in the slot.

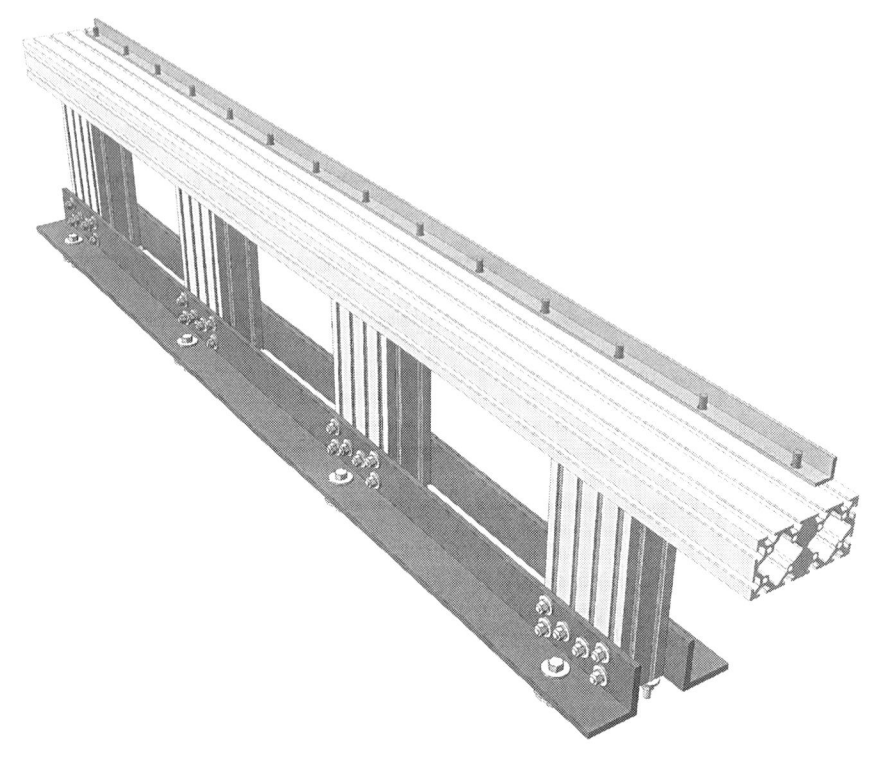

Figure 4.28

Place a 1/4" washer, 1/4" lock nut, and 1/4"-20 hex nut on the bolts, as shown in Figure 4.29. Only finger tighten the nuts. Once you have the top rail nice and snug, proceed with the rail mounted on the bottom of the beam.

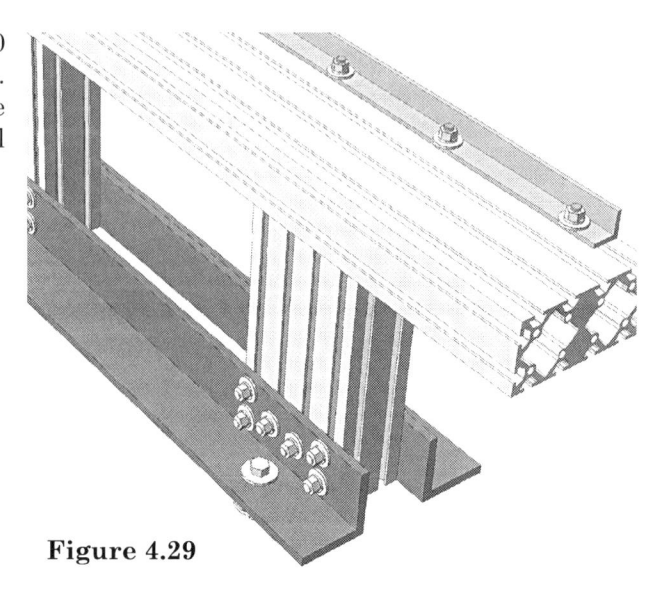

Figure 4.29

Step 19 - Align Rails

The best way to align the Y-rails is to clamp some sort of straight edge to the beam. Figure 4.30 shows a piece of scrap steel angle being used. Clamp a straight edge to both ends and one to the middle. Make sure the nuts holding the Y-rail are loose enough that the Y-rail can move.

Once clamped in place, make sure the Y-rails are snug against the straight edge and tighten the nuts on either end and in the middle. Make sure you get the nuts on the bottom rail as well. Once tight, move the clamps to positions between the nuts you just adjusted and repeat the procedure. The goal here is to work your way through each nut.

Figure 4.30

Adjustments

Table

This completes the construction of your KRMx01 CNC table. Later you will add a clamp table that will become your actual routing surface.

If you are painting your CNC, feel free to paint the table top.

You won't be making frequent adjustments to the table surface, however there are two important adjustments that need to be made now before proceeding. The two beams should be parallel to each other. That's to say, the front of the beams should be the same distance apart as the rear of the beams. The two beams should be the same distance from the table and the front of the beam and the rear of the beam should be the same distance from the table.

The heads of all the carriage bolts on the table top should be below the surface so they wont interfere with your clamp table.

Rails

While the rails are now mounted and ready for the carriages, it is important that you condition the rails. Conditioning the rails was covered in Chapter 1.

Before conditioning, the rails should be flush with the outside edge as described earlier. If your beams are parallel to each other and the rails are flush with the outside edge they will be parallel as well. You can check the distance between the two rails at the front and rear of the rails.

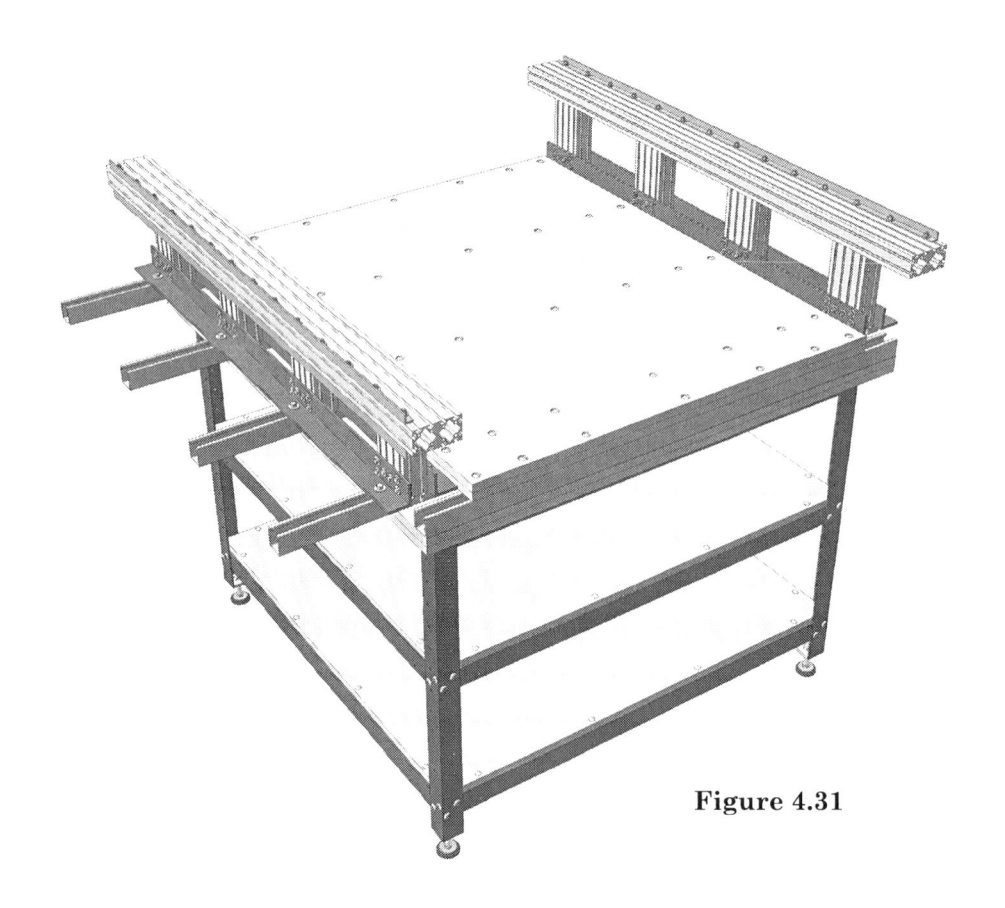

Figure 4.31

Chapter 5

Y-carriage Construction

The KRMx01's carriage system is what sets it apart from other DIY CNC routers. Each carriage is 100% steel, and fully adjustable. The KRMx01 CNC also utilizes dual ACME nuts on each carriage to reduce wear and increase accuracy.

The Y axis consists of two such carriages which you are going to build in this chapter.

Tools Needed For This Chapter

- 2, 7/16" Wrench's or sockets
- 2, 9/16" Wrenches
- Drill press
- 3/8" Drill bit
- 5/16" Drill bit
- 1/8" Drill bit
- 13/64" Drill bit
- Reciprocating saw
- 1/4" Tap

Tap kits are available at most home centers. These kits include the drill bit, tap and handle. You can also purchase individual taps and bits.

Components Needed For This Chapter

- 24, 3/8" Washers (see text)
- 8, 3/8" Split lock washers
- 16, 3/8-16 Hex nuts
- 8, 3/8-16 x 1-1/2" Hex bolts
- 24, 1/4-20 x 1" Hex bolts
- 32, 1/4-20 Hex nuts
- 56, 1/4" Washers
- 32, 1/4" Split lock washers
- 8, 1/4-20 x 1-1/2" Hex bolts
- 4, 1/2-10 ACME 5 Start nut (CNC Router Parts #CRP109-00)
- 2, 2" x 2" x 3/16" X 24" Steel angle
- 1, 1" x 1" x 1/8" x 36" Steel angle
- 8, V groove bearings (VXB #Kit8407)
- 16, 3/16" Washers.

Chapter Estimates
Cost: $175
Time: Long Weekend

Prerequisites

Before starting this chapter cut the 2, 2" x 2" x 3/16" x 24" pieces of steel angle in half. You will need to use the reciprocating saw with a metal cutting blade. These will become your main carriage components.

Cut the 36" piece of 1" x 1" angle into four pieces. They should be 6-7/8" each. These will form the basis for your carriage supports.

The best way to cut the steel angle is to clamp a small piece of scrap along your cut line, as shown in Figure 5.1.

For the best results, use a reciprocating saw to cut one side of the angle. Then move your guide block to the other side and cut.

Once the steel angle is cut, use a rotary grinder or file to clean up all the edges.

Figure 5.1

Step 1 - Create Initial Cuts in Main Carriage Components

The main carriage components are all very similar. In this step you are going to drill the holes and cut the slots that are common to all four. The Carriage Components are symmetrical so the cuts on the left side are the same as those on the right side.

Start by marking the drill holes on one side of the angle with a permanent marker, then dent them with a steel punch. Use drill press and a 1/8" bit to drill pilot holes into the positions shown in Figure 5.2.

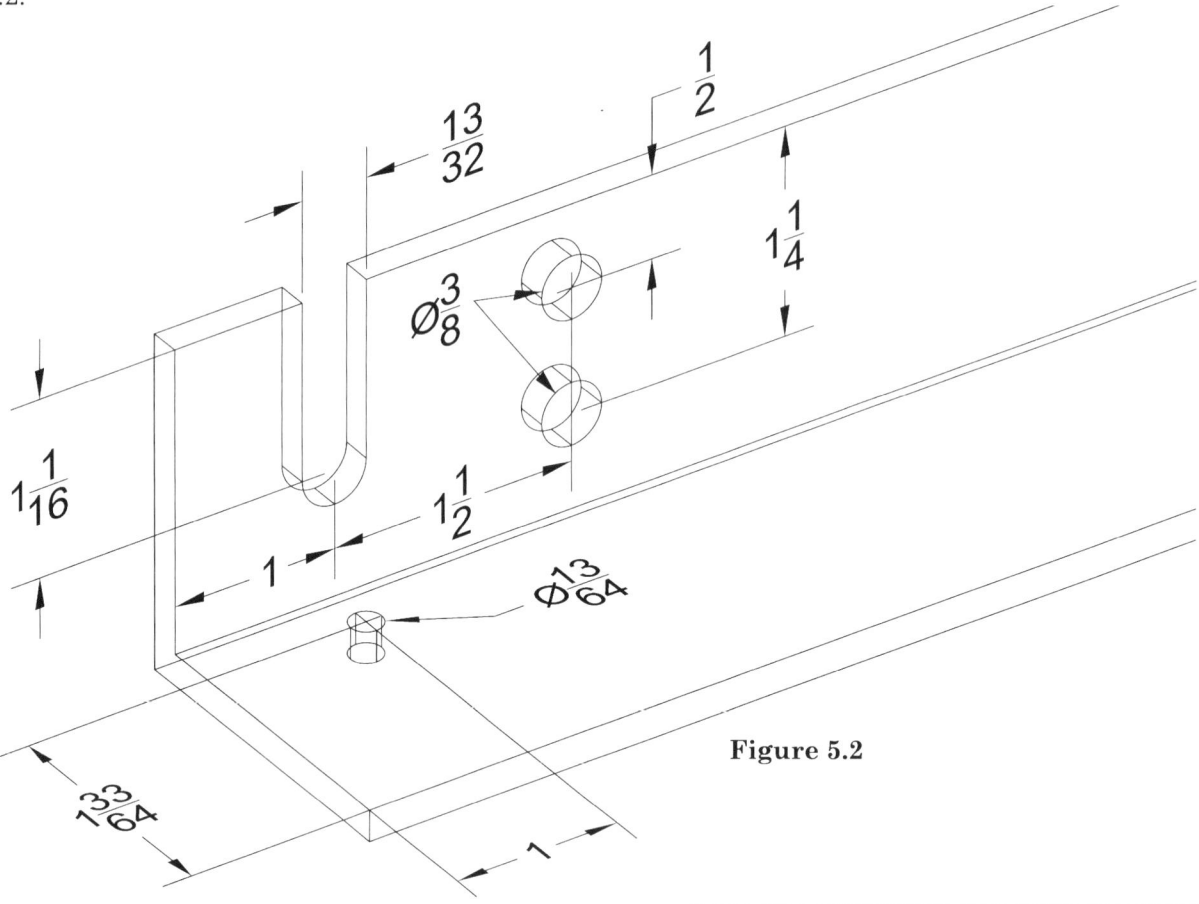

Figure 5.2

Once the three pilot holes are drilled, drill the holes again with the full size bits. Two of the holes are 3/8". The other is 13/64". The 13/64" hole is actually a #7 drill bit and is used when we want to tap a hole to 1/4". It is extremely important that the 13/64" hole is straight. Once the three holes on one side are drilled, repeat the process on the other side.

To cut the slots, first drill a 3/8" hole, then use a straight edge to mark the cut lines, as shown in Figure 5.3. Once marked, use the reciprocating saw to cut along the lines.

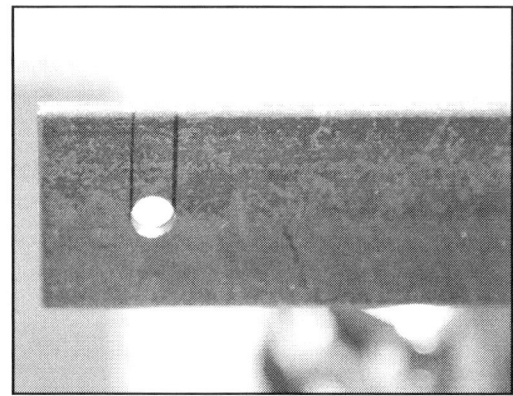

Figure 5.3

66   *Chapter 5*   Y-carriage Construction

When your holes have been drilled and your slots cut, the piece should look like the one shown in Figure 5.4. Repeat the process to produce four identical components.

Be sure to clean up your cuts and drill holes. Use a rotary grinder or file to clean up the cuts and a 1/2" drill bit to ream the holes. It's important that all the burs are removed.

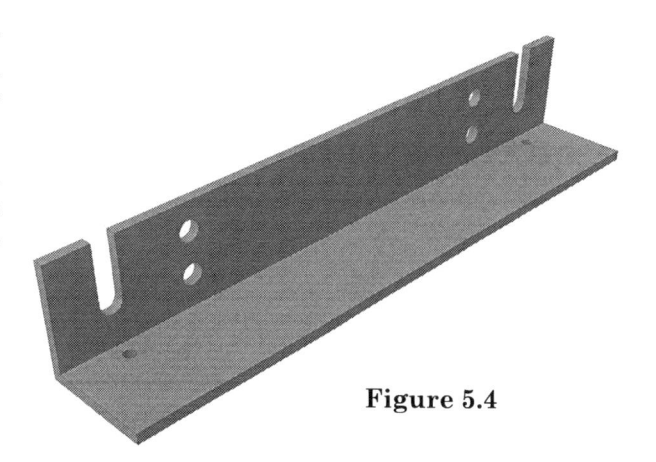

Figure 5.4

Step 2 - Finish the Top Left Carriage Angle

Take one of the common carriage components completed in Step 1 and drill the four holes shown in Figure 5.5. As before, mark, dent, and drill pilot holes before drilling the actual sizes shown. Use a piece of masking tape to mark this piece as "Top Left Carriage".

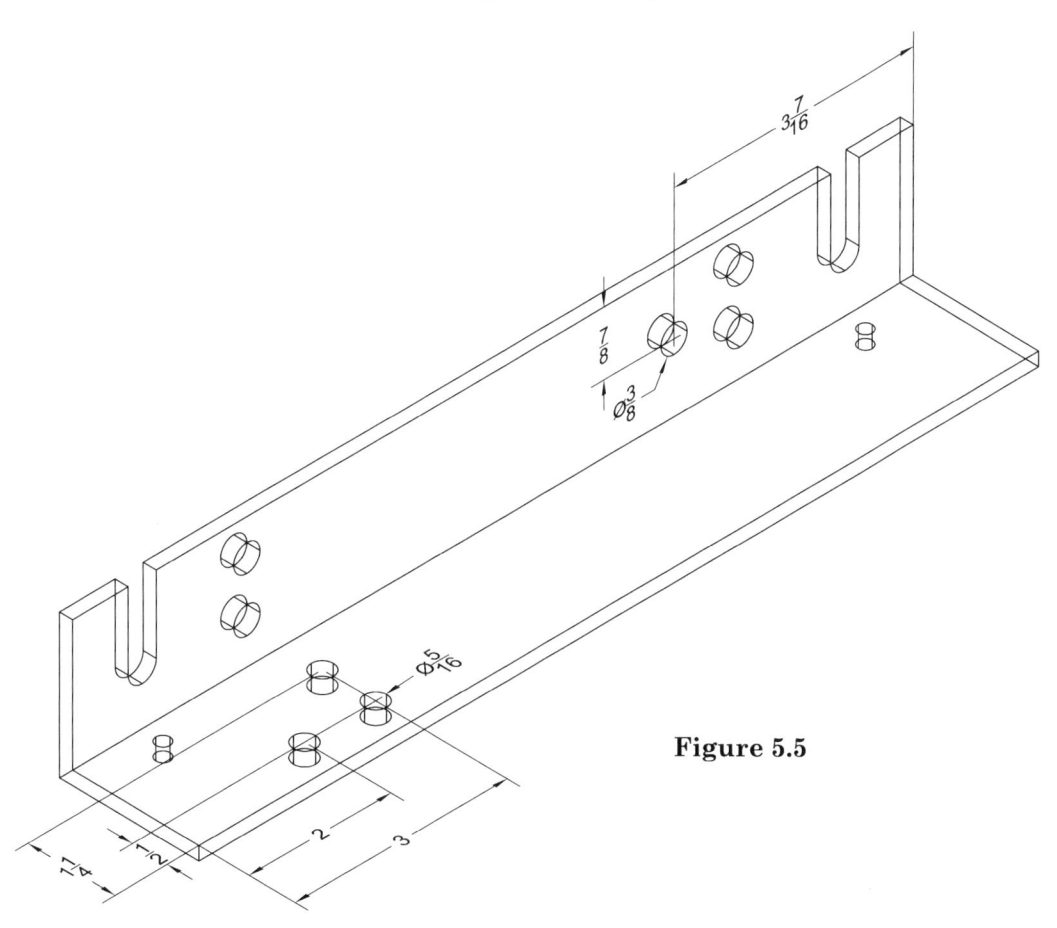

Figure 5.5

Building the KRMx01 CNC **67**

Step 3 - Finish the Top Right Carriage Angle

Take one of the common carriage components completed in Step 1 and drill the three holes shown in Figure 5.6. As before, mark, dent, and drill pilot holes before drilling the actual sizes shown. Use a piece of masking tape and mark this piece as "Top Right Carriage".

Use masking tape and mark the two remain carriage components as "Bottom Carriage".

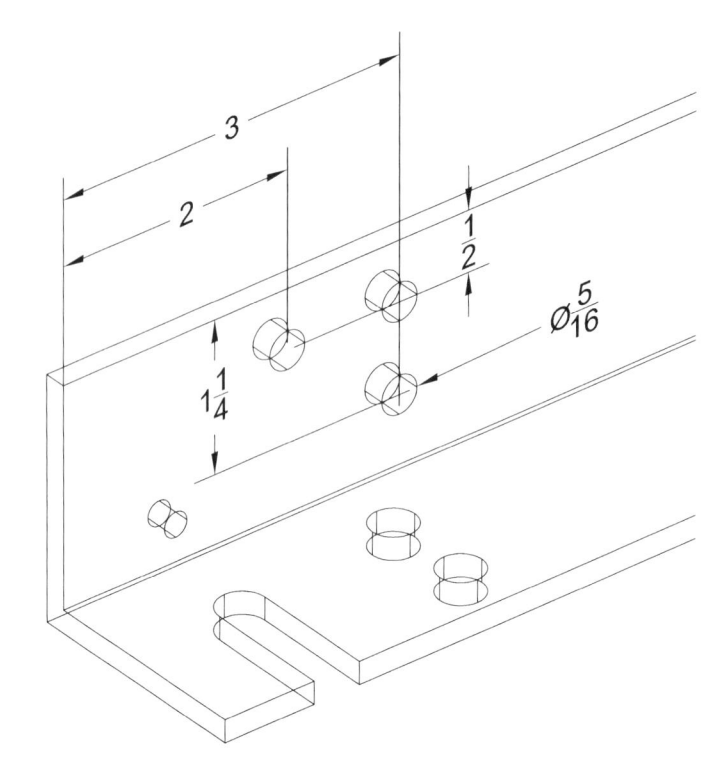

Figure 5.6

Step 4 - Drill the Holes in the Carriage Supports

Take one of the four 6-7/8" carriage support pieces and mark and drill the six holes shown in Figure 5.7. They should all be 5/16" in diameter.

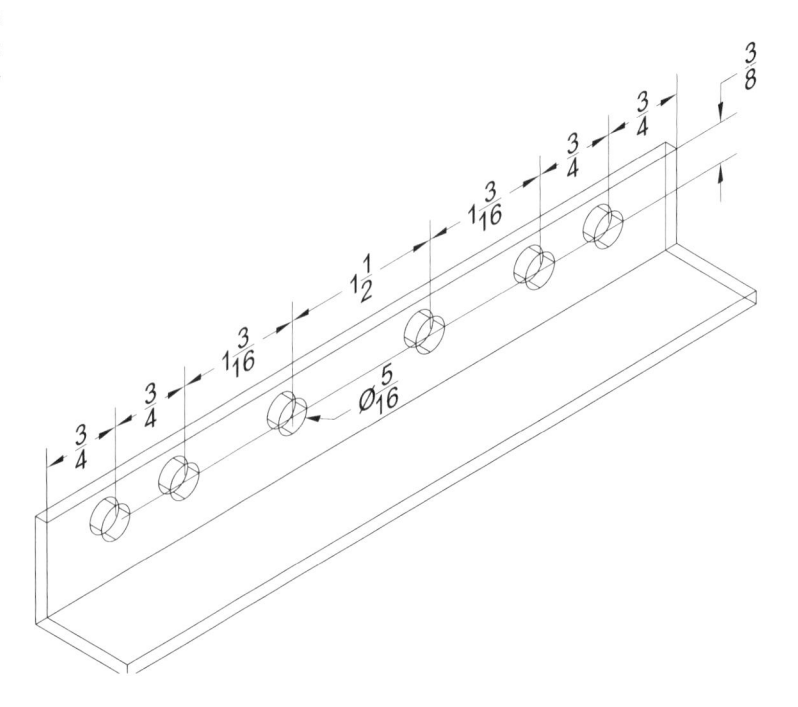

Figure 5.7

68   *Chapter 5*   Y-carriage Construction

The completed support should look like the one shown in Figure 5.8.

Repeat on the remaining three carriage supports.

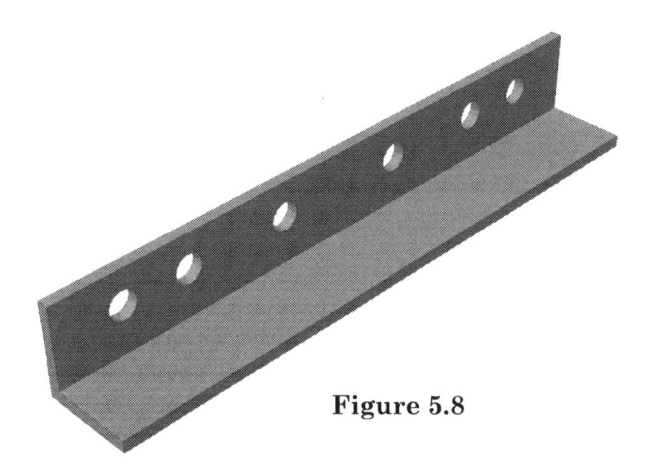

Figure 5.8

Step 6 - Tap the Holes in Main Carriage Components

In the four components you created in Step 1, there are a total of eight, 13/64" holes. These holes hold the V-bearing adjustment bolts and need to be tapped with a 1/4" tap.

Add a little oil to the hole and be sure to back out the tap frequently to clear the chips. It is important that the threads you are creating be as straight as possible, so keep the tap perpendicular to the hole, as shown in Figure 5.9.

Figure 5.9

Tip

To create perfectly straight threads, you can place the tap in your drill press. Then use your hand to turn the chuck. The drill press will keep the tap perpendicular to the hole. You still need to use oil and back out the tap to clear the chips.

Important: don't ever turn on the drill press when doing this operation. To be safe, unplug the tool or remove the safety key if your drill press has one.

Step 7 - Assemble the Carriage Frame

To assemble the frame you need to attach the supports to the main frame components, as shown in Figure 5.10. Start by inserting a 1/4" washer onto a 1/4" x 1" hex bolt. Then insert the bolt into the a carriage support and frame component. Slip on a washer, lock washer, and nut. Finger tighten.

Note that this is the right carriage, so use the carriage frame labeled "Top Right Carriage" and one of the "Bottom Carriage" components when assembling this frame.

The main frame components should be 6-7/8" from outer edge to outer edge. The supports should be square to the frame components.

It is important that the support be flush with or below the top frame. If it sticks up, it could interfere with the X-beam. If you can't readjust the support, use a rotary grinder to trim the support to make it flush. Once you are happy with the frame structure, use a 7/16" wrench and socket to tighten all the bolts.

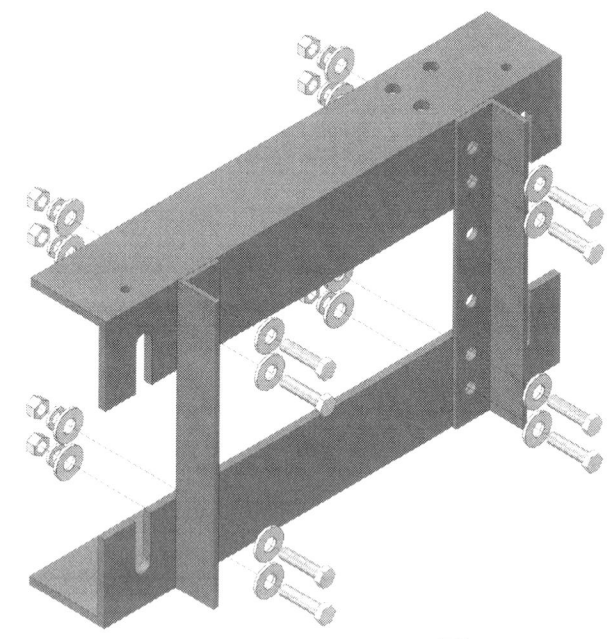

Figure 5.10

Repeat the process of building the left carriage, using the frame labeled "Top Left Carriage" and the remaining "Bottom Carriage".

Step 8 - Attach the Adjustment Bolts

As shown in Figure 5.12, assemble the bolts first by placing a 1/4-20 hex nut, 1/4 lock washer, and 1/4" washer onto a 1/4-20 x 1-1/2 hex bolt. Do this with all eight, adjustment bolts.

Next, screw the bolt into the threaded holes shown in Figure 5.13. Tighten the bolts, and using a digital caliper adjust the nut so that it is .20 from the underside of the bolt head, as shown in Figure 5.11. The goal here is to have the bolt protruding through the frame by a consistent amount. The V-bearing assembly will rest against this bolt.

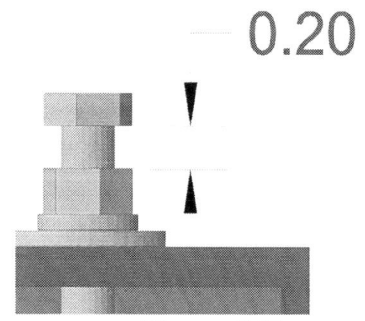

Figure 5.11

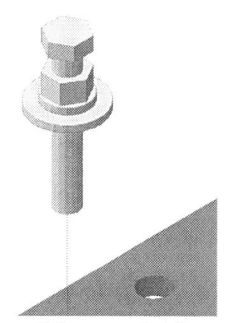

Figure 5.12

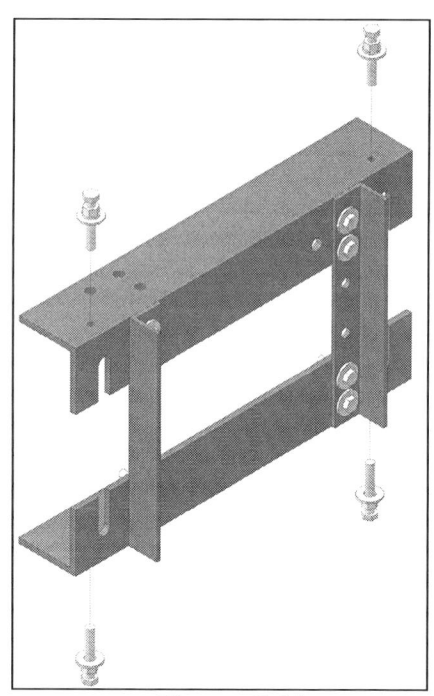

Figure 5.13

70　　Chapter 5　　Y-carriage Construction

Step 9 - Attach the ACME Nuts

Each carriage should have two ACME nuts attached. The nuts are attached to the carriage support, as shown in Figure 5.14, and utilize 2, 1/4-20 x 1" hex bolts on each nut.

Take a 1/4"-20 x 1" hex bolt and insert it through a 1/4" washer and the top of the ACME nut, and through the support bracket, as shown in Figure 5.14.

On the reverse side, slip on a 1/4" washer, lock washer, and hex nut. Finger tighten only.

You can use 1/4" washers on the ACME nuts as shown, but a 3/16" washer will fit a 1/4" bolt and does not distort the ACME nut when tightened. Use two 3/16" washers in place of the 1/4" washer.

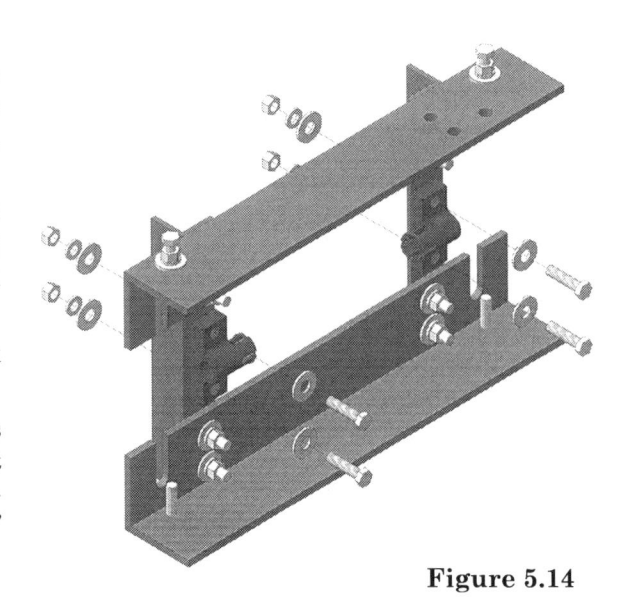

Figure 5.14

Step 10 - Attach the V-bearings

To install the V-bearings you must first attach the bearing to a 3/8-16 x 1-1/2" hex bolt. Place the bearing on the bolt, followed by a 3/8" lock washer and hex nut, as shown in Figure 5.17.

To attach to the carriage, add two 3/8" washers to the bolt/bearing assembly and insert into the slot on the carriage, as shown in Figure 5.15. Add a 3/8" washer and hex nut. Finger tighten only. The flat portion of the hex bolt on the bearing assembly should be pushed snugly up against the adjustment bolt, as shown in Figure 5.16.

Figure 5.15

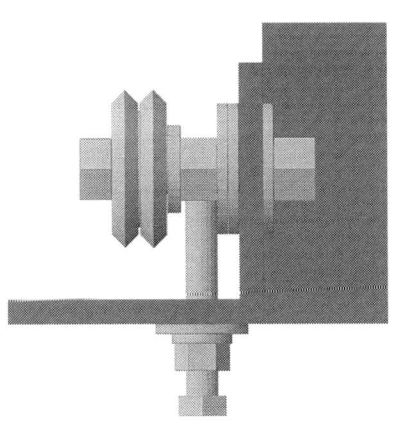

Figure 5.16

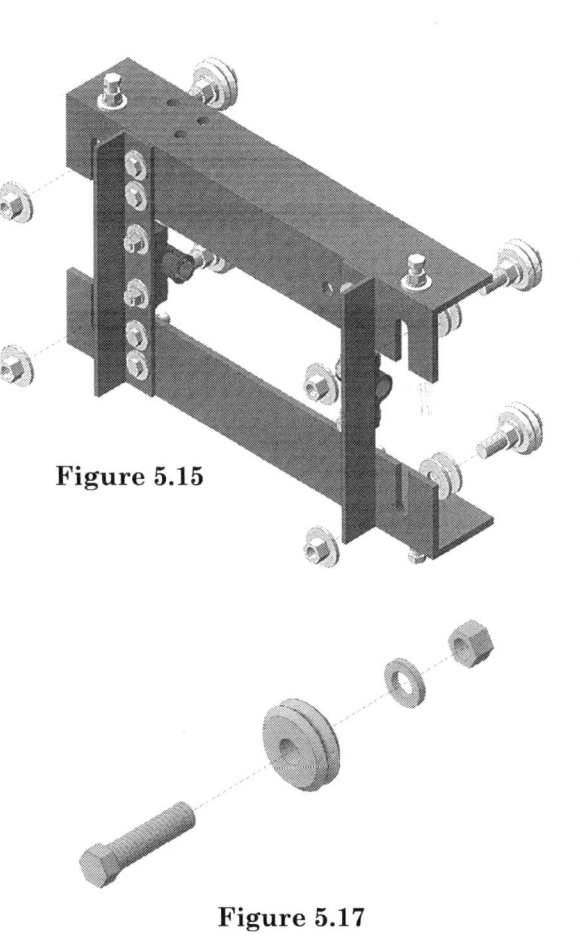

Figure 5.17

Building the KRMx01 CNC

The Y-carriage assemblies are now complete. They should look like the two carriages shown in Figure 5.18.

Important!

Before proceeding to the following steps, you need to condition the Y-rails as outlined in Chapter 1.

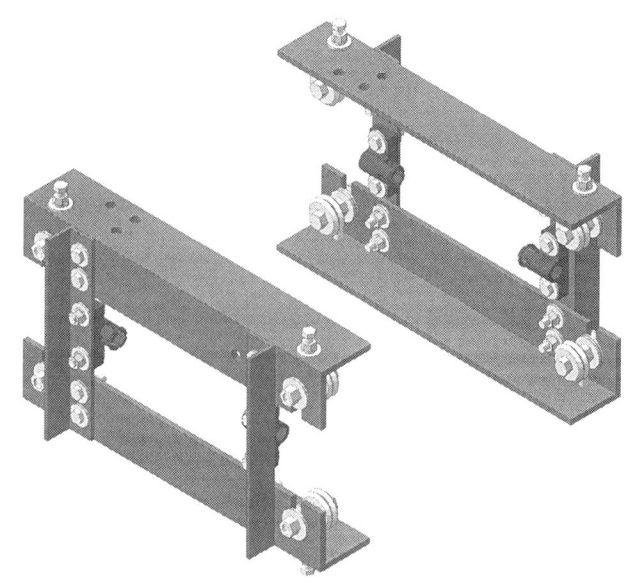

Figure 5.18

Step 11 - Prep the Y-carriages

Loosen the nuts on the two lower adjustment bolts, as shown in Figure 5.19. Back the adjustment bolts out about 1/8". Loosen the outside nut on the lower bearings and drop them down until they have contact with the adjustment bolts. Tighten all four of the bearing bolts.

Repeat on the other carriage. The goal here is to loosen the bearings enough so that they simply slip on to the Y-rails. You will tighten them later in the chapter.

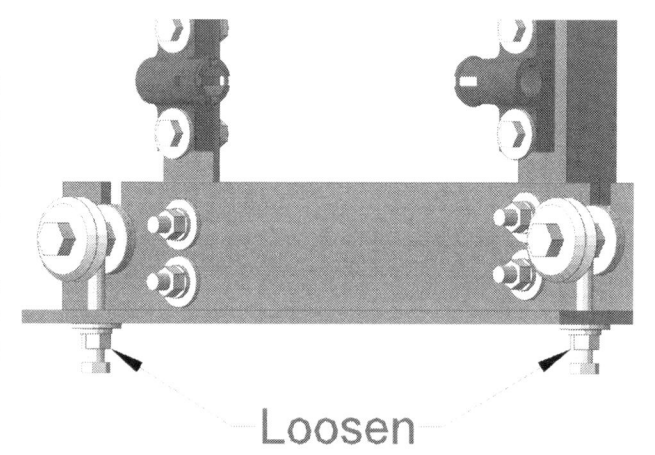

Figure 5.19

Step 12 - Attach the Y-carriages

Slip the right carriage onto the rails by lining up the V-groove on the bearing with the rail, as shown in Figure 5.20. If its too tight you may need to loosen and lower the lower bearings a little more.

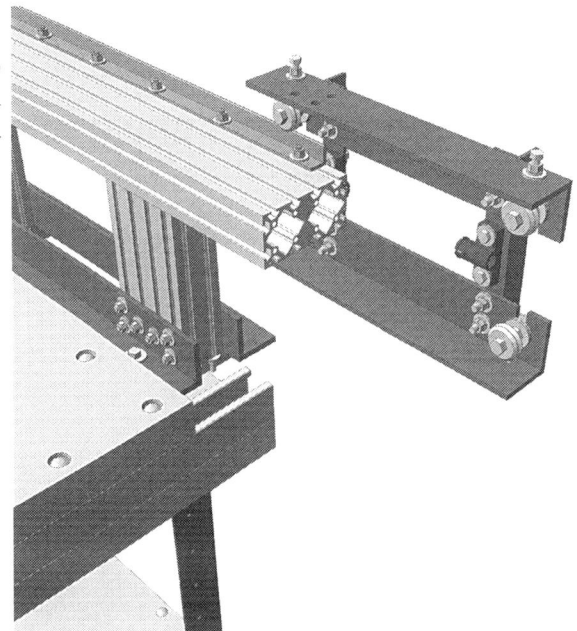

Figure 5.20

Step 13 - Adjust the Lower Bearings

Move the lower bearings up until they come into contact with the lower rail. Tighten the bearing nut on the lower bearings until the bearing is snug, but not tight. Adjust the lower adjustment bolts until they push the bearings against the rail. The goal here is to adjust the play out of the rail, but not so tight that the carriage does not slide smoothly.

Grab the front of the cariage and pull it up. If you feel play or there is any rattling, the lower bearing is too loose. Tighten the adjustment bolt about a quarter of a turn and re-test. If you tighten too much, you will have to back off the adjustment bolt and loosen the V-bearing nut and start all over with the process.

Repeat the process on the rear of the carriage then move to the other carriage. When you are happy with the carriages and they are sliding smoothly, the process is complete.

Figure 5.21

Building the KRMx01 CNC   **73**

Adjustments

As a starting point you should try to get the top of the carriages set to the same height both at the front of the carriage and the rear of the carriage.

The upper bearing adjustment bolts are used to adjust the height of the carriage. The lower bearing adjustment bolts are used to provide the tension on the carriage against the rails. When adjusting the upper adjustment bolts the lower bolts should be backed off first. Once the upper bolts are where you want them, you can then re-tension the lower bolts.

In most cases when adjusting the bearings you will need to loosen the bearing bolts. It is recommended you have your bearing bolts snug when tightening the adjustment bolts.

Figure 5.22

Chapter 6

X-beam

The KRMx01 CNC utilizes a gantry that has a very low center of gravity. This gives the CNC more rigidity. It also simplifies its construction greatly.

Tools Needed For This Chapter

- 2, 7/16' Wrenches
- Drill press
- 11/32" Drill bit
- 1/8 Drill bit

Components Needed For This Chapter

- 1 piece of 80/20 10 Series 2" x 4" X 56" T-slotted extrusion
- 2, 3/4" x 3/4" x 48, 1/8" Thick aluminum angle
- 30, 1/4-20 x 3/4" Carriage bolts
- 30, 1/4-20 Hex nuts
- 30, 1/4" Washers
- 30, 1/4" Split lock washers
- 4, 1/4-20 x 1" Carriage bolts
- 4, 1/4" Washers
- 4, 1/4" Split lock washers
- 4, 1/4-20 Hex nuts
- 2, 1/4-20 x 1-1/2" Carriage bolts

Chapter Estimates

Cost: $10
Time: Half day

Prerequisites

If you did not purchase the 80/20 kit, before starting this chapter, you need to make sure you have your 56" X-beam cut.

You will need 18, 1/4-20 x 3/4" bolts to complete this chapter. However, in the next chapter you will need an additional 12 hex bolts to attach the rails, so it may be advantageous to test fit the bolts now to ensure they fit into the T-slots.

If your local home center does not have 48" aluminum angle in stock you may have to purchase a longer piece and cut it down.

Important!

When purchasing your aluminum rail, be sure to check each piece for dents, bends, and gouges.

Step 1 - Prep X-beam for Assembly

Insert 16 of the 1/4-20 x 3/4" carriage bolts into the lower front T-slot of the X-beam, as shown in Figure 6.1. Insert and additional two bolts, one on each end, into the lower rear T-slot.

Figure 6.1

The three bolts on each end of the X-beam should be positioned, as shown in Figure 6.2. The front two are 1-3/4" and 2-1/2" from the ends. The rear bolt is 2-1/2" from the ends. This is only an approximation as you can shift them as needed when you insert the beam into the Y-carriages.

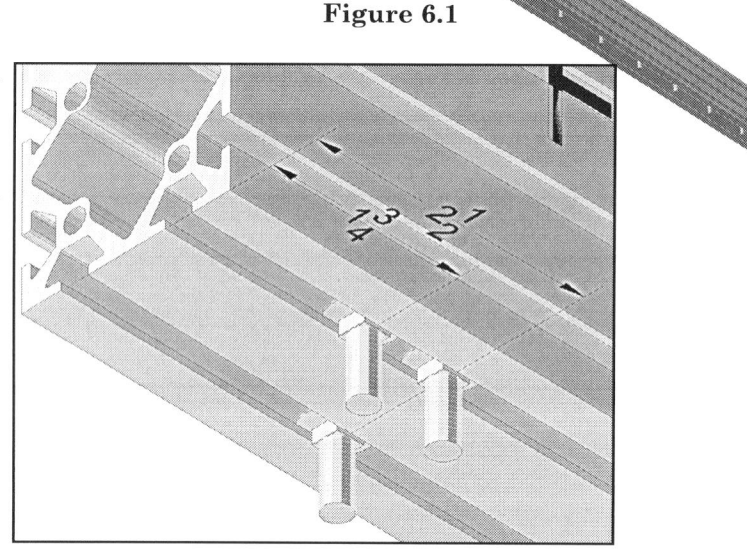

Figure 6.2

Step 2 - Insert the X-beam Into the Y-carriages

Slip the three bolts on each end of the X-beam into the three holes at the rear of each Y-carriage. Note that you want to adjust both ends so that you have the same amount overhanging. If your Y-beams are positioned properly, the overhang should be just a little over and inch, as shown in Figure 6.3

The actual overhang is not important, but it must be at least 1" or the motor mounts wont clear the Y-carriage supports later.

You need to add a 1/4" washer, 1/4" lock washer, and 1/4-20 hex nut to each of the bolts under the X-beam as shown. These are a very tight fit, so you will need an open ended 7/16" wrench to access the bolts. Snug the bolts only, you will need to square the X-beam with the Y-beam in the next step.

Note that some of the components have been left off the drawing for clarity only.

Figure 6.3

78   Chapter 6   X-beam

Step 3 - Square the X-beam

To square the X-beam to the Y-carriage you will need a square. You can use just about any square, but the larger the better. It is recommended you use a rafter square like the one shown in Figure 6.4.

Don't nit pick over this adjustment. Just get it close. Later you will need to square the actual router to the table so you will be fine tuning all adjustments.

Nudge the X-beam as necessary, then tighten the bolts.

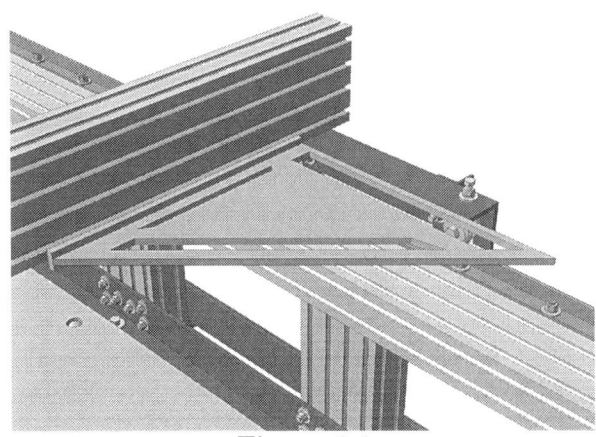

Figure 6.4

Step 4 - Layout X-rails

The rail holes are symmetrical. The six holes on the right side of the rail are exactly the same on the left. Mark both sides, as shown in Figure 6.5. The best way to mark the holes is with a fine tip permanent marker, then to dent with a center punch. The placement along the length is not critical. The distance from the edge *is* critical, and should be as close to 1/4" as possible.

All holes are 11/32", but use a 1/8" bit to drill pilot holes first. Drill the holes as you did with the Y-rails. Be sure to clean all burs.

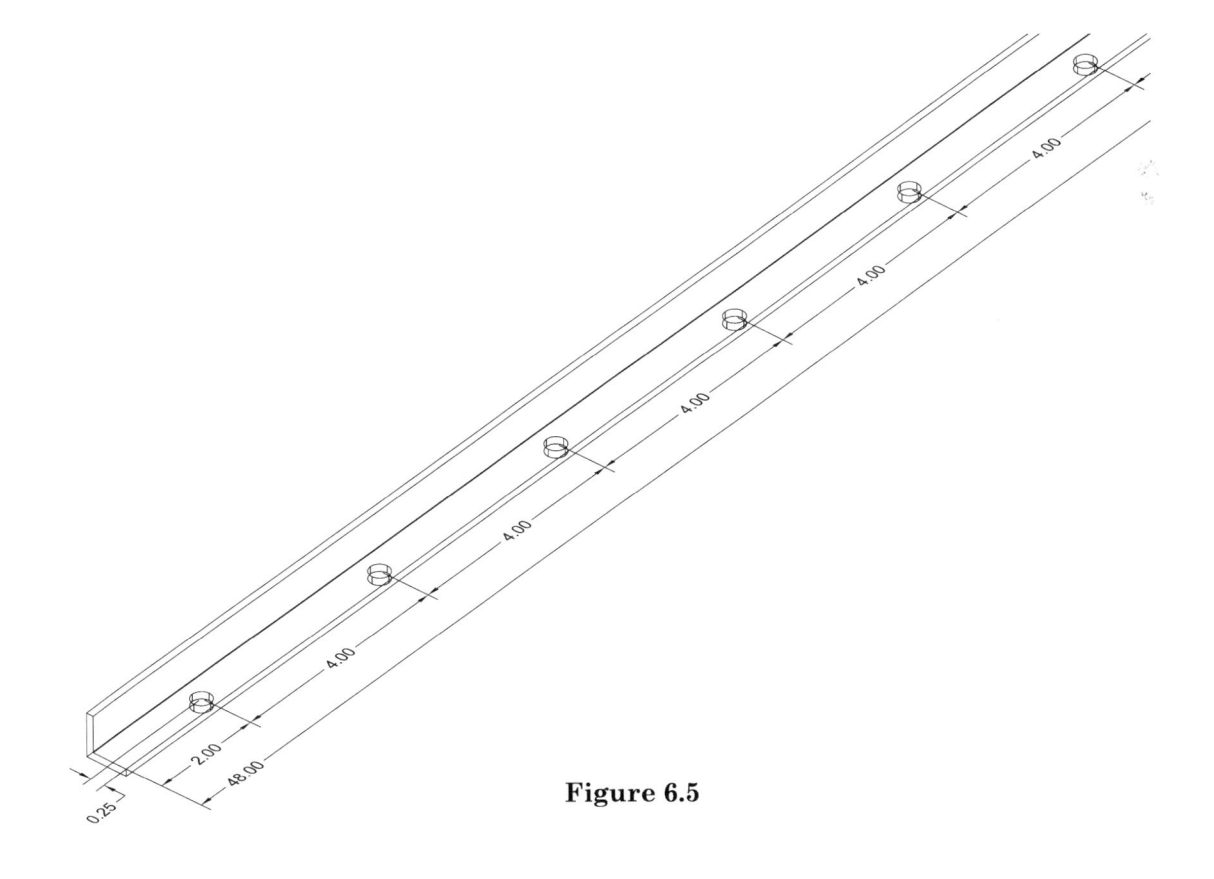

Figure 6.5

Building the KRMx01 CNC

Step 5 - Layout Mounting Bolts

Slip 14 of the 3/4" bolts into the slot on Y-beam, as shown in Figure 6.6. You can slip them in from either the side of the beam. If a bolt is too tight to slide in the slot, don't force it. Try twisting the bolt 90 degrees and inserting it. If it still does not fit, try another bolt.

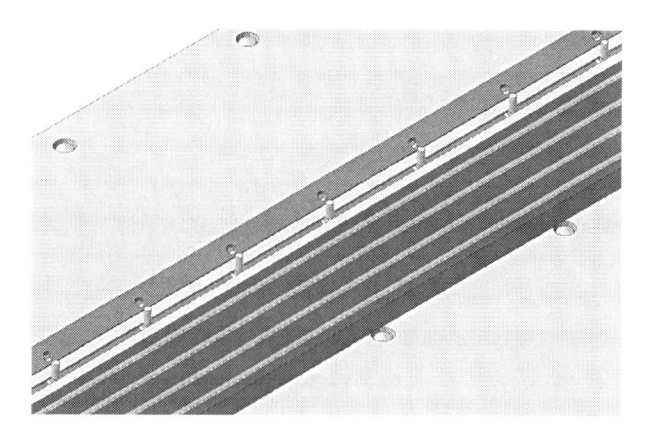

Figure 6.6

Step 6 - Attach Rails

Slip the rail over the bolts, as shown in Figure 6.7. Be sure the rail is 4" from the edges of the beam.

Once you have the bolts positioned for the top rail, proceed with positioning bolts for the bottom rail.

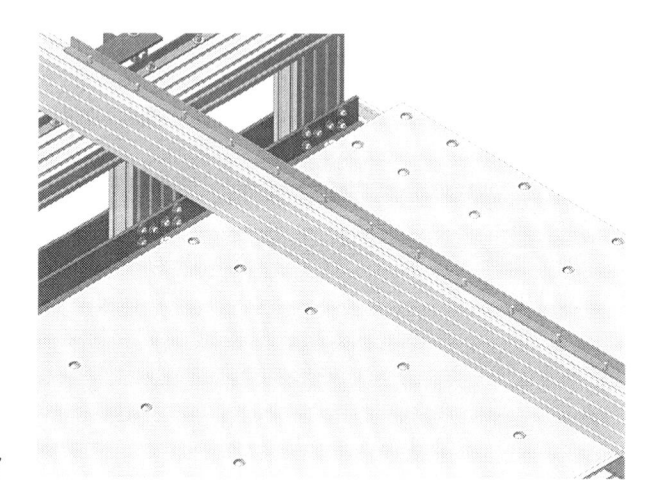

Figure 6.7

Place a 1/4" washer, 1/4" lock nut, and 1/4"-20 hex nut on the bolts, as shown in Figure 6.8. Only finger tighten the nuts. Once you have the top rail nice and snug, proceed with the rail mounted on the bottom of the beam.

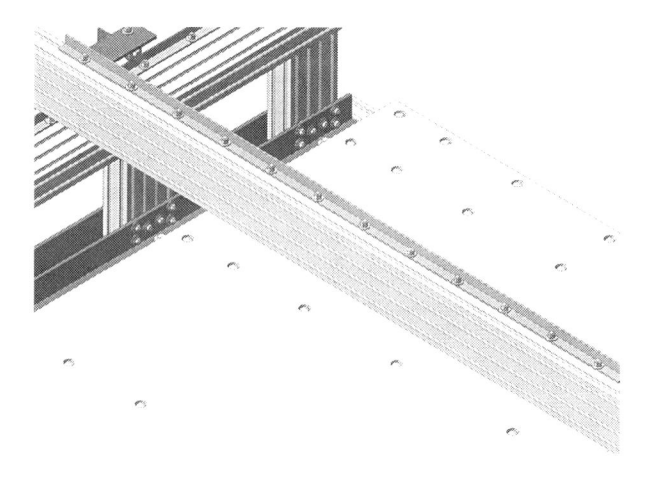

Figure 6.8

Step 7 - Align Rails

The best way to align the X-rails is to clamp some sort of straight edge to the beam. Figure 6.9 shows a piece of scrap steel angle being used. Clamp a straight edge to both ends and one to the middle. Make sure the nuts holding the Y-rail are loose enough that the X-rail can move.

Once clamped in place, make sure the X-rails is snug against the straight edge, and tighten the nuts on either end and in the middle. Make sure you get the nuts on the bottom rail as well. Once tight, move the clamps to positions between the nuts you just adjusted and repeat the procedure. The goal here is to work your way through each nut.

Figure 6.9

Adjustments

Your KRMx01 CNC is starting to take shape, but before moving forward be sure to condition the X-rails as outlined in Chapter 1. The rails should be coplanar. That is to say, they should both be flush with the edge of the X-beam.

The X-beam needs to be perpendicular to the table, and the front of the X-beam needs to be at a perfect 90 degree angle from the table. First you adjust the face. This is done by placing a framing square on the table and against the front face of the X-beam. Do this on both ends of the beam. If either side is off, raise or lower one end of the Y-carriage closest to where you are measuring. Note that changing one end will slightly affect the opposite end, so go back and forth several times.

Once the X-beam is square with the table, measure the distance between the bottom of the beam to the table. If the two ends of the beam are not the same you will need to raise or lower one of the Y-carriages. When adjusting the carriage make sure you make the exact same adjustment on the front and rear of the carriage.

The KRMx01 utilizes a dual drive system on the Y axis. This will allow you to tweak the X-beam so that it is square with your cutting surface. This is more important then having the X-beam square with the Y-beam. You still want them close, but once you add the homing switches, they will be used to control the motors so that the cuts you make are square.

Important!

Before proceeding insert two 1/4-20 x 1" carriage bolts into the top slot as shown in Figure 6.10. Add a 1/4" washer, lock washer and 1/4-20 hex nut to each bolt. These can be used later to add upgrades, such as homing or limit switches.

Then, insert a 1/4-20 x 1-1/2" carriage bolt into the top slot as shown in Figure 6.10. This will be used to attach the X brace upgrade later.

Add these bolts to both the left front and right front sides of the X-beam.

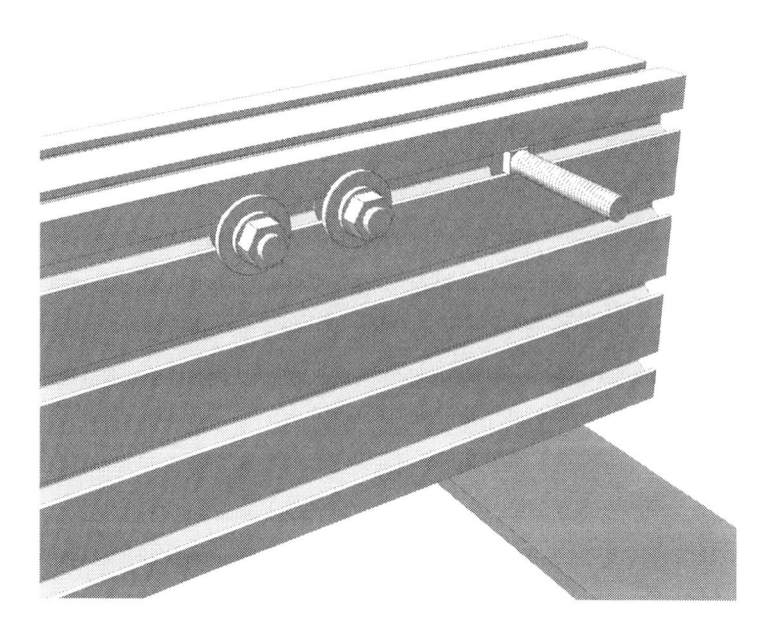

Figure 6.10

Chapter 7

X-carriage

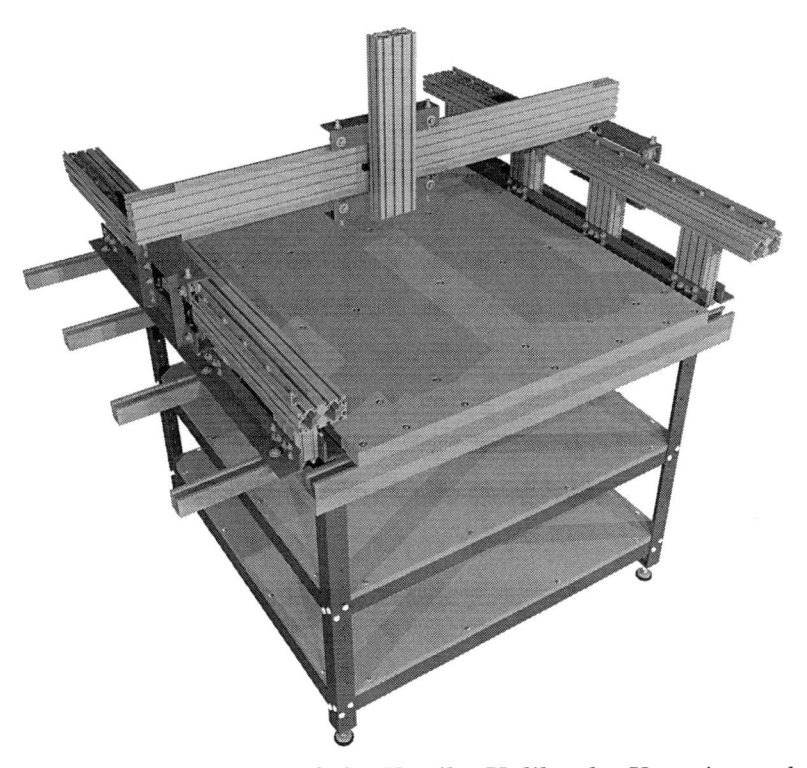

The X-carriage rides on top of the X-rails. Unlike the Y-carriages there are no support rails. The main X-carriage components are connected to a 17" piece of T-slot aluminium extrusion. This extrusion forms the Z-beam of your CNC.

Tools Needed For This Chapter

- 2, 7/16" Wrenches or sockets
- 2, 9/16" Wrenches (used to tighten V-bearing bolts)
- Drill press
- 3/8" Drill bit
- 1/8" Drill bit
- 13/64" Drill bit
- Reciprocating saw
- 1/4" Tap

Components Needed For This Chapter

- 1, 17" piece of 80/20 extrusion (previously purchased)
- 8, 1/4-20 x 3/4" Carriage bolts
- 4, 1/4-20 x 1" Carriage bolts
- 4, 1/4-20 x 1-1/2" Hex bolts
- 16, 1/4-20 Hex nuts
- 16, 1/4" Washers
- 16, 1/4" Split lock washers
- 2, 1/2-10 ACME 5 start nut (CNC Router Parts #CRP109-00)
- 2, 2" x 2" x 3/16" X 12" Steel angle
- 4, V Groove bearings (VXB #Kit8407)
- 8, 3/16" Washers
- 2, 3/4" x 3/4" x 1/8" x 15-1/2" Aluminum angle (cut form scrap, see text)
- 24, 3/8" Washers (see text)
- 4, 3/8" Split lock washers
- 8, 3/8-16 Hex nuts
- 4, 3/8-16 x 1-1/2" Hex bolts

Chapter Estimates

Cost: $90
Time: Weekend

Prerequisites

Before starting this chapter, cut the 2" x 2" x 3/16" x 24" pieces of steel angle in half. You will need to use the reciprocating saw with a metal cutting blade. These will become your X-carriage components.

Your 17" piece of 80/20 extrusion should have already been cut.

You will need to have two pieces of 3/4" x 3/4" x 1/8" x 15-1/2" Aluminum angle. This can be cut from the scrap end of the Y-rails you cut earlier.

Step 1 - Create Initial Cuts in X-carriage Components

The upper and lower carriage components are identical.

Start by marking the drill holes on one side of the angle with a permanent marker, then dent them with a steel punch. Use a drill press and an 1/8" bit to drill pilot holes into the positions shown in Figure 7.1.

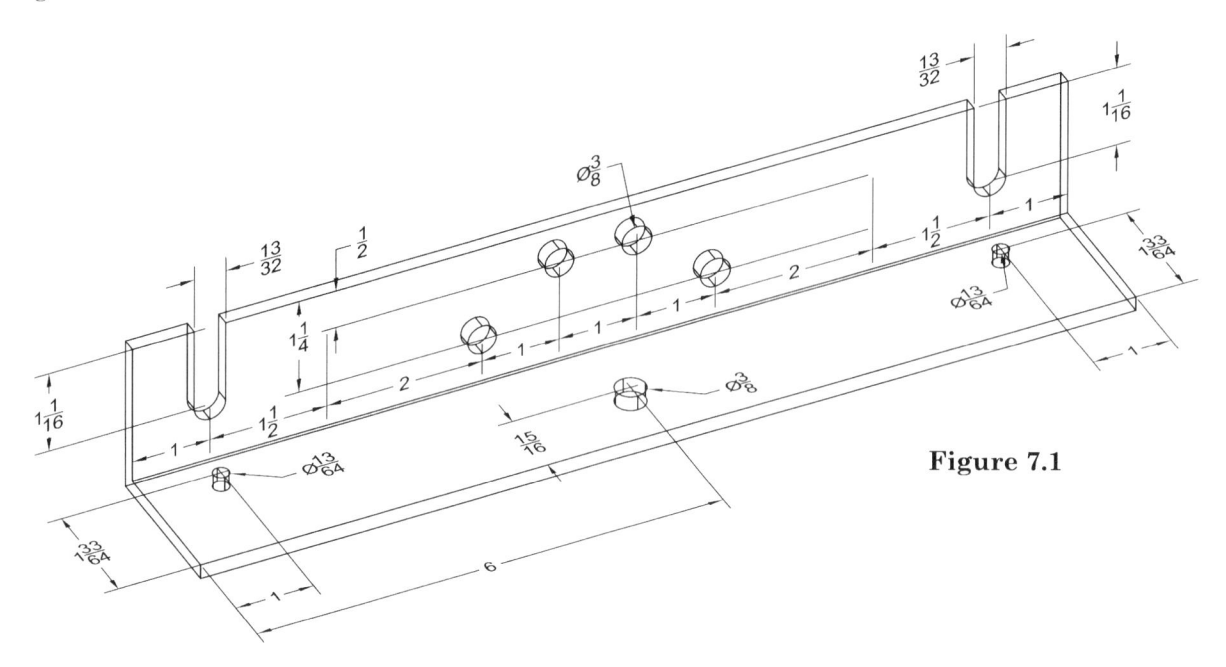

Figure 7.1

As with the Y-carriage, all the holes should be 3/8" except for the two small holes on the end marked 13/64". For those, use a #7 drill bit (13/64"). It is extremely important that the 13/64" hole is straight.

To cut the slots, first drill a 3/8" hole, then use a straight edge to mark the cut lines, as shown in Figure 7.2. Once marked, use the reciprocating saw to cut along the lines.

You probably have noticed that the X-carriage is similar to the Y-carriage. They are actually identical, save for the holes in the center. More importantly, you only need two components for the X-carriage.

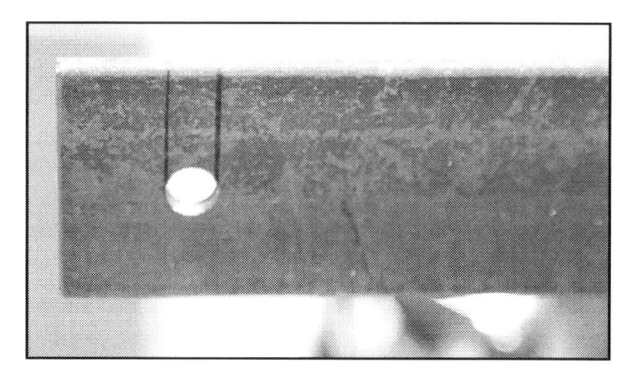

Figure 7.2

When your holes have been drilled and your slots have been cut, the piece should look the one shown in Figure 7.3. Repeat the process to produce the other carriage component.

Be sure to clean up your cuts and drill holes. Use a rotary grinder or file to clean up the cuts and a 1/2" drill bit to ream the holes. It's important that all the burs are removed.

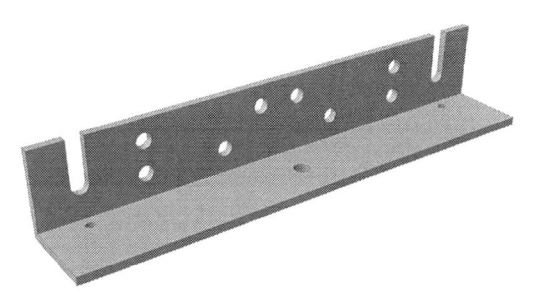

Figure 7.3

Step 2 - Tap the Holes in Y-carriage Components

In the two components you created in Step 1, there are a total of eight, 13/64" holes. These holes hold the V-bearing adjustment bolts and need to be tapped with a 1/4" Tap.

Just like you did with the Y-carriage, add a little oil to the hole and be sure to back out the tap frequently to clear the chips. It is important that the threads you are creating be as straight as possible as shown in Figure 7.4.

Figure 7.4

Step 3 - Insert Mounting Bolts

Insert four, 1/4-20 x 3/4" carriage bolts into the 17" extrusion, followed by four, 1/4-20 x 1" carriage bolts, and finally four more, 1/4-20 x 3/4" carriage bolts as shown in Figure 7.5. Figure 7.6 shows the bolt positions from the bottom of the extrusion. This is only a rough guide, as you will set the exact positions in the steps that follow.

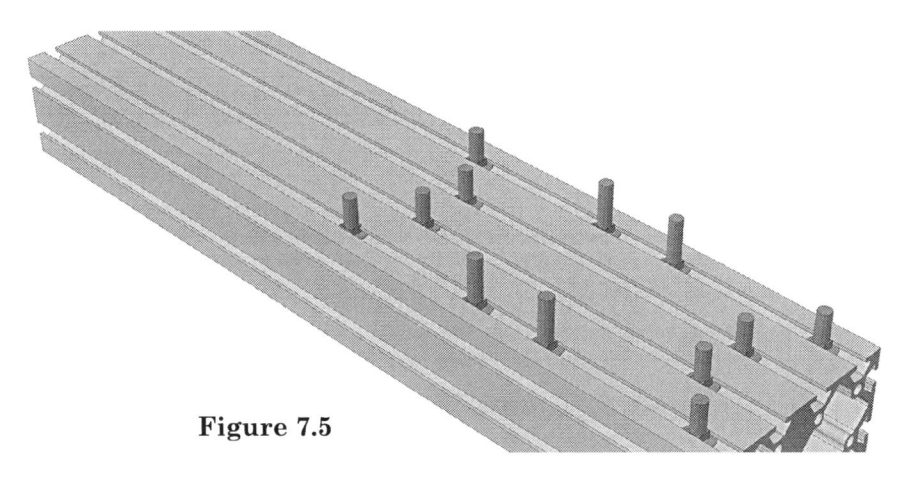

Figure 7.5

Building the KRMx01 CNC **87**

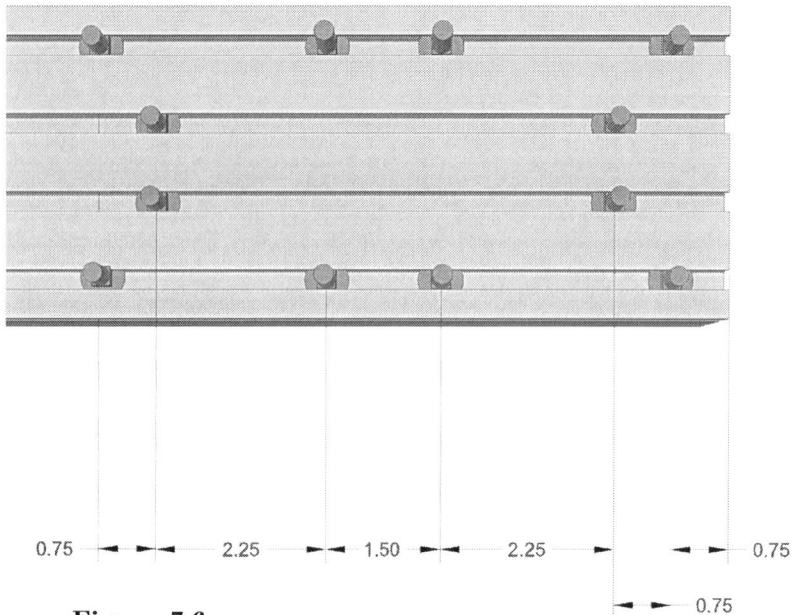

Figure 7.6

Step 4 - Attach the Carriage Components

Place the two carriages components over the bolts, then add a 1/4" washer, 1/4" split lock washer, and a hex nut, as shown in Figure 7.7. Finger tighten only. They should be 9" apart from outside edge to outside edge. They should also be square with the extrusion. Tighten once you have them in the proper position.

Place the two ACME nuts over the 1" bolts, then add two, 3/16" washers, a 1/4" split lock washer, and a hex nut as shown in Figure 7.8. Finger tighten only. The edge of the lead nut should be roughly 1-1/2" from the carriage component as shown. In a pinch you can use 1/4" washers on the ACME nuts, but a 3/16" washer will also fit a 1/4" bolt and does not distort the nut when tightened.

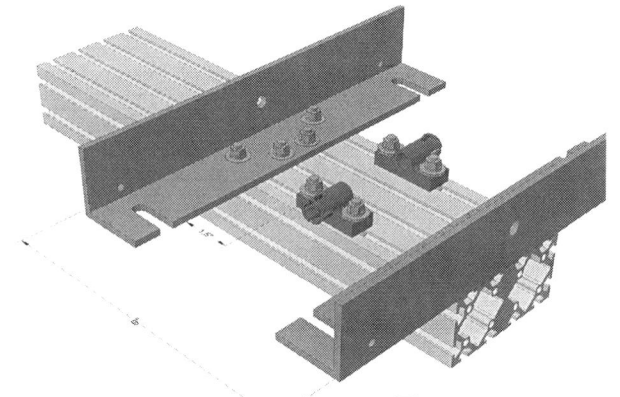

Figure 7.7

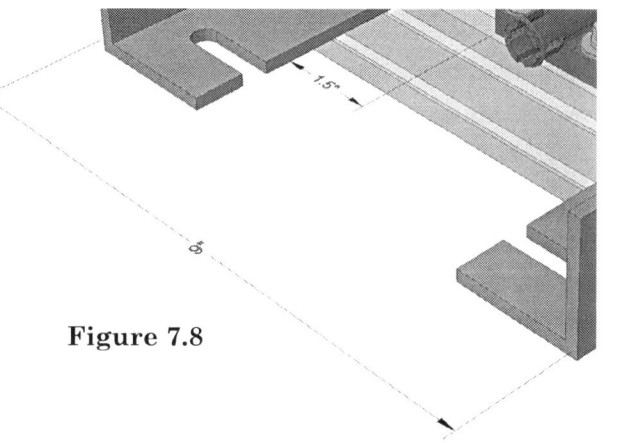

Figure 7.8

Step 5 - Adjustment Bolts and V-bearings

Assemble the adjustment bolts first by placing a 1/4-20 hex nut, 1/4 lock washer, and 1/4" washer onto a 1/4-20 x 1-1/2 hex bolt. Do this with all four adjustment bolts.

Next, screw the bolt into the threaded holes shown in Figure 7.10. Tighten the bolts, and using a digital caliper, adjust the nut so that it is .20 from the underside of the bolt head. The goal here is to have the bolt protruding through the frame by a consistent amount. The V-bearing assembly will rest against this bolt.

To install the V-bearings you must first attach the bearing to a 3/8-16 x 1-1/2" hex bolt. Place the bearing on the bolt, followed by a 3/8" lock washer and hex nut, as shown in Figure 7.11.

To attach to the carriage add two 3/8" washers to the bolt/bearing assembly and insert into the slot on the carriage as shown in Figure 7.9. Add a 3/8" washer and hex nut. Finger tighten only. The flat portion of the hex bolt on bearing assembly should be pushed snugly up against the adjustment bolt.

Figure 7.9

Figure 7.10

Figure 7.11

Step 6 - Attach X-carriage to X-rails

To attach the X-carriage to the X-rails you need to back out the lower adjustment bolts. Loosen the lower V-bearing nut and lower it about 1/2" or so. Tilt the X-carriage and set the top V-bearings on the X-rails as shown in Figure 7.12. Slide the lower V-bearings up until they come into contact with the lower X-rails. Tighten the V-bearing nut until it's snug, but not tight. You want the nut tight enough to hold the rail in place, but loose enough to allow the adjustment bolt to move the bearing.

Tighten the adjustment bolt until it comes into contact with the V-bearing.

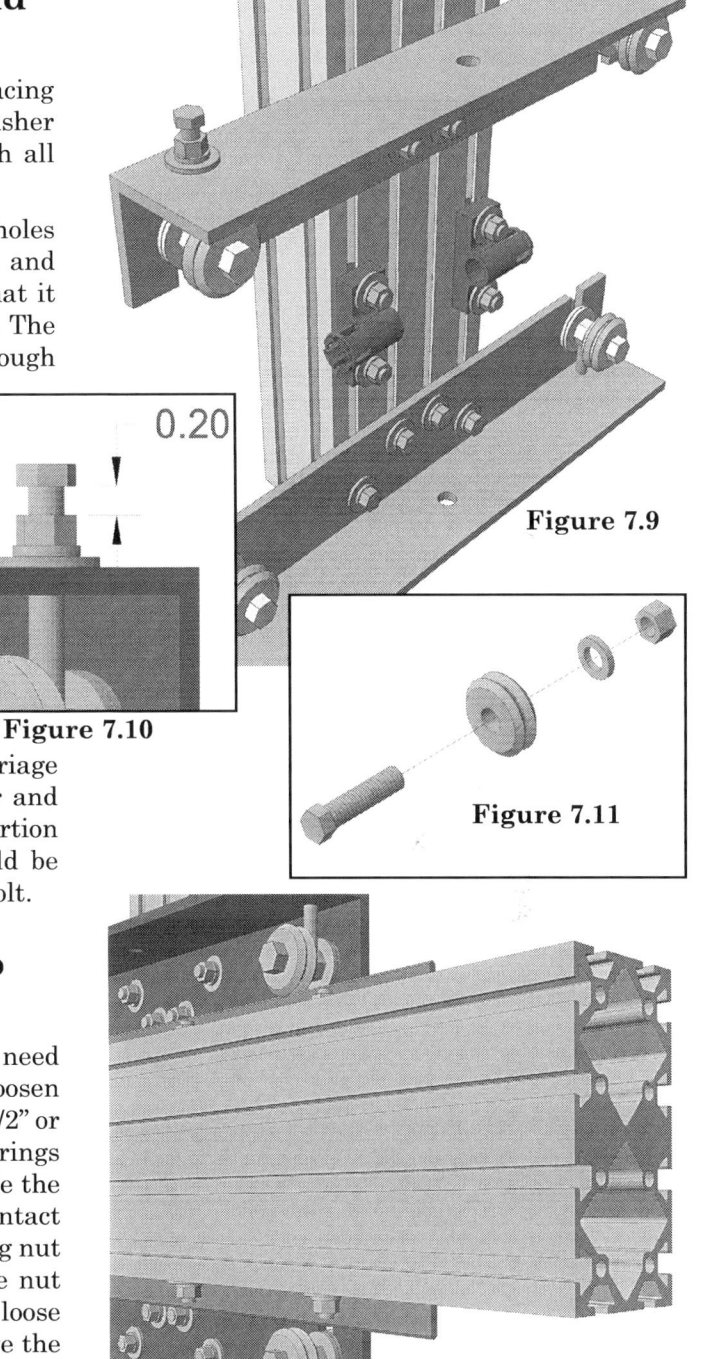

Figure 7.12

Building the KRMx01 CNC   **89**

Step 7 - Layout the Z-rails

The Z-rail holes are not symmetrical, so they need to be marked as shown in Figure 7.13. The best way to mark the holes is with a fine tip permanent marker, then to dent with a steel punch. The placement along the length is not critical. The distance from the edge *is* critical and should be as close to 1/4" as possible.

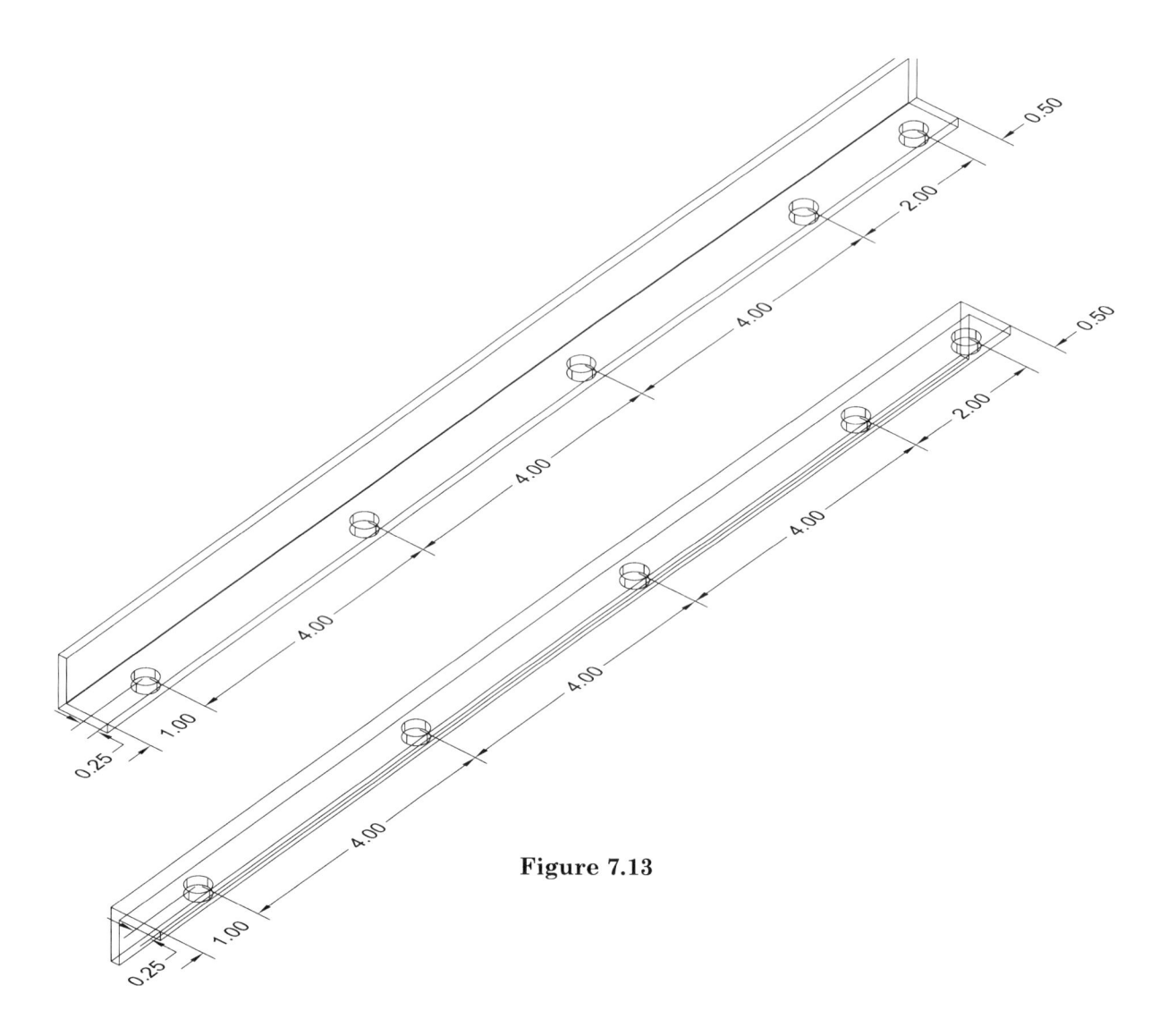

Figure 7.13

Step 8 - Drill the Z-rails

Use a drill press with a fence to drill the holes in your aluminum angle. It is important that all the holes be the same distance from the outer edge.

Use a 1/8" drill bit to drill pilot holes, then drill the final hole diameters with a 11/32" drill bit.

> **Tip**
> Take a scrap piece of MDF or plywood to create a table surface for your stock as shown in Figure 7.14. This will keep the pressure of the drill press from deforming the rail.

Figure 7.14

Step 9 - Attach Z-rails

The Z-rails are installed flush with the bottom of the Z-beam, as shown in Figure 7.15. The end of the angle with the hole 1/2" from the end is on the bottom. Attach the nuts to the bolts and finger tighten. Be sure the flat edge of he Z-rail is flush with the front of the beam.

> **Tip**
> It can be difficult to attach the Z-rails with the Z-beam in a horizontal position as shown in Figure 7.15. Feel free to remove the X-carriage from the X-rails to make it easier to attach the Z-rails.

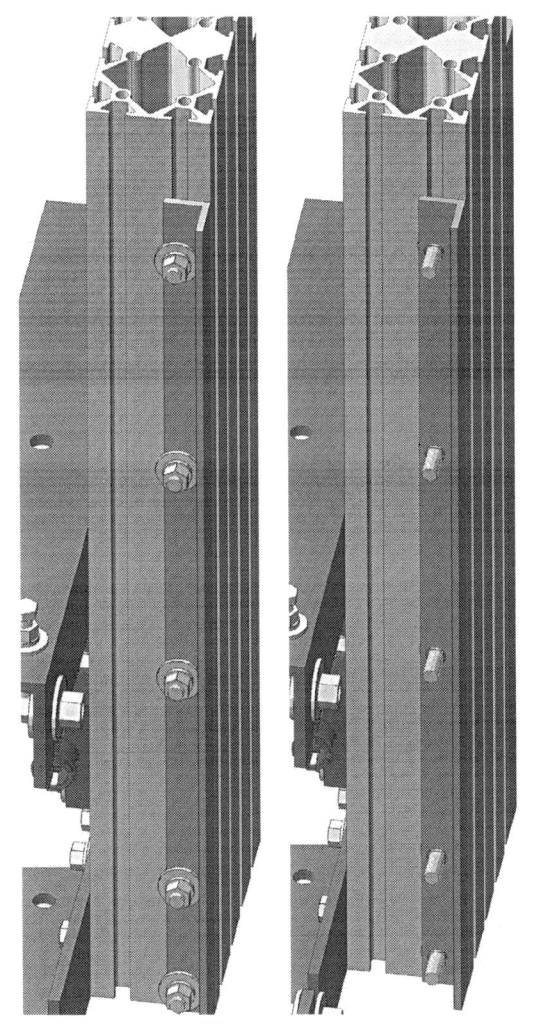

Figure 7.15

Building the KRMx01 CNC

Adjustments

Before moving forward, condition the Z-rails as outlined in Chapter 1.

The two Z-rails must be absolutely perpendicular to the table top. That is to say, they must be 90 degrees to the table on the sides and the front.

The sides are easy to adjust, you just loosen the eight bolts holding the X-carriage components to the Z-beam. Leave them tight enough that the beam is firmly in place, but loose enough so that you can nudge or tap the Z-beam into position.

It is important that before proceeding you are happy with the adjustments of the X-beam. Any adjustments to the Y-carriages can affect the Z-rails.

To adjust a Z-rail, loosen all the nuts on the rail. The bottom-most nut should be snug enough to keep the rail from sliding off the Z-beam. Move the Z-carriage to one side of the table. Now place a framing square against the rail and table. Move the Z-rail against the square and finger tighten the top nut. Move the Z-carriage to the other end of the table, and check that it is square. If it is not, then your X-beam or X-rails needs to be rechecked. Once you are happy with the Z-rail position, tighten all of the nuts and recheck. Repeat the process on the other Z-rail.

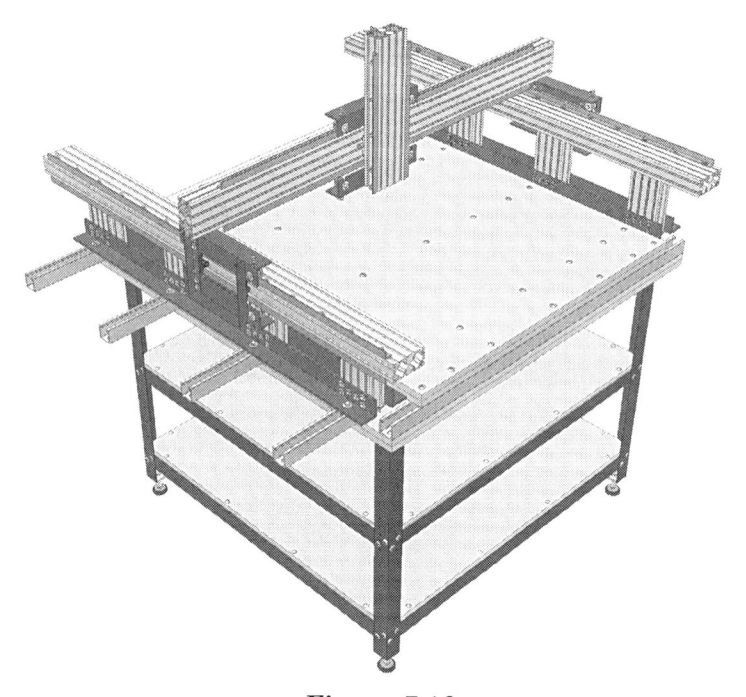

Figure 7.16

Tip

It is extremely important that the two Z-rails be at 90 degrees to the table consistently across the X-beam. This will determine how accurate your CNC cuts.

If you don't have enough play in the Z-rails to make the adjustments you need, widen the holes to 3/8"

Chapter 8

Z-carriage

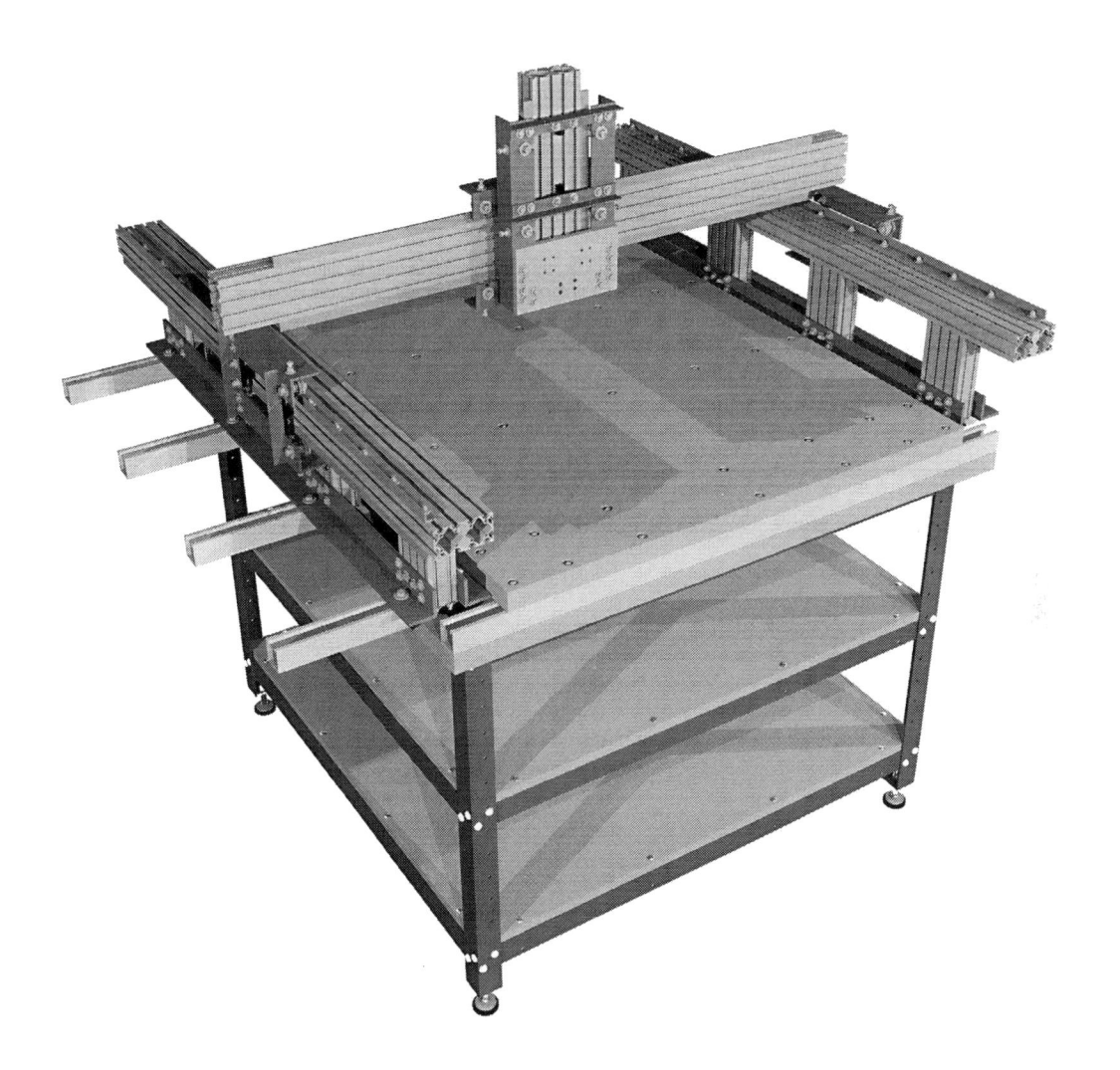

The Z-carriage rides on the Z-rails; it holds the Z-plate, which is what holds the router mount. The Z-plate will allow you to attach a K2CNC router mount and the router of your choice.

Tools Needed For This Chapter

- 2, 7/16" Wrenches or sockets
- 2, 9/16" Wrenches (used to tighten V-bearing bolts)
- Drill press
- 1/8", 3/8", 13/64", 5/16" Drill bits
- Reciprocating saw
- 1/4" Tap
- Rotary grinder with cutting wheel
- Pliers

Components Needed For This Chapter

- 2, 1" x 1" x 1/8" x 8-7/8" Steel angle
- 2, 2" x 2" x 1/8" x 14" Steel angle
- 1, 1/4-20 x 2" Carriage bolt
- 8, 1/4-20 x 3/4" Hex bolts
- 16, 1/4-20 x 1-1/2" Hex bolts
- 4, 1/4-20 x 1" Hex bolts
- 29, 1/4-20 Hex nuts
- 49, 1/4" Washers
- 28 1/4" Split lock washers
- 2, 1/2-10 ACME 5 start nuts (CNC Router Parts #CRP109-00)
- 8, V-groove bearings (VXB #Kit8407)
- 8, 3/16" Washers
- 12, 3/8" Washers (see text)
- 4, 3/8" Split lock washers
- 8, 3/8-16 Hex nuts
- 4, 3/8-16 x 1-1/2" Hex bolts
- KRMx01 Z-plate

Chapter Estimates
Cost: $160
Time: One day

Prerequisites

Before starting this chapter, cut two 14" lengths out of a 2" x 2" x 1/8" x 36" piece of steel angle. You will need to use the reciprocating saw with a metal cutting blade. These will become your main Z-carriage components.

You will also need to cut a 1" x 1" x 1/8" x 24" piece of steel angle into two 8-7/8" pieces. These will be used to form the two Z-carriage supports.

You will also need to purchase a KRMx01 Z-plate from Kronos Robotics, part #KRMX01Z1. This Z-plate, shown in Figure 8,1, will allow you to connect the various K2CNC router mounts.

Purchase the Kronos Robotics Z-plate here:

http://www.kronosrobotics.com/xcart/product.php?productid=16583

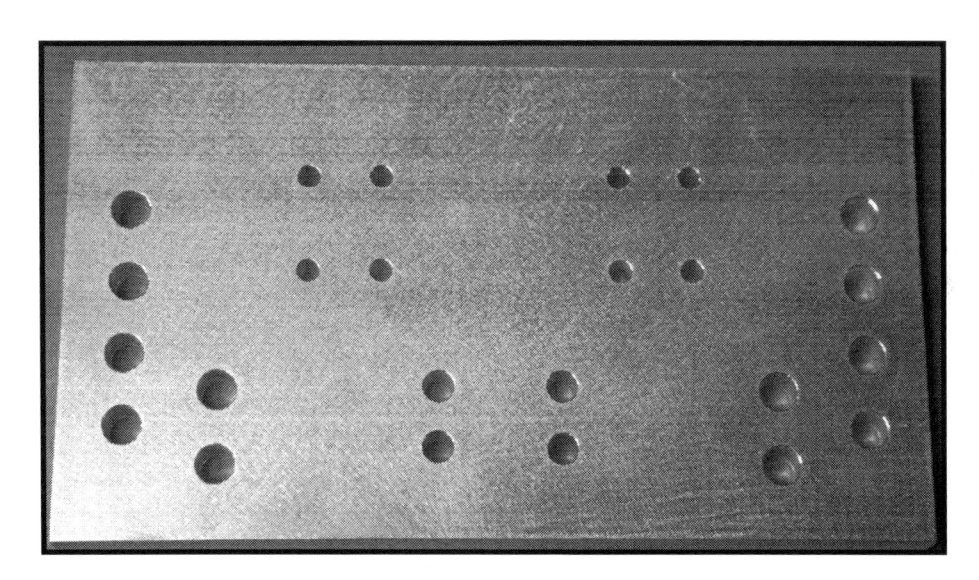

Figure 8.1

Step 1 - Layout the Right Carriage Component

Take one of the 2" x 2" x 1/8" x 14" pieces of steel angle and layout the holes shown in Figure 8.2. All of the larger holes are 3/8" in diameter. The two smaller holes are 13/64".

Use a piece of masking tape and mark this piece "Z-carriage Right"

Note that some of the holes will not be used, and are for future enhancements.

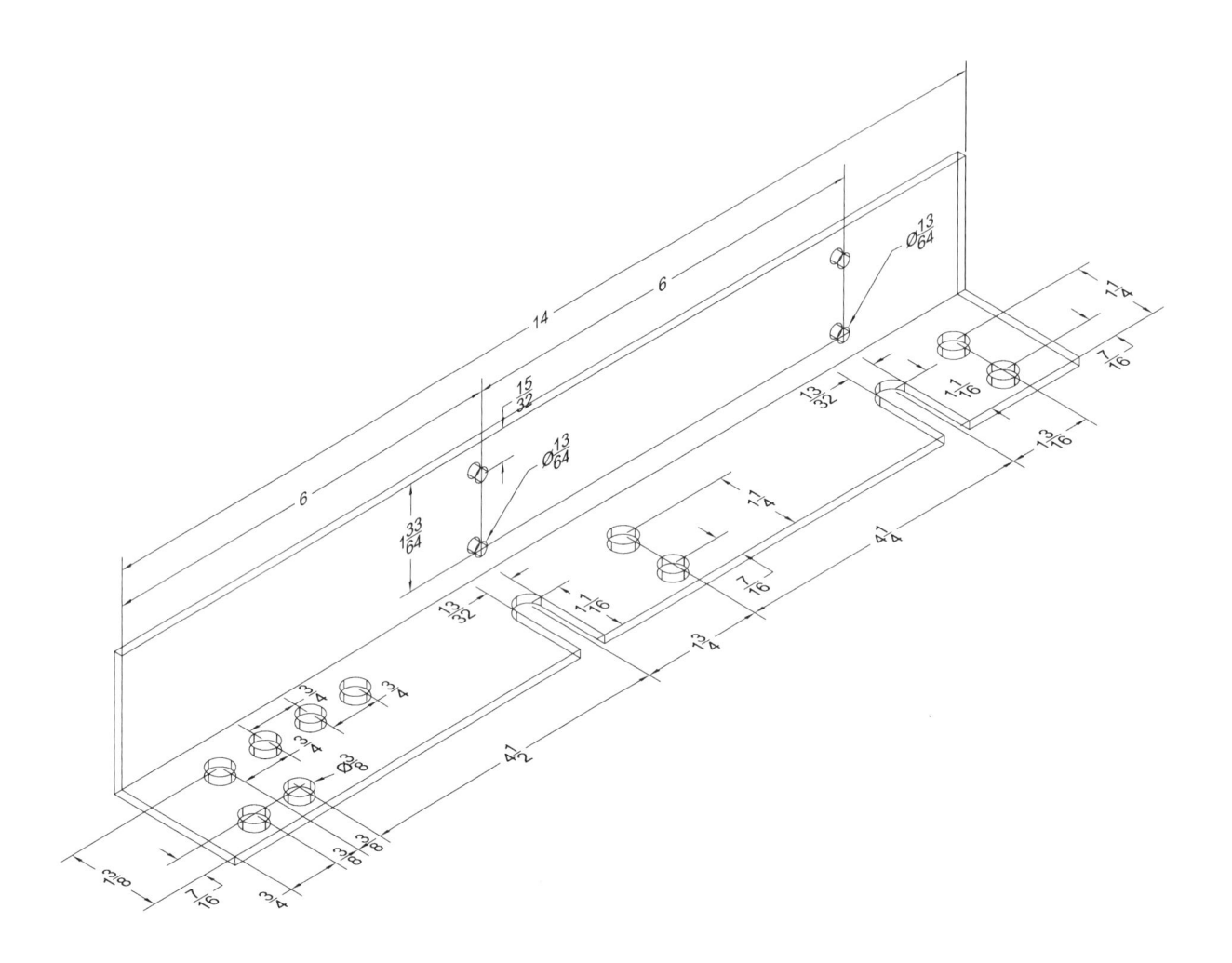

Figure 8.2

Step 2 - - Layout the Left Carriage Component

Take the other 2" x 2" x 1/8" x 14" pieces of steel angle and layout the holes shown in Figure 8.3. All of the larger holes are 3/8" in diameter. The two smaller holes are 13/64". This is a mirrored version of the right carriage component.

Use a piece of masking tape and mark this piece "Z-carriage Left"

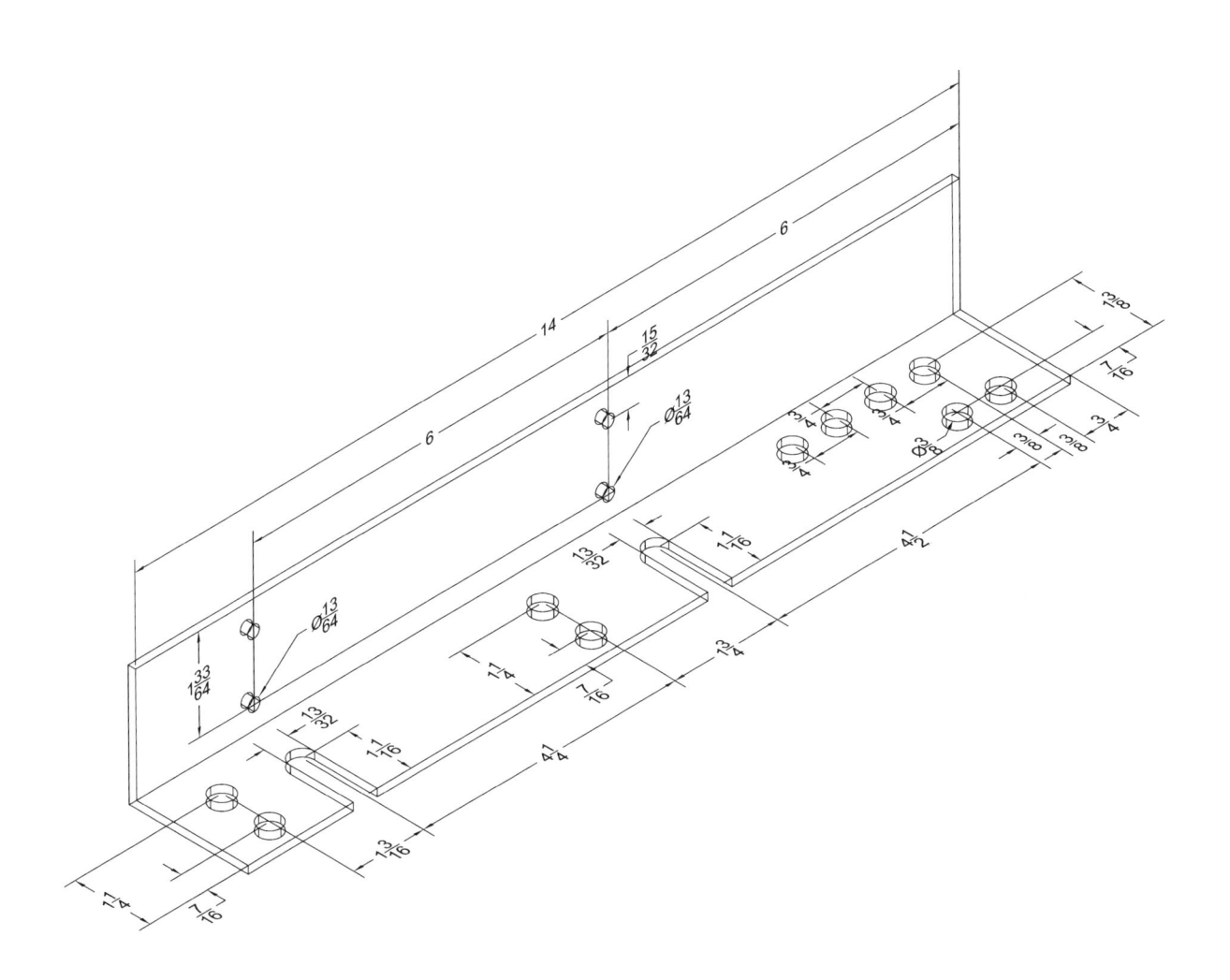

Figure 8.3

Step 3 - Drill Holes and Cut slots

Once marked, dent the steel angle with a center punch. Drill all holes with a 1/8" pilot drill bit first, then follow with the actual diameter drill bit. As with the Y-carriage, all the holes should be 3/8" except for the two small holes on the end marked 13/64". For those, use a #7 drill bit (13/64"). It is extremely important that the 13/64" hole is straight.

To cut the slots, first drill a 3/8" hole, then use a straight edge to mark the cut lines, as shown in Figure 8.4. Once marked, use the reciprocating saw with metal cutting blade to cut along the lines. Be sure to clean the cuts with a file or rotary grinder.

Once the slots have been cut and the holes drilled, the two carriage components should like the two shown in Figure 8.5.

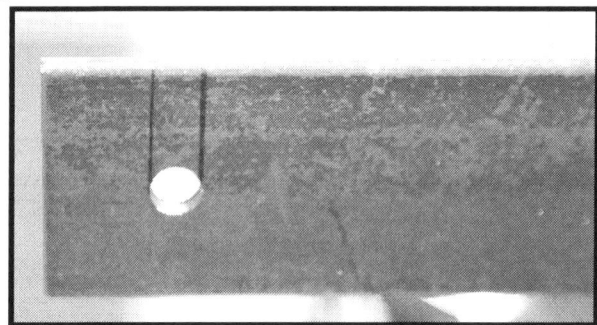

Figure 8.4

Step 4 - Tap Holes

In the two components you created in Steps 1 and 2, there are a total of eight, 13/64" holes. These holes hold the V-bearing adjustment bolts and need to be tapped with a 1/4" Tap, shown in Figure 8.6.

Just like you did with the previous carriages, add a little oil to the hole and be sure to back out the tap frequently to clear the chips. It is important that the threads you are creating be as straight as possible.

Figure 8.6

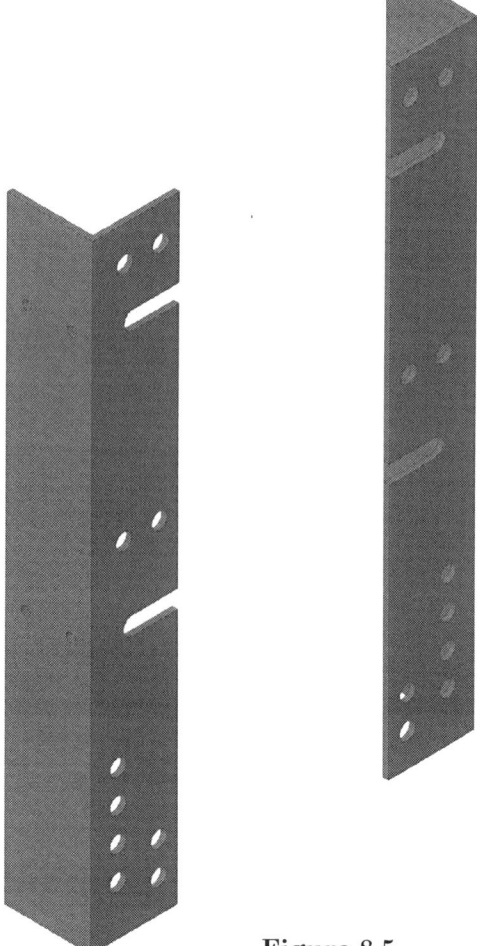

Figure 8.5

98   Chapter 8   Z-carriage

Step 5 - Layout the Z-carriage Supports

There are two Z-carriage support brackets. Using two pieces of 1" x 1" x 1/8" x 8-7/8" steel angle stock, mark and layout as shown in Figure 8.7. All the holes should be 5/16" in diameter.

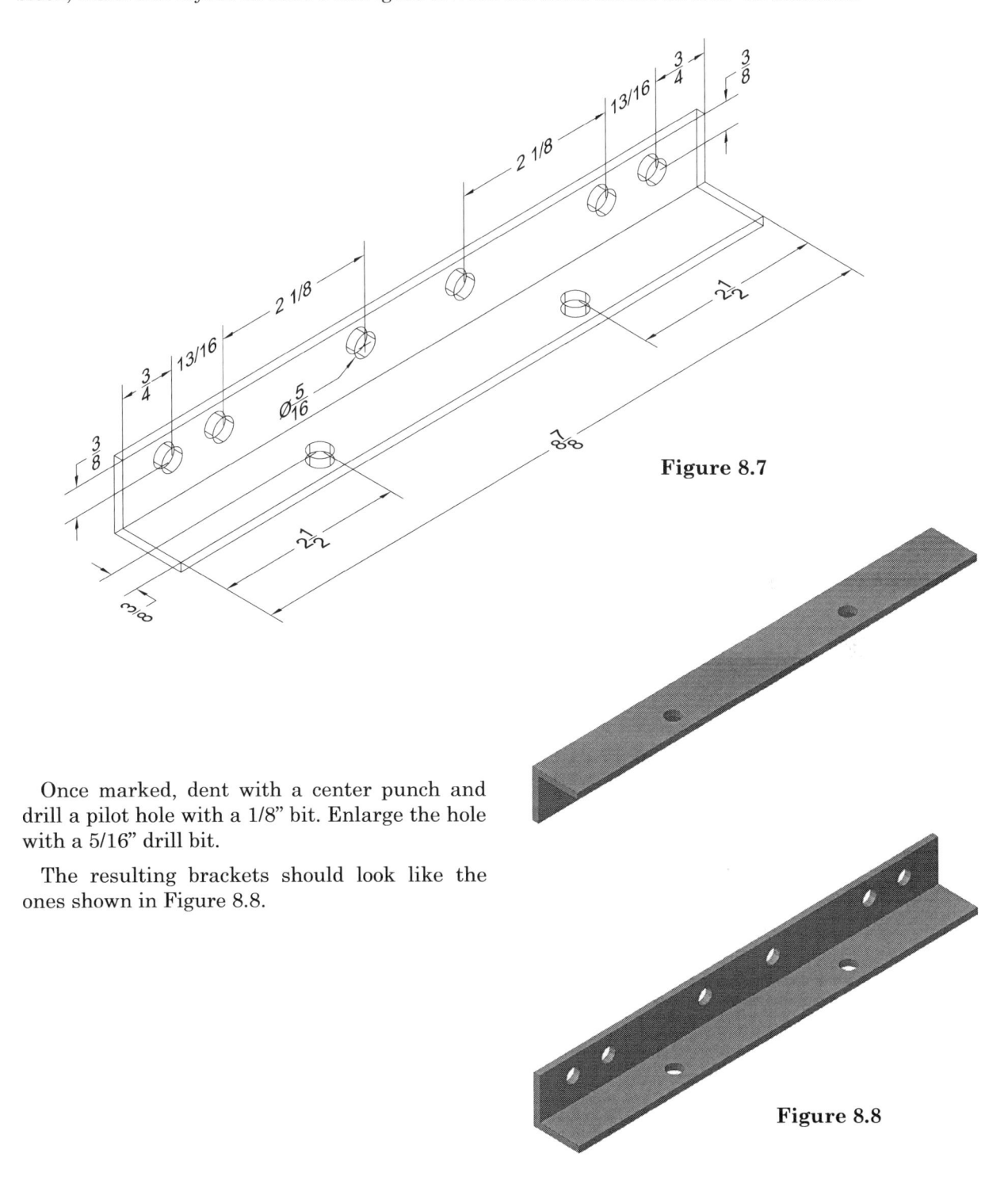

Figure 8.7

Once marked, dent with a center punch and drill a pilot hole with a 1/8" bit. Enlarge the hole with a 5/16" drill bit.

The resulting brackets should look like the ones shown in Figure 8.8.

Figure 8.8

Building the KRMx01 CNC

Step 6 - Assemble Z-carriage

Using 8, 1/4"-20 x 3/4" hex bolts, and 12, 1/4-20 x 1-1/2" hex bolts, attach the Z-carriage support brackets and Z-plate to the main Z-carriage upright brackets as shown in Figure 8.9.

Start by adding a 1/4" washer to each of the hex bolts, then insert the bolts into the holes shown. Insert a 1/4" washer, lock washer, and hex nut onto each bolt. Finger tighten only.

The ends of the supports should be flush with the main brackets. The Z-plate should be flush with the bottom of the main brackets. All brackets should be parallel to each other and square .

Once you are satisfied with the layout, tighten all bolts.

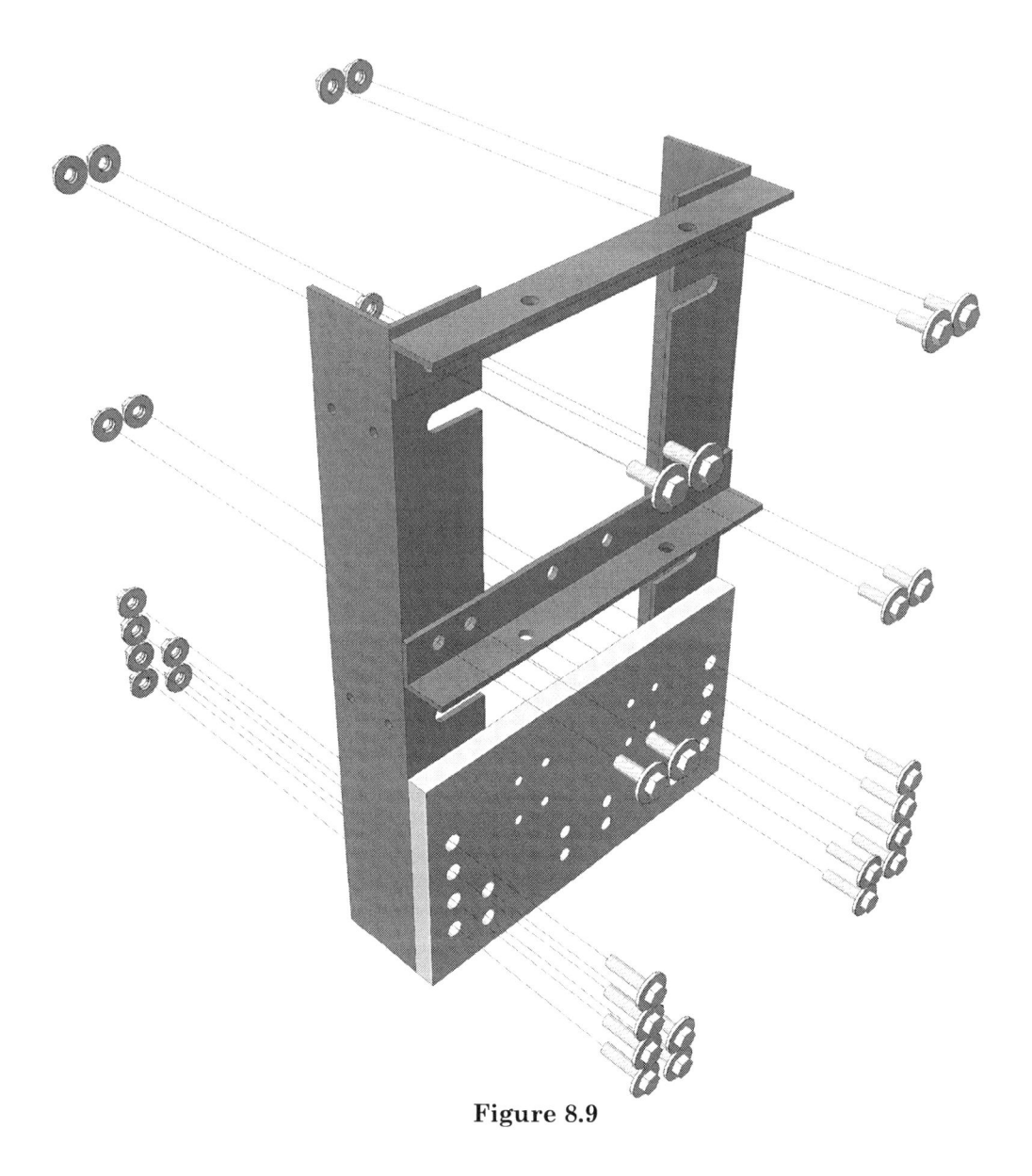

Figure 8.9

Step 7 - Attach ACME Nuts

Insert two 3/16" washers onto four, 1/4-20 x 1" hex bolts. Next, slip the bolt through a hole in the ACME nut and through the carriage brackets as shown in Figures 8.10 and 8.11. Add a 1/4" washer, a 1/4" lock washer and a 1/4" hex nut to each bolt and finger tighten.

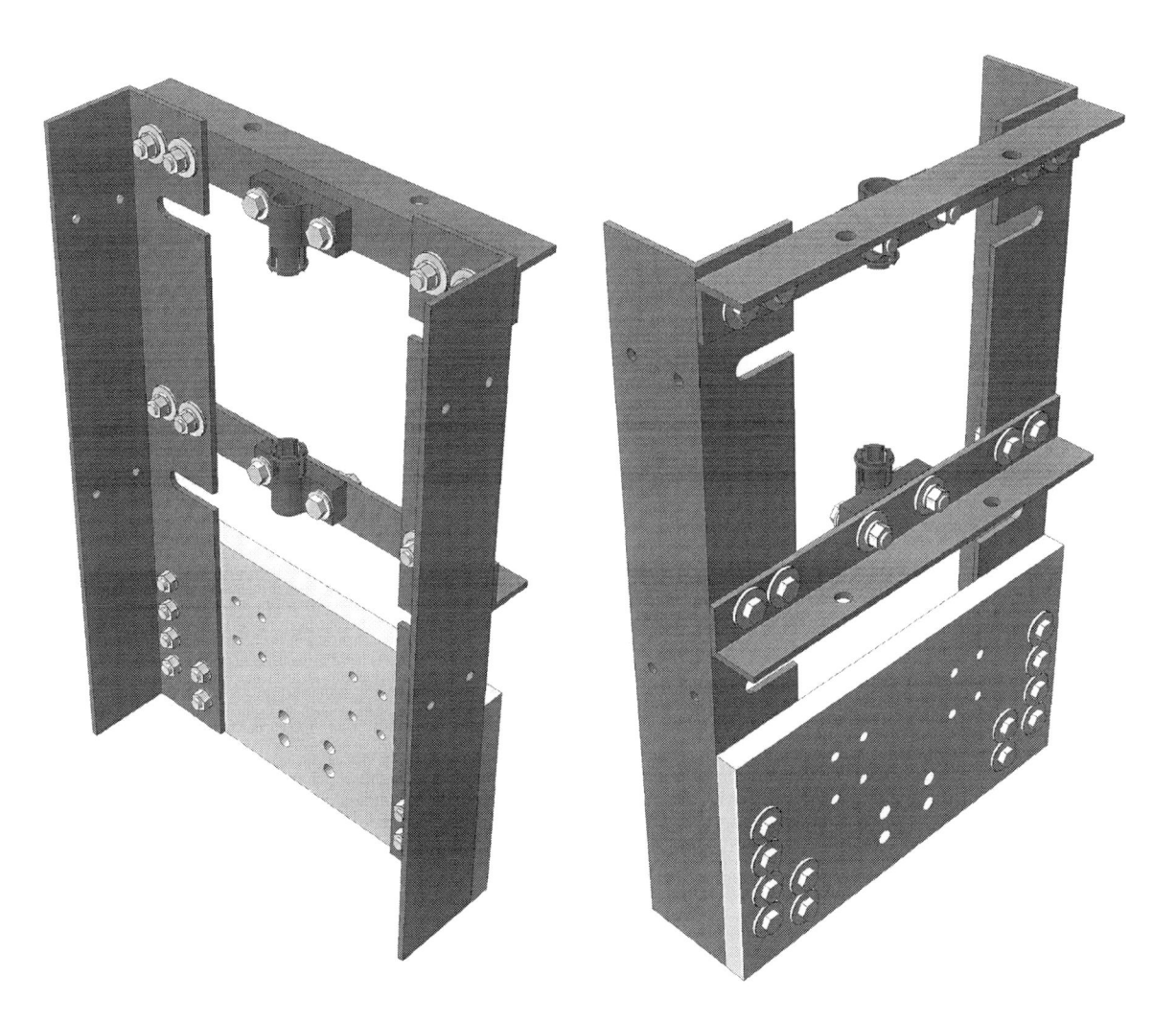

Figure 8.10

Figure 8.11

Step 8 - Add Carriage Adjustment Bolts

Add a 1/4" hex nut, a 1/4" lock washer, and a 1/4" washer to each of the four, 1/4-20 x 1-1/2" hex bolts. The nut should be adjusted so that it's about .2" from the head as shown in Figure 8.12. Insert the bolt assembly into each of the threaded holes you tapped in the Z-carriage.

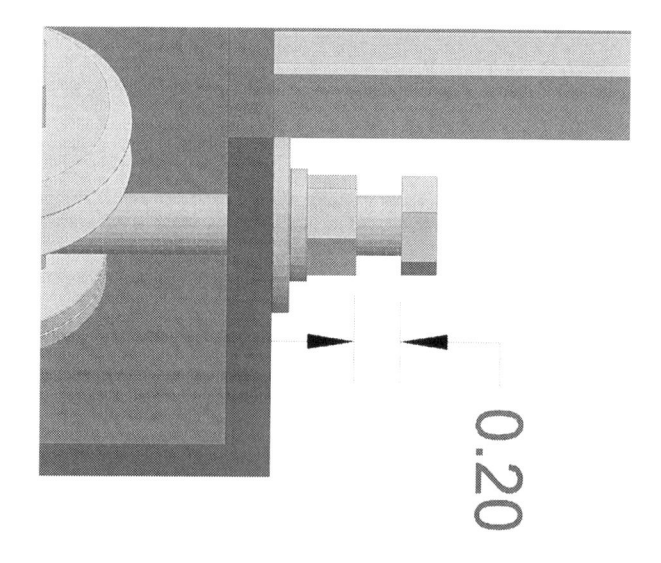

Figure 8.12

Step 9 - Assemble V-bearings

To install the V-bearings, you must first attach the bearing to a 3/8-16 x 1-1/2" hex bolt. Place the bearing on the bolt, followed by a 3/8" lock washer and hex nut as shown in Figure 8.13. Tighten.

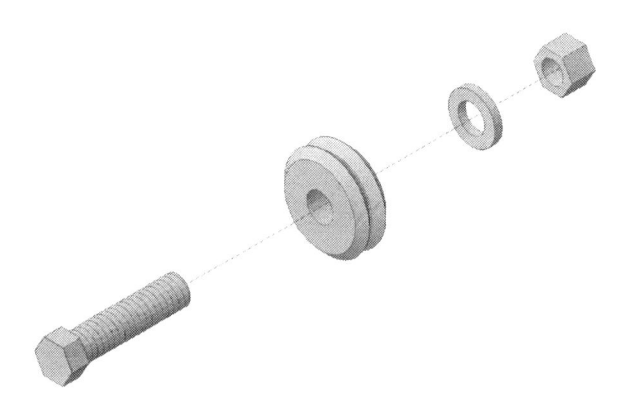

Figure 8.13

Step 10 - Add V-bearings

Add two 3/8" washers to the bolt/bearing assembly and insert the assembly into the slot on the carriage as shown by the arrow in Figure 8.14. Add a 3/8" washer and hex nut. Finger tighten only. The flat portion of the hex bolt on the bearing assembly should be pushed snugly up against the adjustment bolt..

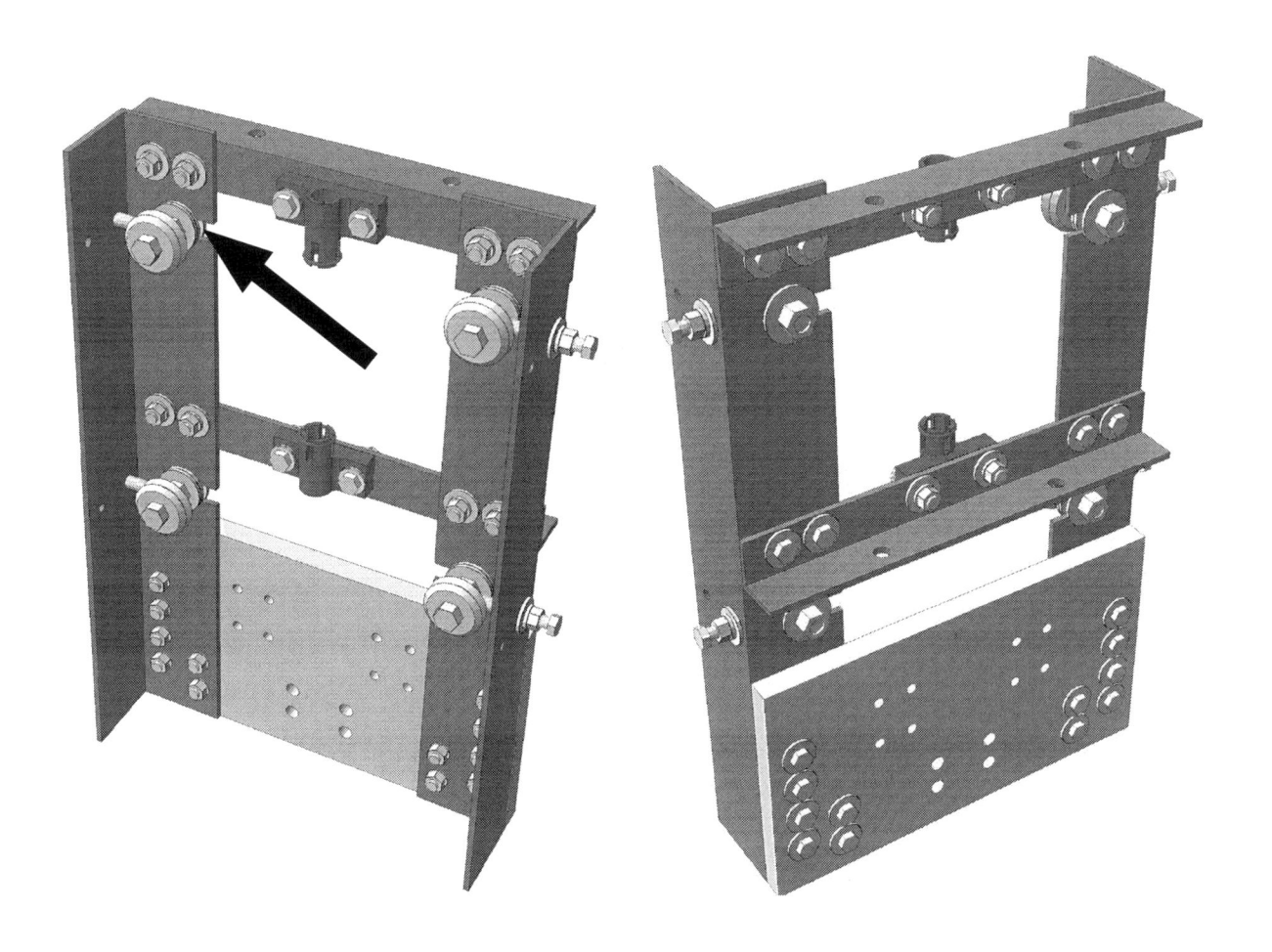

Figure 8.14

Figure 8.14 shows the front and back view of the completed Z-carriage assembly.

Step 11 - Attach the Z-carriage to the Z-rail

Slip the lower two V-bearings over the Z-rails as shown in Figure 8.15. If the V-bearings are too tight, you may need to back out an adjustment bolt and move the V-bearing.

Proceed by sliding the upper V-bearings over the Z-rails.

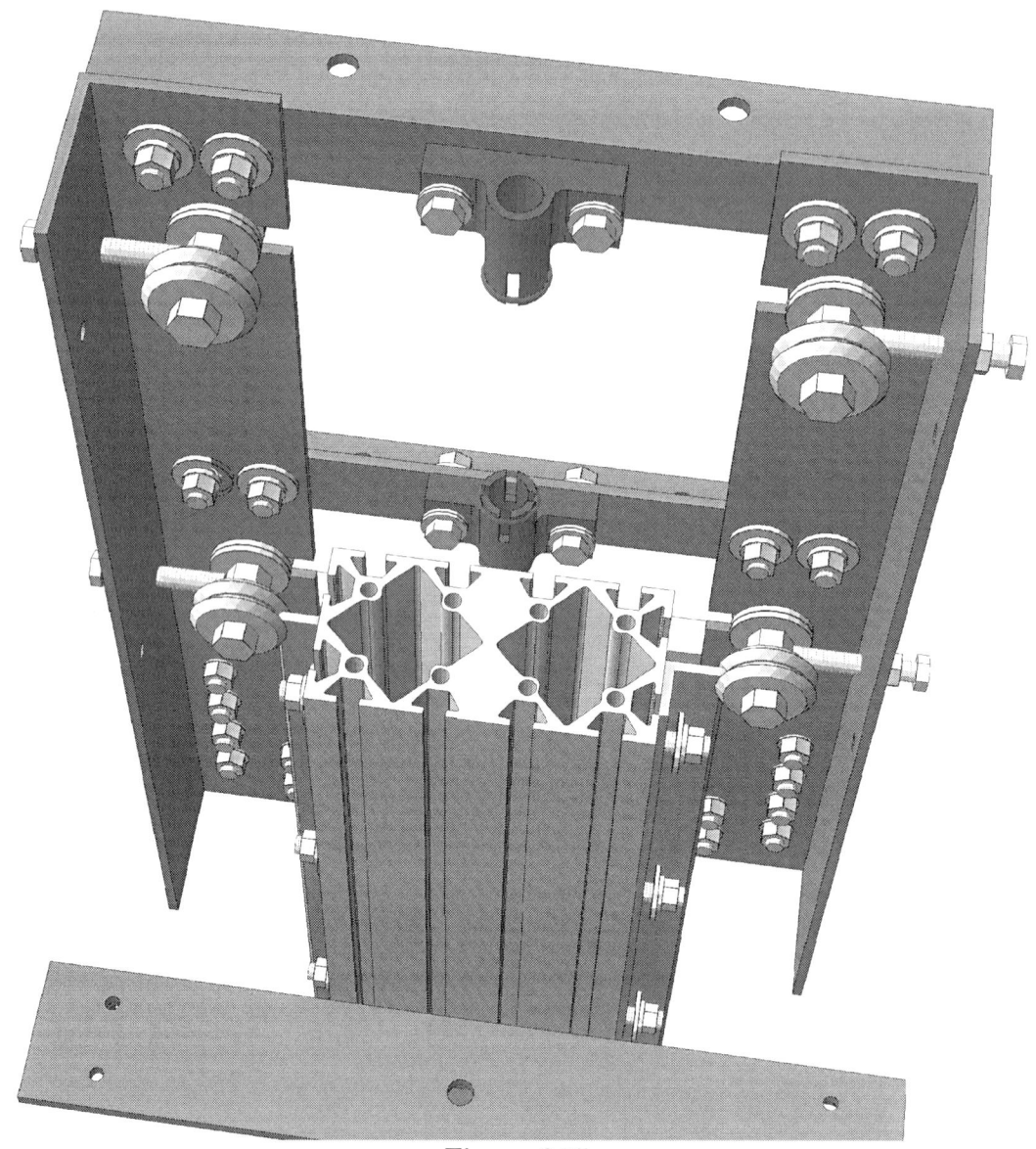

Figure 8.15

Step 12 - Attach the Z-carriage Stop

Until the ACME screws are installed on the Z-axis, the carriage will fall through to the table top. For the time being add a 1/4-20" x 2" carriage bolt, washer, and nut to the bottom of the extrusion as shown in Figure 8.16. Let the Z-carriage rest on the bolt. Later, you will remove the bolt.

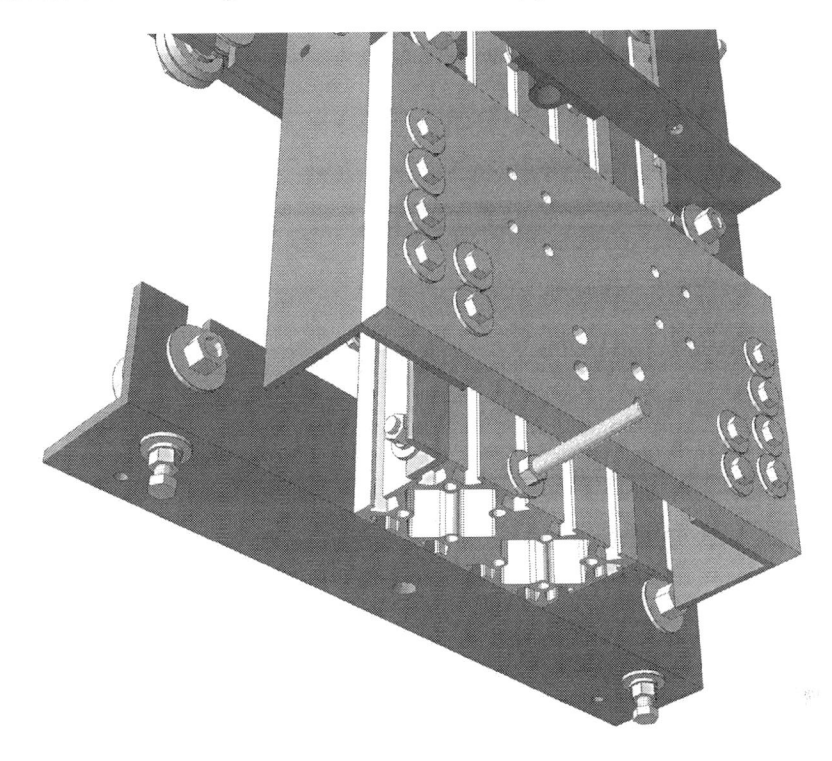

Figure 8.16

Figure 8.17, shows the completed Z-carriage in-place.

The four upper holes in the Z-plate are used to mount one of the various K2CNC mounts available from K2CNC. Please note, in order to mount the K2CNC router mount you will need 8, #10-24 x 1-1/4 machine screws. You will also need 8 #10-24 hex nuts and lock washers.

Figure 8.17

Building the KRMx01 CNC

Adjustments

The sides of the Z-carriage can be squared by adjusting the bearing adjustment bolts. To do this you would loosen the bolts on both sides of the top or bottom depending on which you wanted to change.

The following is an example of how to make an adjustment to the top bearings on the Z-carriage.

1. Loosen top adjustment bolts on both sides. Leave the bottom adjustment bolts in place.
2. Loosen the bearing bolts and back the bearings away from the rail.
3. Tighten the bearing bolts. Use a wrench, but don't overdo it. You want them snug only.
4. Now place a square up against the carriage . Place and hold one of the bearings against the rail.
5. Slowly adjust the adjustment bolt on the bearing you are holding until the carriage is 90 degrees with the table.
6. Tighten the same bearing bolt fully.
7. Slowly tighten the adjustment bolt on the opposite side until the rail is snug against the rail.

If you check the opposite side of the carriage with a square and it's off, it may be that the two sides of the Z-carriage are not parallel. If this is the case, it is best to remove the carriage and adjust it properly, as outlined in the previous steps.

Since the Z-rails are perpendicular to the table, the Z-carriage front should be perpendicular to the table. If it is not, then you need to go back and look at your bearing hardware.

Note that you can compensate for a small discrepancy later when you attach the router.

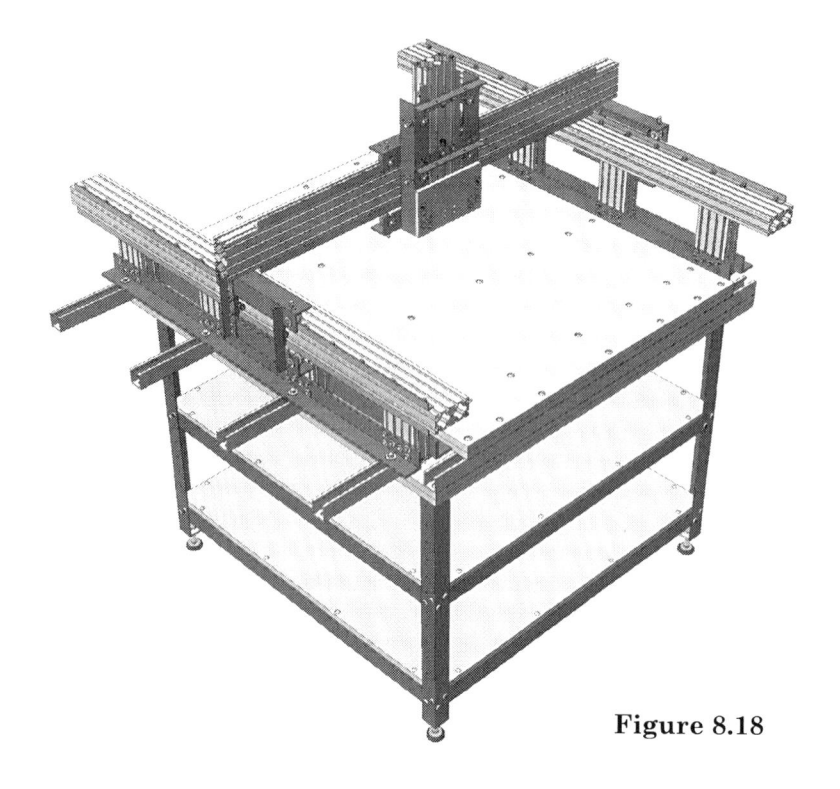

Figure 8.18

Chapter 9

Motor Mounts

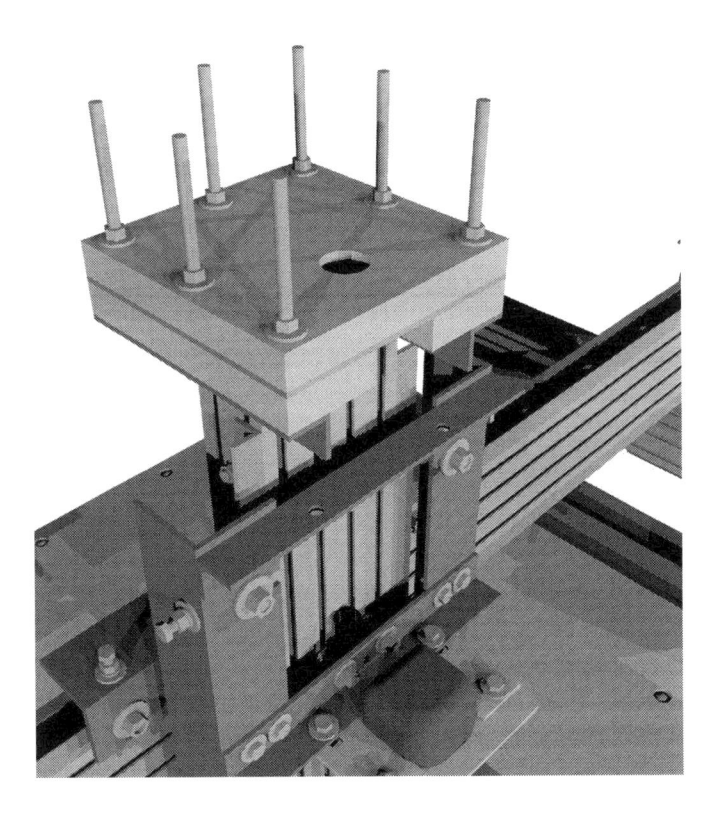

The KRMx01 CNC utilizes a very simple, ridged bearing block system, which supports easy access to the motor couplings and shaft collars.

Tools Needed For This Chapter

- Drill press
- 3/8" Drill bit
- 1-1/8" Forstner bit
- 1" Forstner bit
- Scroll saw (jig saw)
- Reciprocating saw

Components Needed For This Chapter

- 18, 6" x 6" x 3/4" Blocks cut from particle board or similar material
- 13, 6" x 6" x 1/8" Blocks cut from hard board
- 12, 1" x 1" x 1/8" x 6" Steel angle
- 2, 1" x 1" x 1/8" x 4" steel angle
- 62, 1/4-20 x 3/4" Carriage bolts
- 127, 1/4-20 Hex nuts
- 184, 1/4" Washers
- 81, 1/4" Split lock washers
- 26, 1/4-20 x 4-1/2" Hex bolts (full thread)
- 35, 1/4-20 x 2-1/2" Hex bolts
- 7, 1/4-20 x 5" Carriage bolts
- 7, 1/2" ID x 1-1/8" OD bearings

The 1/2" bearings can be purchased from www.cncrouterparts.com and VXB.com.

Chapter Estimates
Cost: $72
Time: Weekend

Prerequisites

You need 18, 6" x 6" x 3/4" blocks to create the motor mounts. You also need 13, 6" x 6" x 1/8" pieces for your bearing stop block.

The 3/4" blocks are cut from a 2' x 4' x 3/4" sheet of particle board or MDF. The 1/8" blocks are cut from a sheet of 2' x 4' x 1/8 tempered hard board.

Shown in Figures 9.1 and 9.2 are examples of cut lists for the various blocks cut from two, 2' x 4' sheets. Feel free to cut them in any way you wish. In many cases you can probably get your local home center to cut them for you if you don't have access to a table saw.

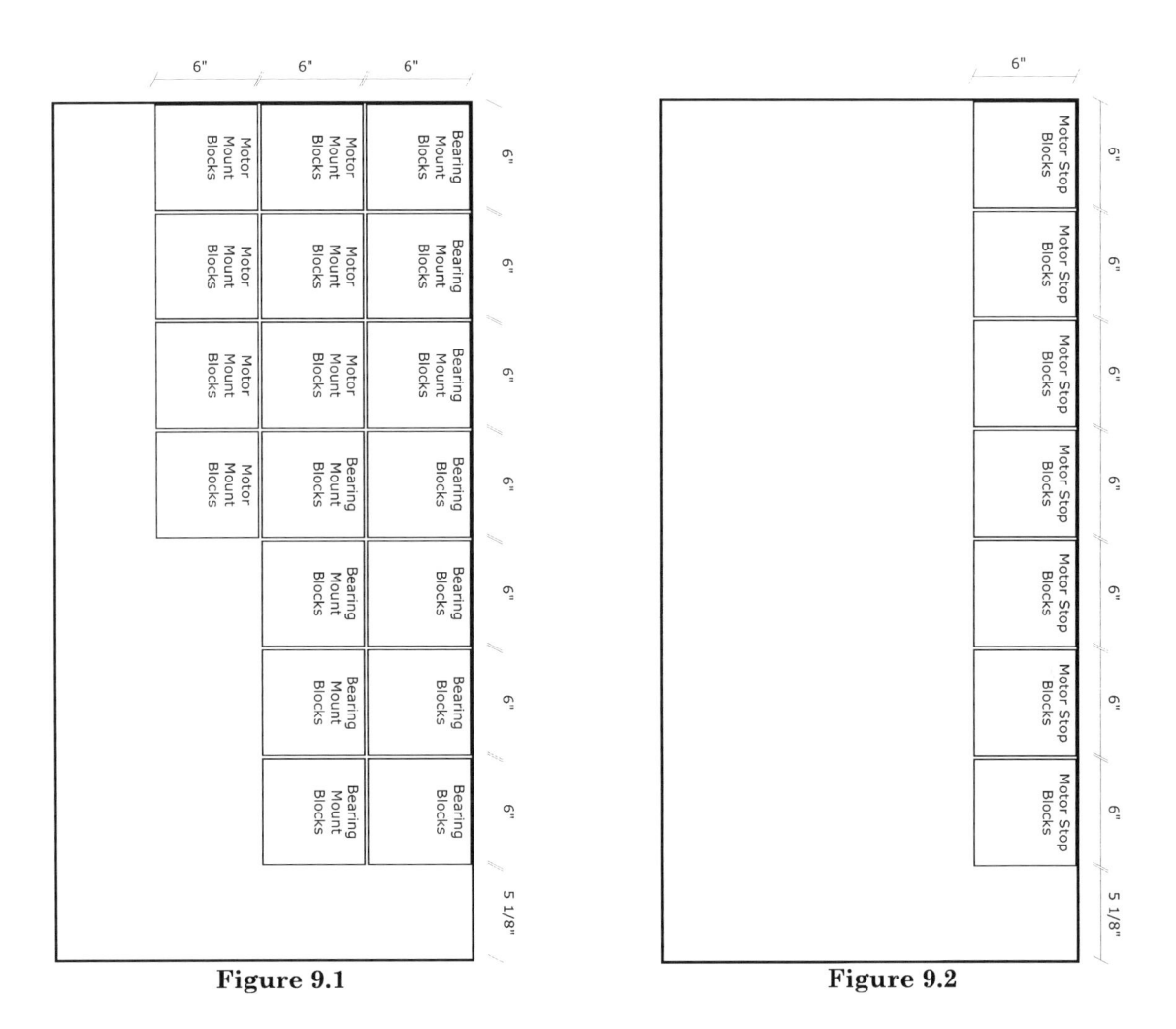

Figure 9.1

Figure 9.2

Cut 18, 6" sections from a piece of 1" x 1" x 1/8" steel angle. You can't use a 12" section to cut these parts, as the saw kerf will not allow you to get two full 6" parts. Start with a larger piece. If you use a 24" piece you will have some scrap left over that can be used for backup, in case you make a mistake.

You also need to cut two, 4" sections of 1" x 1" x 1/8" steel angle. You can use some of the waste from the 6" pieces to get these.

Building the KRMx01 CNC

Introduction to Motor Mounts

The complete drive train for a KRMx01 beam consists of a motor/bearing block on one end and a bearing block on the other. Between them runs an ACME screw that drives the carriage via the ACME nuts connected to the screw.

The motor/bearing group shown in Figure 9.3 utilizes three of the 15, 6" x 6" x 3/4" blocks and one, 6" x 6" x 1/8" block.

While the ways that they are attached to the beam may vary, the actual blocks are the same. Two of the 3/4" blocks and the 1/8" block hold the 1/2" bearing in place. The remaining block is used to mount the motor.

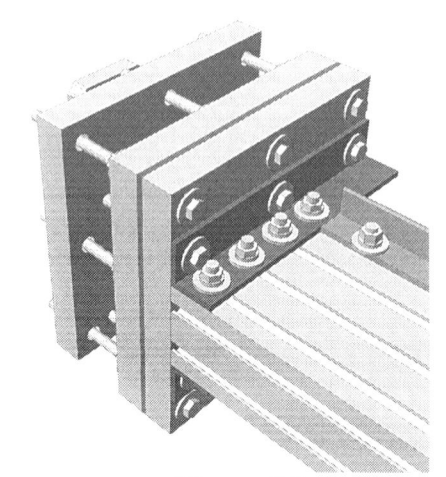

Figure 9.3

The bearing group shown in Figure 9.4, utilizes two of the 15, 6" x 6" x 3/4" blocks and one, 6" x 6" x 1/8" block.

Essentially this block is the bearing portion of the motor/bearing group shown on the left.

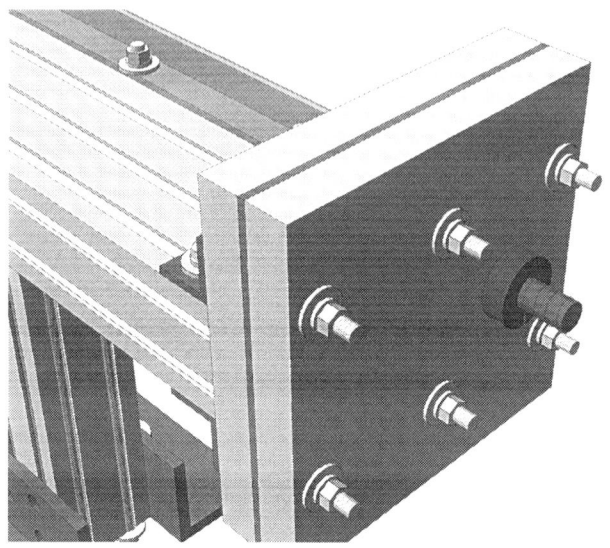

Figure 9.4

This lay out holds true for all but the Z-beam. The Z-beam only has a single motor/bearing block as shown in Figure 9.5. It is short enough, and with the dual ACME nuts, has more than enough support for the ACME screw.

In this chapter you are going to build and install the bearing portion of the motor/bearing block for the Z axis. In a later chapter you will attach the motor and its mounting block.

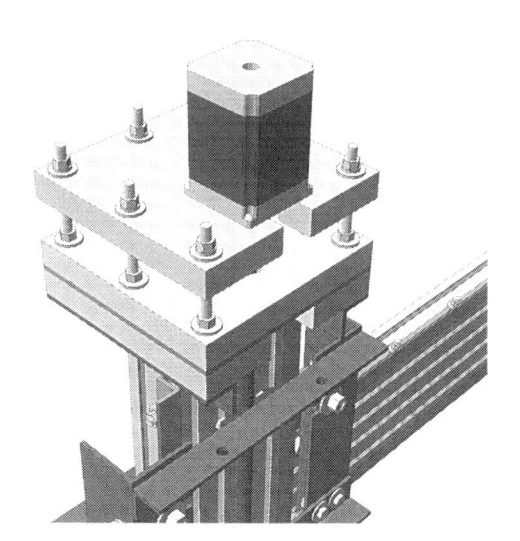

Figure 9.5

110   *Chapter 9*   Motor Mounts

Z Motor Mount
Step 1 - Layout the Z Bearing Block

Take one of the 6" x 6" x 3/4" blocks and mark the holes shown in Figure 9.6.

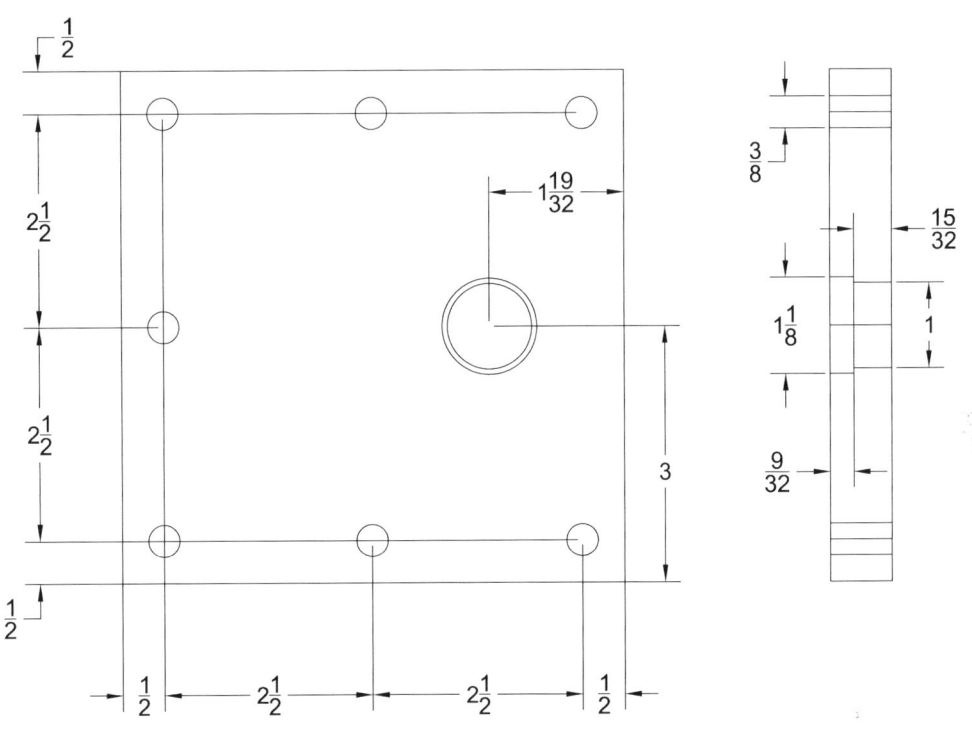

Figure 9.6

Tip

Since almost every block shares the seven outside holes and some sort of cut referenced to the shaft location, it makes sense to create a cardboard template to mark these locations. Do this by cutting a 6" x 6" piece of cardboard, then place small X's at the center of each hole, as indicated in the layout drawing shown in Figure 9.6. Next, use a steel punch to create a small hole at each of the X's. You can then lay the template over a 6" x 6" block and mark each hole with a punch. The finished template should look like the one shown in Figure 9.7.

Figure 9.7

Step 2 - Drill the Z Bearing Block

Using a 3/8" drill bit, drill the seven outside holes into the block, as shown in Figure 9.8. The larger hole is used to hold the bearing. Start by using a 1-1/8" Forstner bit to drill a pocket 9/32" deep. Then using a 1" Forstner bit, drill the rest of the way through.

When drilling the 9/32" pocket, it's important that you don't drill too deep. You can always go back and add to the pocket as needed. The goal is to have the bearing slightly exposed outside the pocket. If the pocket is too deep the bearing will wiggle back and forth and result in excessive backlash.

Once the block is complete, label it "Z Bearing Block".

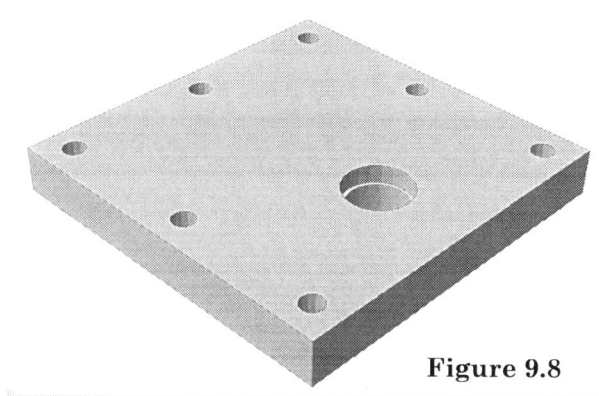

Figure 9.8

Tip

Use a piece of scrap 3/4" stock to drill a test pocket. You can then set the depth stop on your drill press to get a perfect depth. Note that it's better if the pocket is too shallow than too deep.

The outside holes are all 3/8", however the bolts used to mount the bearing blocks are 1/4". This is done to give the block a little play when we mount the lead screws.

Step 3 - Layout the Z Bearing Mount

Take one of the 6" x 6" x 3/4" blocks and mark the holes indicated in Figure 9.9. The large notch can be larger than the dimensions shown, but it can not be smaller. You can also make it a square notch if you like. This slot is to give you access to the 1/2" shaft collars for adjustment.

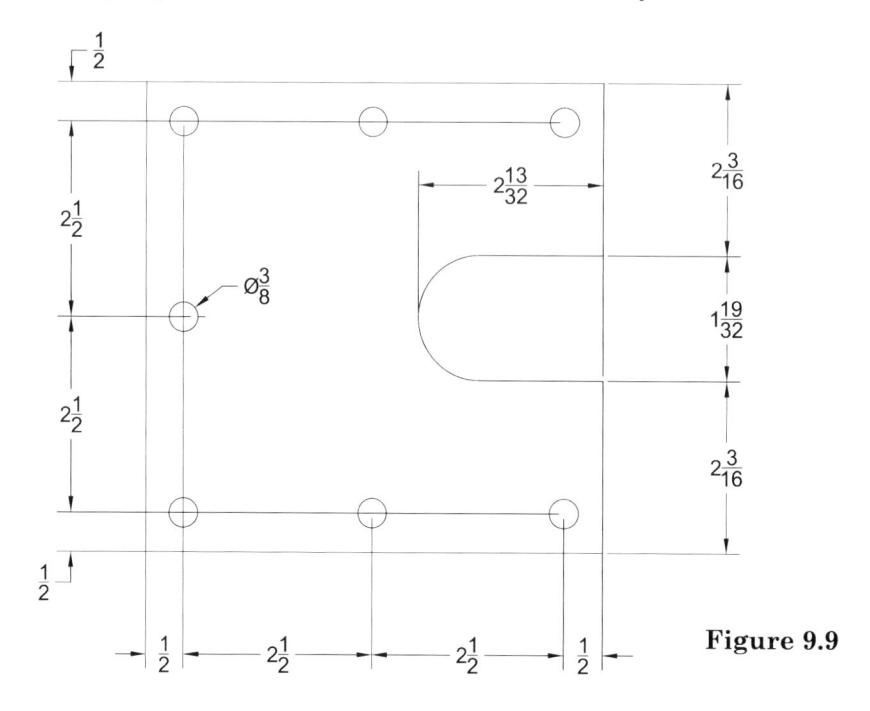

Figure 9.9

Chapter 9   Motor Mounts

Step 4 - Cut the Z Bearing Mount

As before, drill the outside holes with a 3/8" drill bit. Use a jigsaw, band saw, or scroll saw to cut the slot as shown in Figure 9.10.

Once the block is complete, label it "Z Bearing Mount Block".

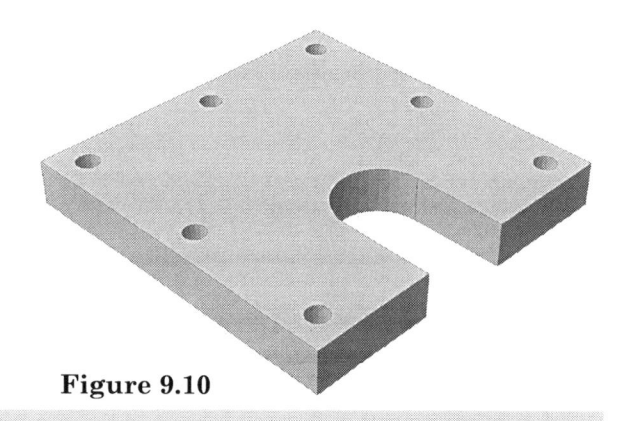

Figure 9.10

Tip

An easy way to cut the slot is to drill a 1-5/8" hole 3" from the upper and lower edge and 1-5/8" from the left edge. Then mark two lines perpendicular to the upper and lower quadrant of the hole. You can cut the two lines with any saw that suites you. You can even use your reciprocating saw to cut the two slots.

Note if dimensions are slightly larger, this is OK.

Step 5 - Layout the Z Motor Mount

Take another 6" x 6" x 3/4" block and mark the holes indicated in Figure 9.11. The large hole is to allow a NEMA 23 motor to fit. It can be slightly larger, but not smaller. The slot is to allow access to the motor coupler. The smaller 7/32" holes will be used to mount the motor in a later chapter.

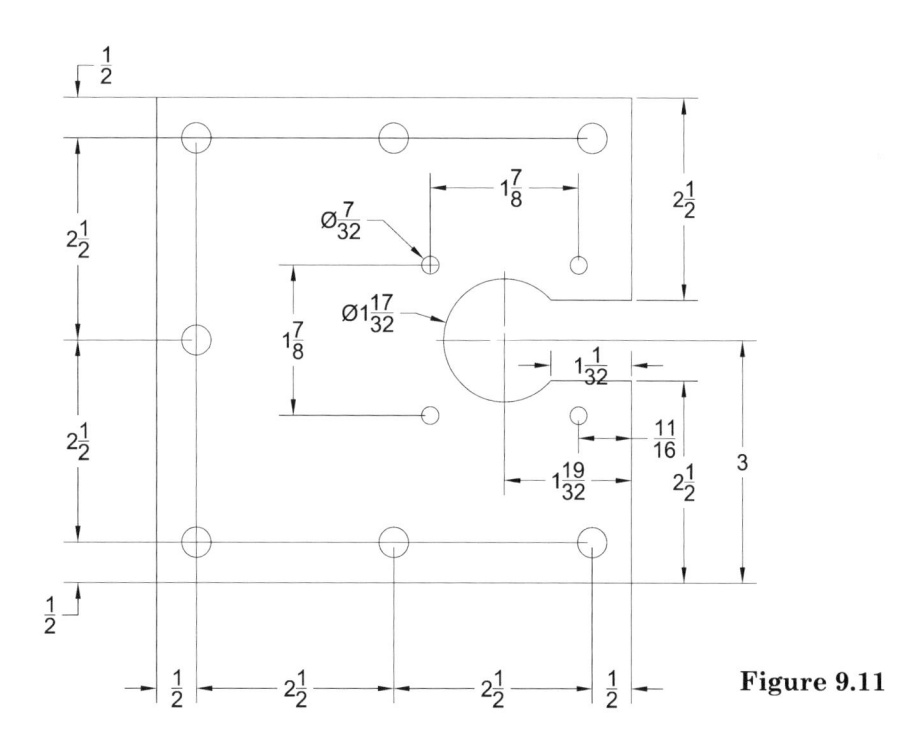

Figure 9.11

Building the KRMx01 CNC

Step 6 - Drill the Z Motor Mount

Again, drill the outside holes with a 3/8" drill bit. Drill the smaller holes with a 7/32" drill bit. Use a jigsaw, band saw, or scroll saw to cut the slot as shown in Figure 9.12.

Once the block is complete, label it "Z Bearing Motor Block".

This part will not be used in this chapter. In a later chapter you will use it to mount your Z stepper motor.

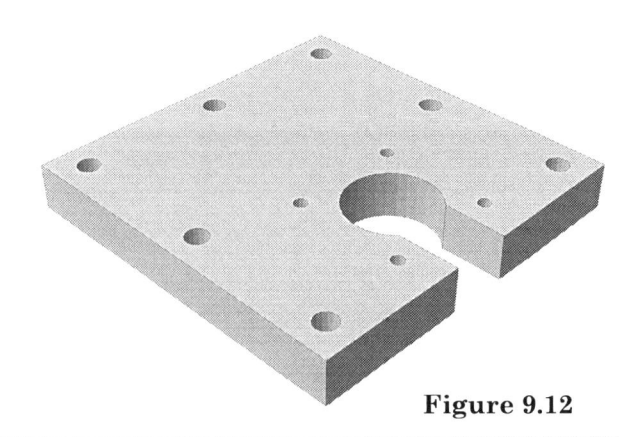

Figure 9.12

Tip
Similar to the last tip, an easy way to cut the slot is to drill a 1-5/8" hole into the location shown on the layout drawing. Then mark the two lines and cut them with your reciprocating saw.

Step 7 - Layout the Z Bearing Stop

Take one of the 6" x 6" x 1/8" blocks (hardboard) and mark the holes indicated in Figure 9.13. The large diameter hole is 1".

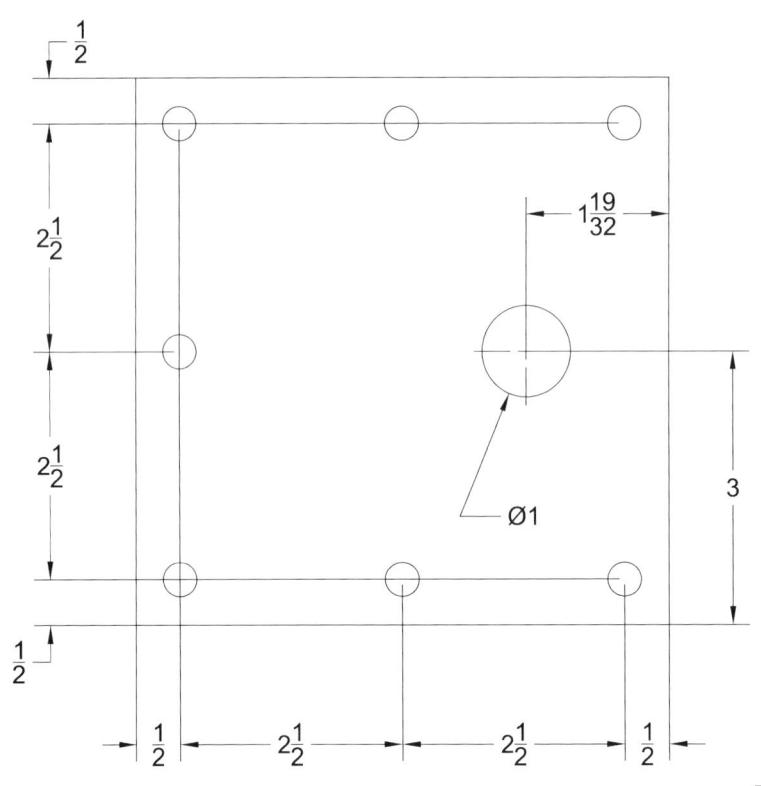

Figure 9.13

114   Chapter 9   Motor Mounts

Step 8 - Drill the Z Bearing Stop

Drill the outside holes with a 3/8" drill bit. Use a 1" Forstner bit to drill the larger hole as shown in Figure 9.14.

Once the block is complete, label it "Z Bearing Stop Block".

The bearing stop block will be sandwiched between the bearing block and the bearing mount. Its job is to hold the bearing in place.

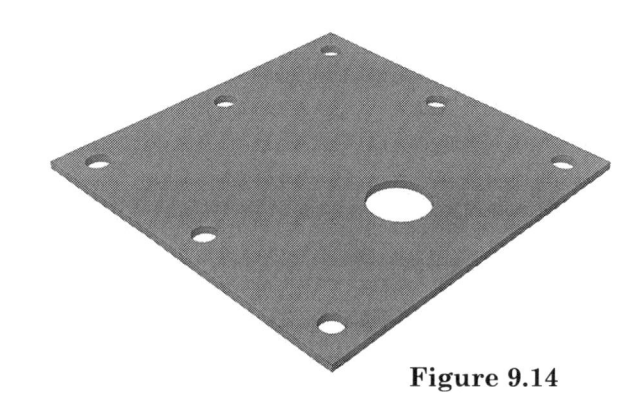

Figure 9.14

Step 9 - Layout the Z Bearing Bracket

Take the two pieces of 1" x 1" steel angle and mark the holes shown in Figure 9.15.

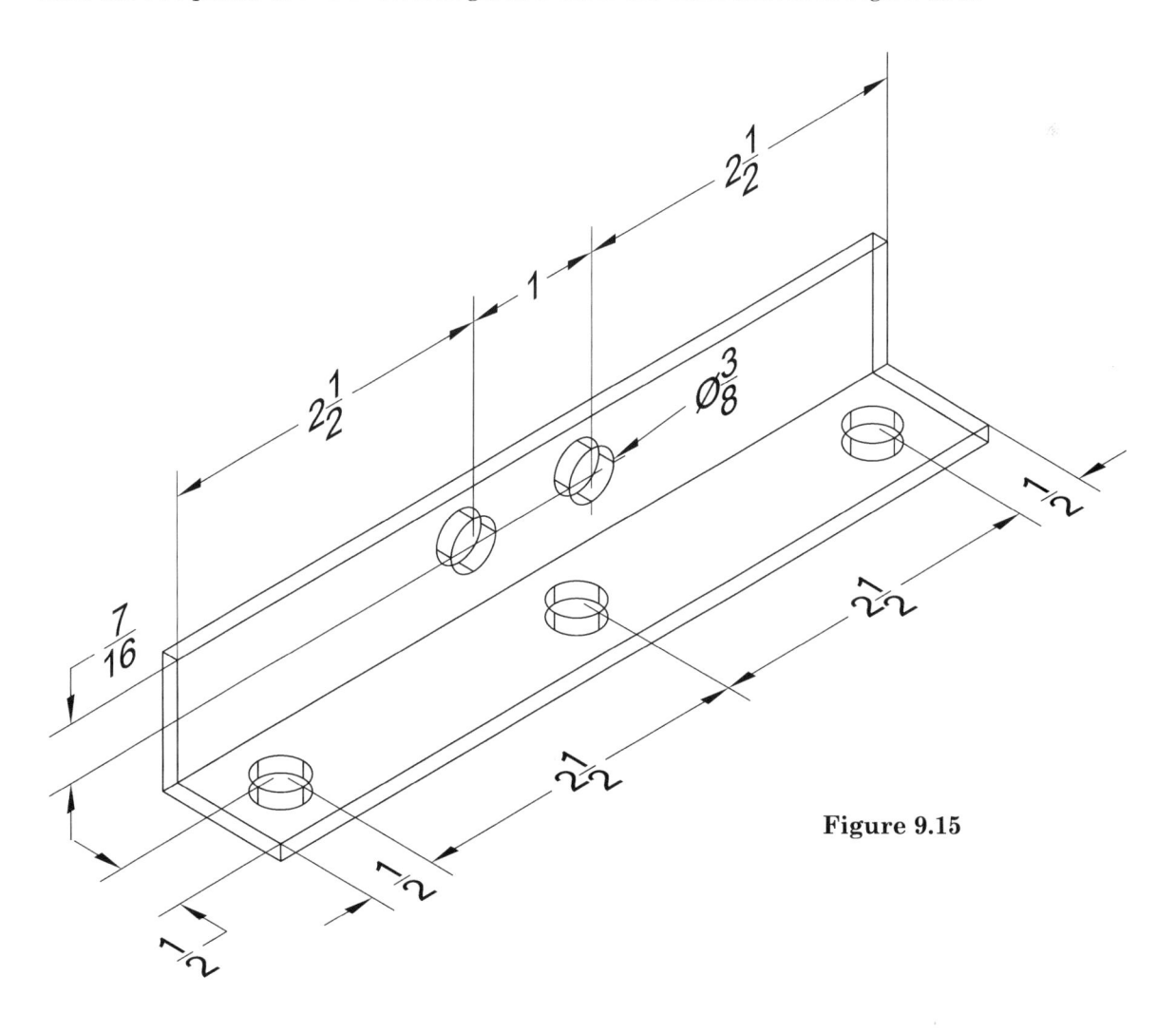

Figure 9.15

Building the KRMx01 CNC

Step 10 - Drill the Z Bearing Bracket

Using the techniques from previous chapters, dent and drill the five, 3/8" holes into the 1" x 1" steel angle as shown in Figure 9.16. These are the bearing mounting brackets. They are used to attach the bearing block to the extrusion. You will need two of these for the Z bearing block.

Figure 9.16

Step 11

Start by inserting two, 1/4-20 x 3/4" bolts into the side slots on the top of the extrusion, as shown in Figure 9.17.

Add a 1/4" washer, lock washer, and hex nut to the bolts and finger tighten. You want the top of the angle to be flush with the top of the extrusion.

Take a piece of scrap or one of your blocks and place it on the top of the extrusion. Butt the top of the steel angle against the block and tighten the nuts.

Repeat on the opposite side as shown in Figure 9.18.

Figure 9.17

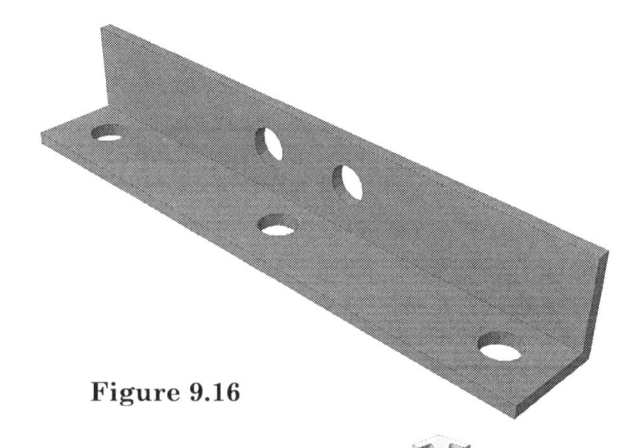

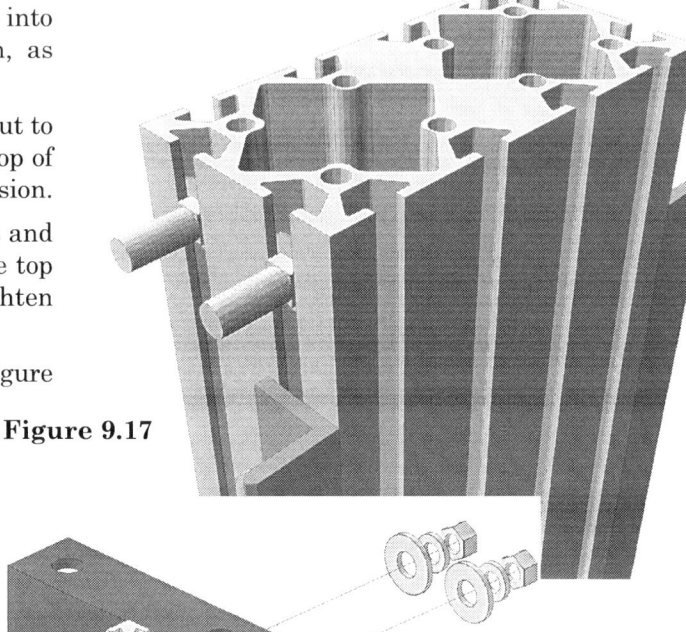

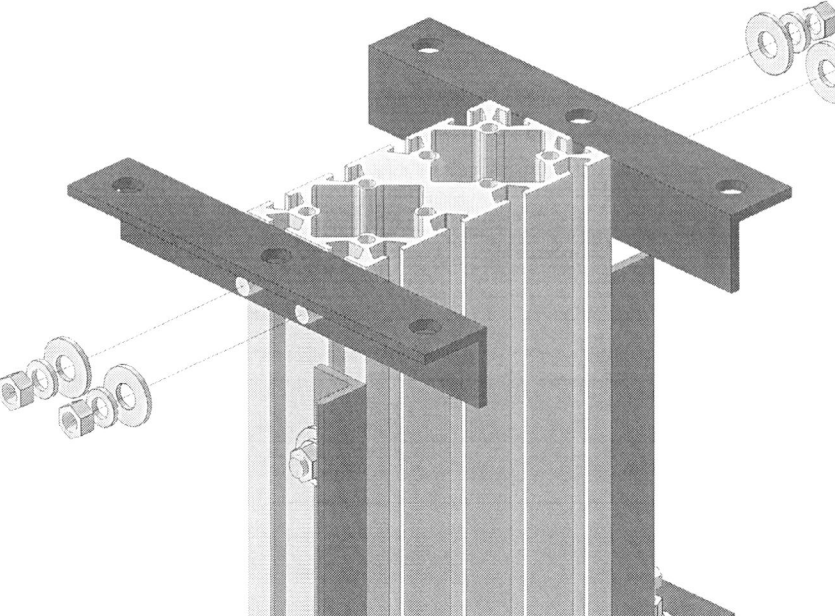

Figure 9.18

Step 12

Place the 1/2" bearing in the pocket on the Z bearing block. Next, sandwich the 1/8" bearing stop in between the bearing block and bearing mount as shown in Figure 9.19. The exposed end of the bearing should be facing the inside, toward the bearing stop, as shown in Figure 9.20.

Set the assembly on top of the bearing brackets and insert a 4-1/2" bolt, with a washer, through the bottom of the bracket and up through the assembly.

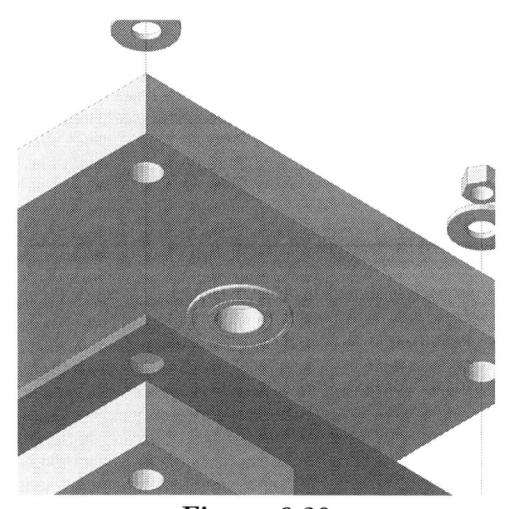

Figure 9.20

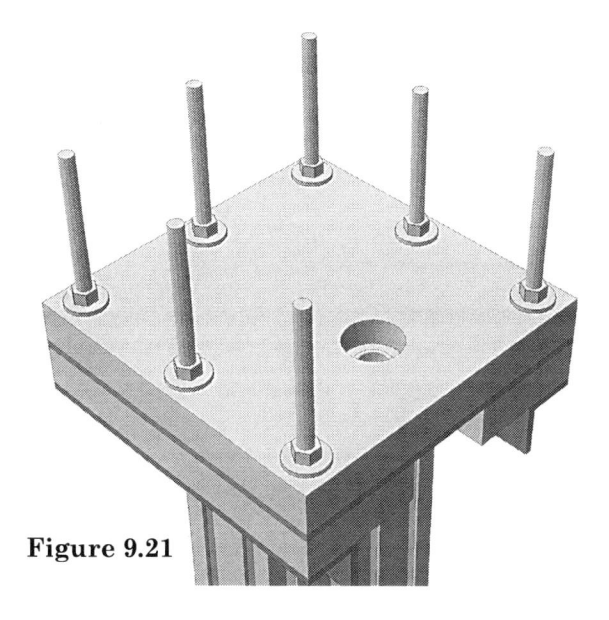

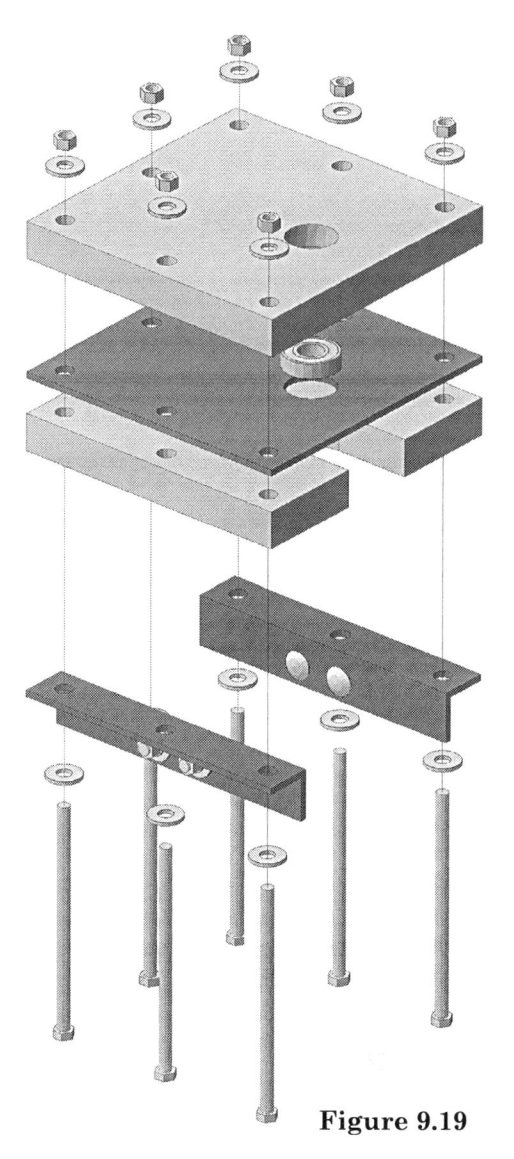

Figure 9.19

Place a 1/4" washer and hex nut onto each bolt as shown in Figure 9.21. Finger tighten only at this point. You want the bearing block to be movable.

Figure 9.21

Building the KRMx01 CNC **117**

Y Motor Mounts
Step 1 - Layout the Y Bearing Blocks

Take four of the 6" x 6" x 3/4" blocks and layout the holes that need to be drilled.

You will need two blocks with the layout shown in Figure 9.22. These will be used on the rear of the Y axis. Eventually the outside holes will be used to hold the motor mounts. These will be added in a later chapter.

Once cut label these "Y Bearing Block Rear".

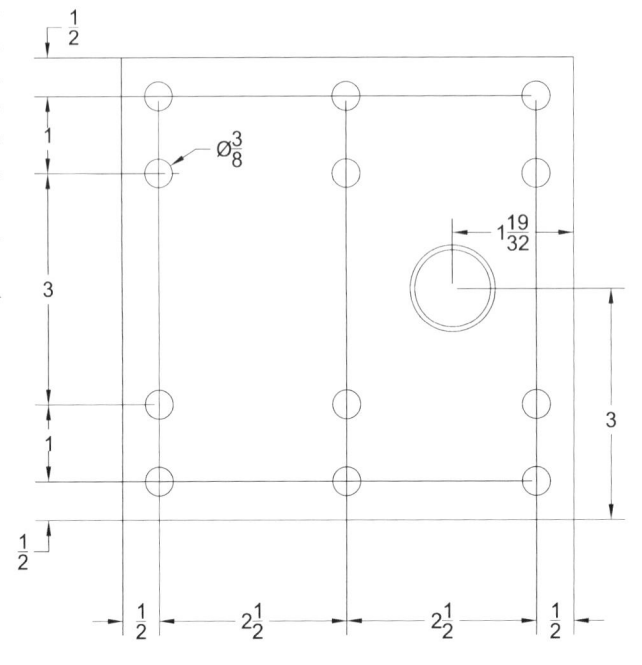

Figure 9.22

Additionally, you will need two blocks with the layout shown in Figure 9.23. The blocks will be mounted on the front of the Y axis.

Notice that these are identical to the previous two blocks with outer 6 holes removed.

Once cut, label these "Y Bearing Block Front"

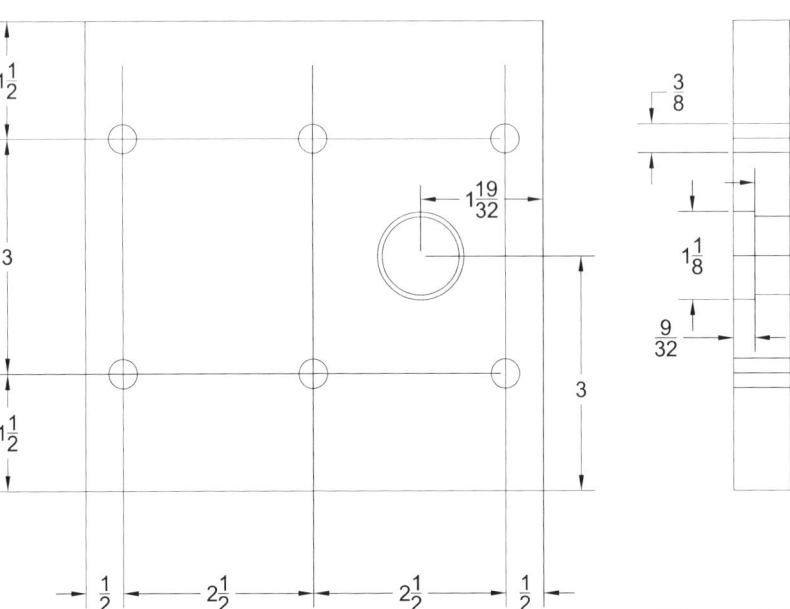

Figure 9.23

Step 2 - Drill the Y Bearing Block

As in the last chapter, use a 3/8" drill bit to drill the smaller holes shown in Figure 9.24. The larger hole are used to hold the bearing. Start by using a 1-1/8" Forstner bit to drill a pocket 9/32" deep. Then using a 1" Forstner bit, drill the rest of the way through.

When drilling the 9/32" pocket, it's important that you don't drill too deep. You can always go back and add to the pocket as needed. The goal is to have the bearing slightly exposed outside the pocket. If the pocket is too deep the bearing will wiggle back and forth and result in excessive backlash.

Once the blocks are complete, label them "Y Bearing Block Rear" and "Y Bearing Block Front". Remember that you will need two of each block.

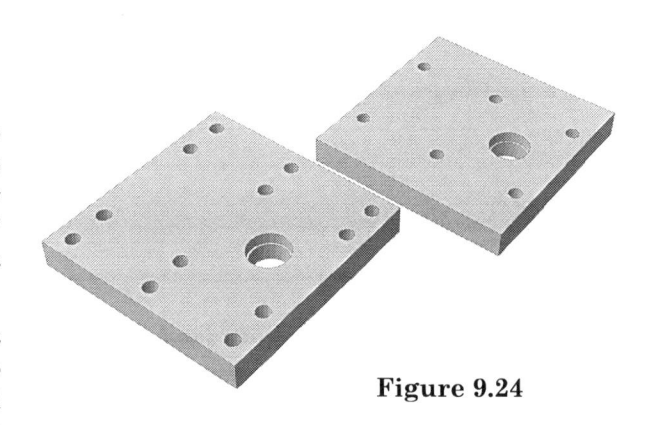

Figure 9.24

Step 3 - Layout the Y Bearing Mounts

As in step 1, take four of the 6" x 6" x 3/4" blocks and layout the holes that need to be drilled as shown in Figure 9.25.

You will need two blocks with the layout shown in Figure 9.25. These will be used on the rear of the Y axis.

The large cutout shown in Figure 9.25 can be larger than the dimensions shown, but not smaller. You can also make it a square notch if you like. This slot is to give you access to the 1/2" shaft collars for adjustment.

Once cut label these "Y Bearing Mount Rear"

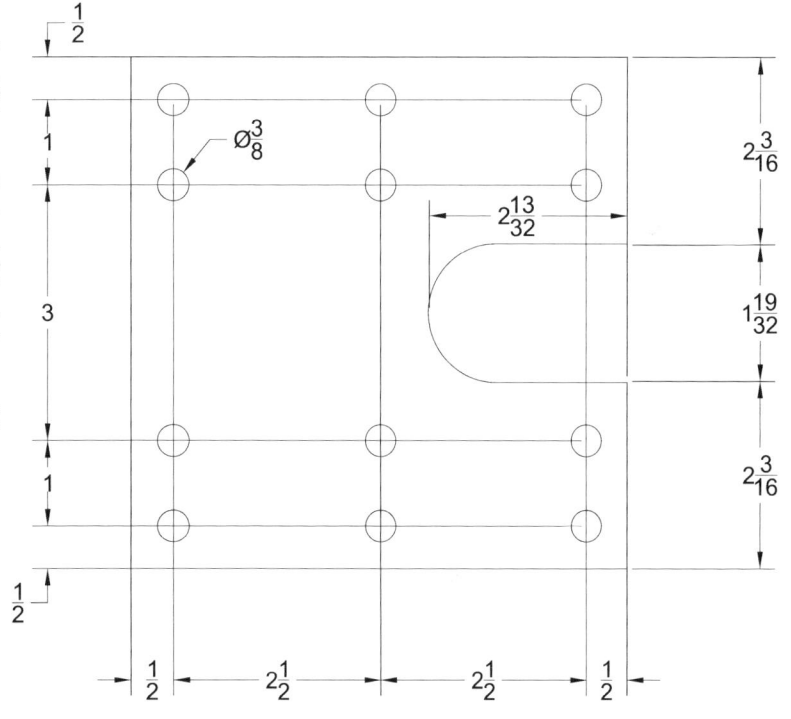

Figure 9.25

Building the KRMx01 CNC

Additionally, you will need two blocks with the layout shown in Figure 9.26. The blocks will be mounted on the front of the Y axis.

Notice that these are identical to the previous two blocks with the outer six holes removed.

Once cut label these "Y bearing mount front".

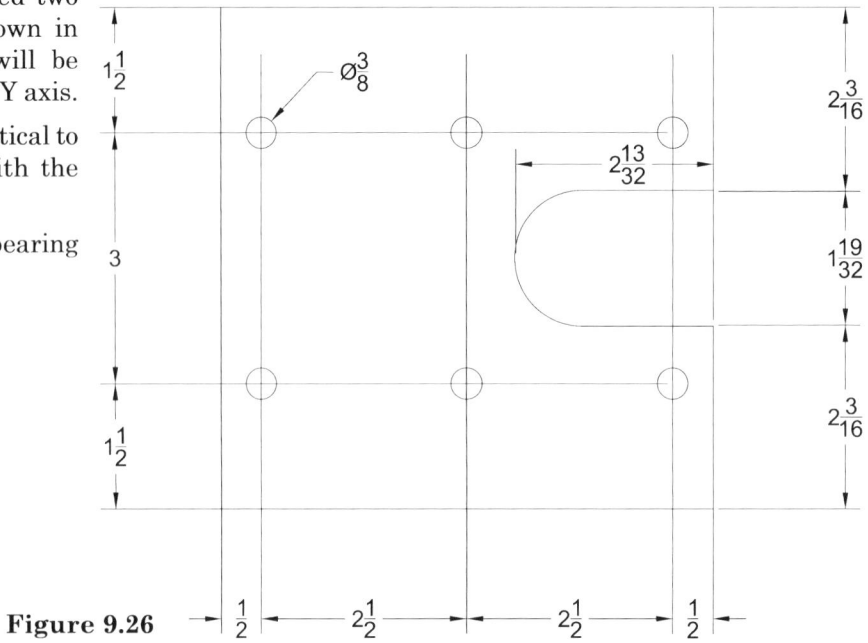

Figure 9.26

Step 4 - Drill the Y Bearing Mounts

As before, drill the smaller holes shown in Figure 9.27 with a 3/8" drill bit. Use a jigsaw, band saw, or scroll saw to cut the larger slot.

Once the block is complete, label it "Y Bearing Mount Rear" and "Y Bearing Mount Front". Use the techniques outlined earlier to help you cut the notches.

Again, keep in mind that you will need two of each of these blocks.

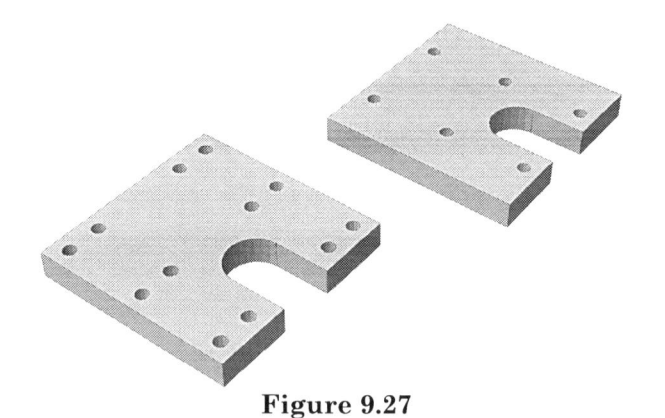

Figure 9.27

Step 5 - Layout the Y Bearing Stops

As before, take four of the 6" x 6" x 1/8" blocks and layout the holes that need to be drilled as shown in Figure 9.28.

You will need two blocks with the layout shown in Figure 9.28. Make sure you use the 1/8" blocks you cut out of the hardboard. These will be mounted on the rear of the Y axis.

Once cut label these " Y Bearing Mount Stop Rear"

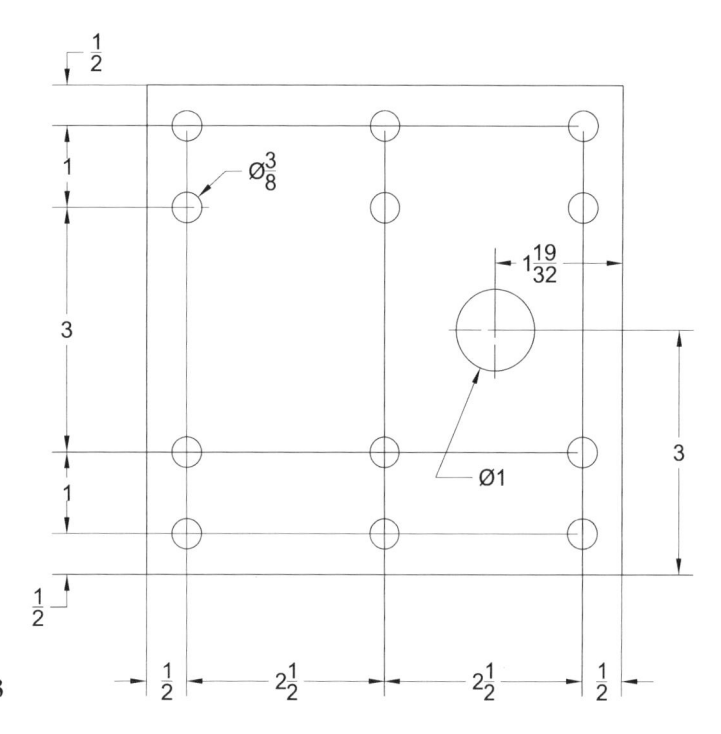

Figure 9.28

Additionally, you will need two blocks with the layout shown in Figure 9.29.

The blocks will be mounted on the front of the Y axis.

Notice that these are identical to the previous two blocks with the outer six holes removed.

Once cut label these "Y Bearing Stop Front"

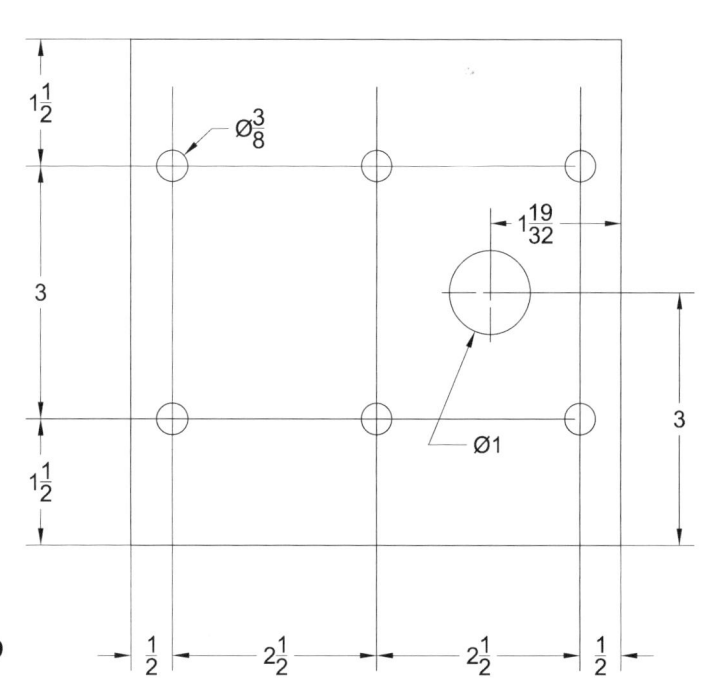

Figure 9.29

Building the KRMx01 CNC   **121**

Step 6 - Drill the Y Bearing Stops

Drill the smaller holes shown in Figure 9.30 with a 3/8" drill bit. Use a 1" Forstner bit to drill the larger hole.

Once the block is complete, label it "Y Bearing Stop Rear" and "Y Bearing Stop Front".

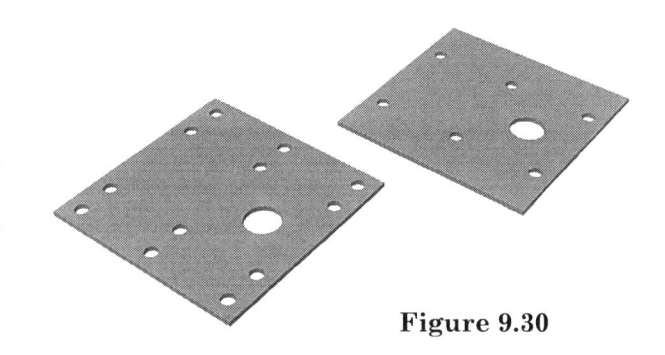

Figure 9.30

Step 7 - Layout the Y Motor Mounts

Take two 6" x 6" x 3/4" blocks and mark the holes indicated in Figure 9.31. The large hole is to allow a NEMA 23 motor to fit. It can be slightly larger, but not smaller. The slot is to allow access to the motor coupler. The smaller 7/32" holes will be used to mount the motor in a later chapter.

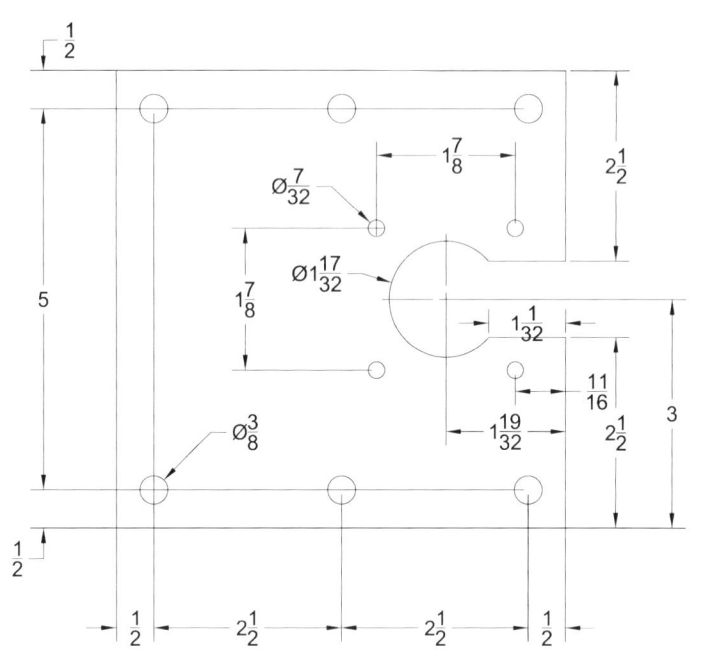

Figure 9.31

Step 8 - Drill the Y Motor Mounts

Drill the outside holes shown in Figure 9.32 with a 3/8" drill bit. Drill the four smaller holes with a 7/32" bit. Use a jigsaw, band saw, or scroll saw to cut the slot.

In a later chapter you will use them to mount your Y stepper motors.

Once the block is complete, label them both, "Y Motor Mount Rear"

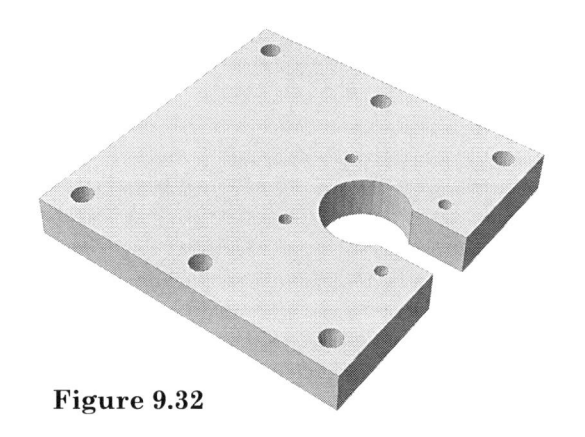

Figure 9.32

Step 9 - Layout the Y Bearing Brackets

Take the eight pieces of 1" x 1" x 6" steel angle and mark the holes shown in Figure 9.33 and 9.34.

Four of the brackets should be marked with the holes shown in Figure 9.33.

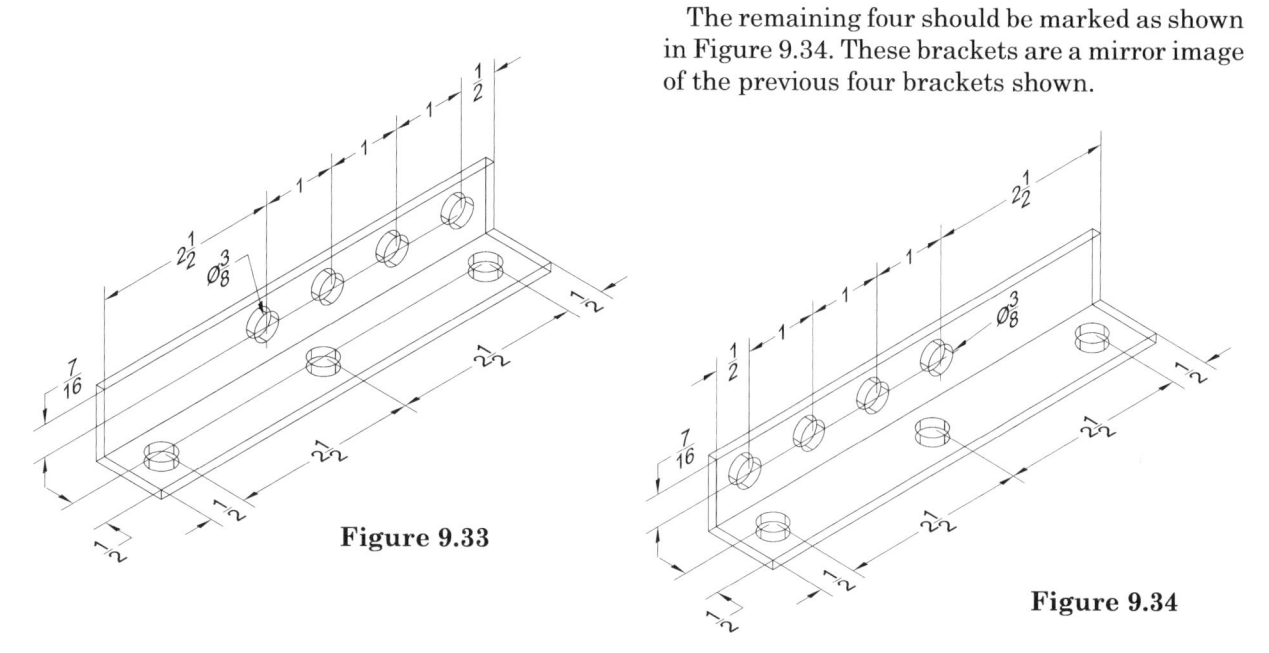

The remaining four should be marked as shown in Figure 9.34. These brackets are a mirror image of the previous four brackets shown.

Figure 9.33

Figure 9.34

Step 10 - Drill the Y Bearing Brackets

Using the techniques from previous chapters, dent and drill the seven, 3/8" holes into each of the 1" x 1" pieces of the cut steel angle. These will be used to mount the motor block assemblies to the Y-beam extrusions. One of each type is used to mount each block. The finished brackets should look lit the two shown in Figure 9.35.

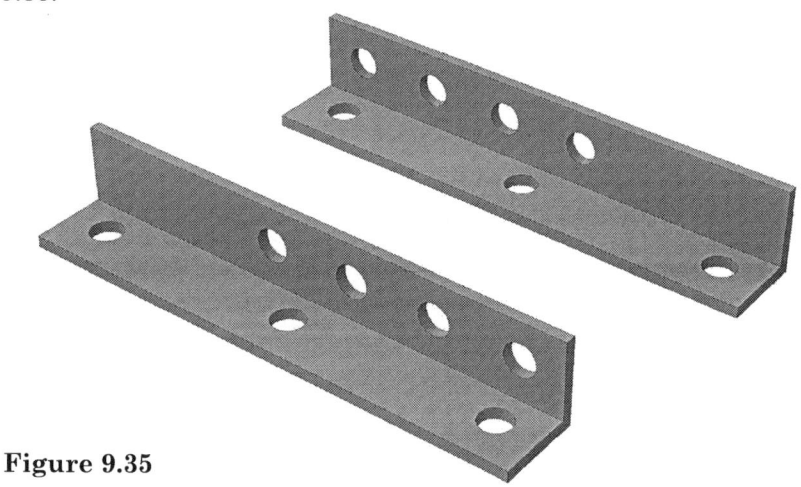

Figure 9.35

Building the KRMx01 CNC **123**

Step 11 - Add Bolts to Y-beam

Start by inserting twelve, 1/4-20 x 3/4" carriage bolts into the slots at the end of the Y-beam extrusion as shown in Figure 9.36.

Four of the bolts will be used later for future upgrades. Make sure that they are in the two slots closest to the inside of the CNC. Slide these bolts towards the center and out of the way for now. Add a washer, lock washer, and hex nut, and tighten them so they don't rattle.

Four bolts will be inserted into the top four slots and four bolts will be inserted into the bottom slots as shown in Figure 9.36.

Repeat this on both ends of both Y-beams.

Figure 9.36

Step 12 - Mount the Bearing Brackets

Add one of the bearing brackets to the bolts on the top, then add 1/4" washers, lock washers, and hex nuts, as shown in Figure 9.37. Only finger tighten.

Repeat for the bracket on the bottom. Note that the brackets are oriented so that they overhang on the outside of the beam as shown in Figure 9.38. Each end will require one of each type of bracket.

You want the top of the angle to be flush with the top of the extrusion.

Take a piece of scrap or one of your blocks and place it on the top of the extrusion. Butt the top of the steel angle against the block and tighten the nuts.

Repeat the bracket attachment on the end of each Y-beam extrusion.

Figure 9.37

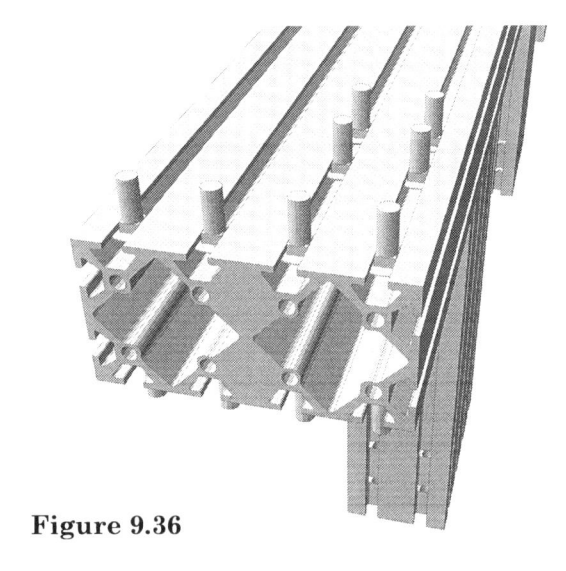

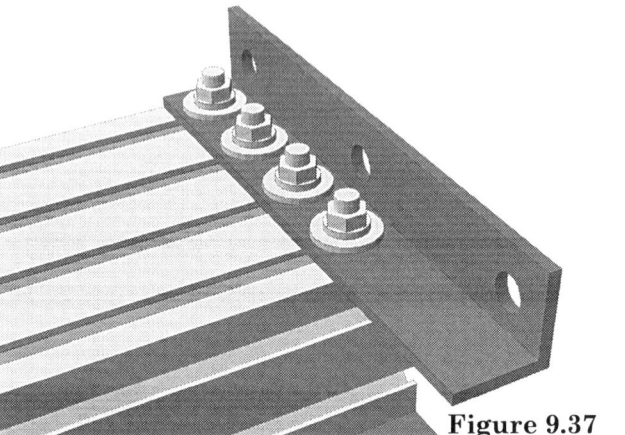

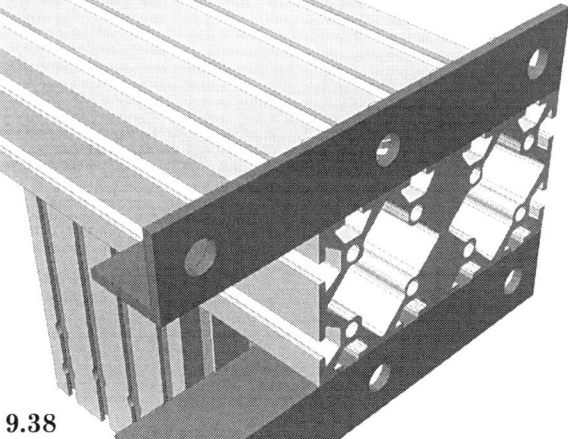

Figure 9.38

Step 13 - Assemble the Rear Bearing Blocks

Place a 1/2" bearing in the pocket on one of the Y bearing blocks marked "Y Bearing Block Rear" as shown in Figure 9.39. Next, sandwich the 1/8" bearing stop (rear), in between the bearing block and bearing mount, (rear). The open exposed end of the bearing should be facing the inside, towards the bearing stop.

Set the assembly against the set of bearing brackets on the rear of the CNC, and insert six, 2-1/2" bolts with washers through the inside of the bracket as shown in Figure 9.39. Next, add a 1/4" washer, lock washer, and hex nut. Finger tighten only.

The side of the blocks with the bearing should be on the outside of the CNC as shown in Figure 9.40. The six holes on the top and bottom of the block will be used in a later chapter to mount the actual motor.

Repeat on the other rear Y-beam. The finished assemblies should look like the one shown in Figure 9.40.

Figure 9.39

Figure 9.40

Step 14 - Assemble the Front Bearing blocks

Place a 1/2" bearing in the pocket on one of the Y bearing blocks marked "Y Bearing Block Front" as shown in Figure 9.41. Next, sandwich the 1/8" bearing stop (front), in between the bearing block and bearing mount, (front). The exposed end of the bearing should be facing the inside, towards the bearing stop.

Set the assembly against the set of bearing brackets on the front of the CNC, and insert six, 2-1/2" bolts with washers through the inside of the bracket as shown in Figure 9.41. Next, add a 1/4" washer, lock washer, and hex nut. Finger tighten only.

The side of the blocks with the bearing should be on the outside of the CNC.

Repeat on the other front Y-beam end. The finished assemblies should look like the one shown in Figure 9.42.

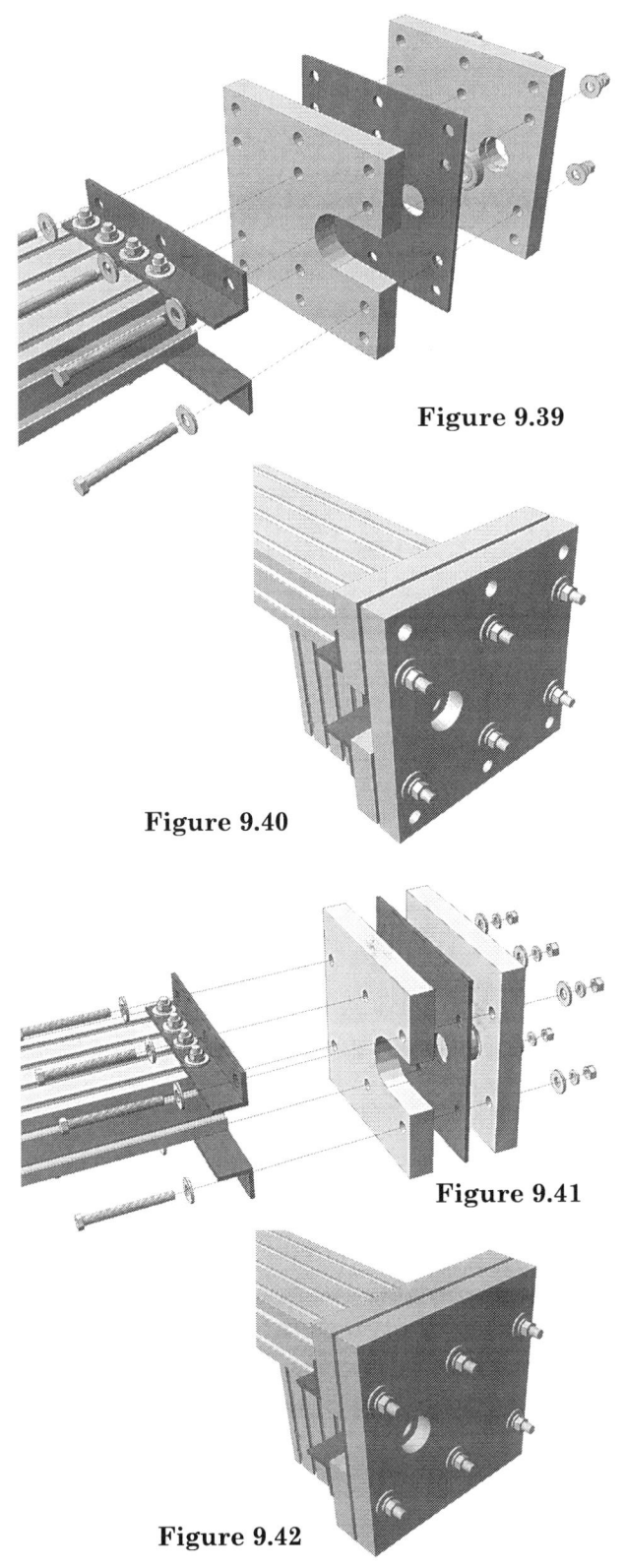

Figure 9.41

Figure 9.42

Building the KRMx01 CNC

X Motor Mounts
Step 1 - Layout the X Bearing Blocks

Take two of the 6" x 6" x 3/4" blocks and layout the holes that need to be drilled as shown in Figure 9.43.

Layout one of the blocks as shown in Figure 9.43. This block will be used on the left side of the X-beam.

Once cut, label these "X Bearing Block Left"

Important!

The open (larger) portion of the large hole is on the side of the block shown in Figure 9.43.

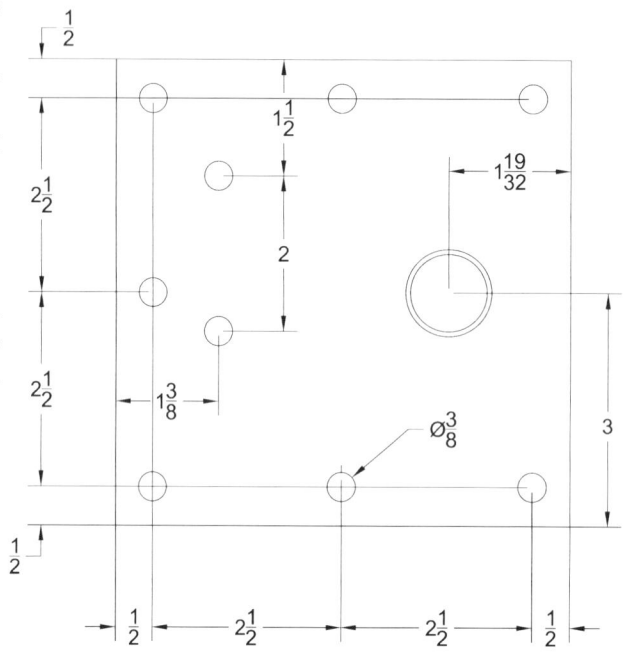

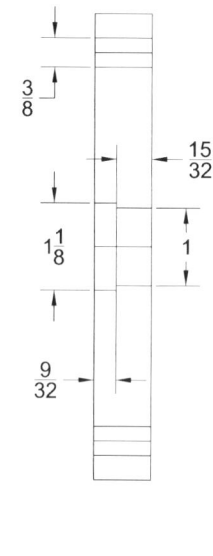

Figure 9.43

Layout on of the blocks as shown in Figure 9.44. This block will be used on the right side of the X-beam.

Once cut, label these "X Bearing Block Right"

Important!

The open (larger) portion of the large hole is on the side of the block shown in Figure 9.44.

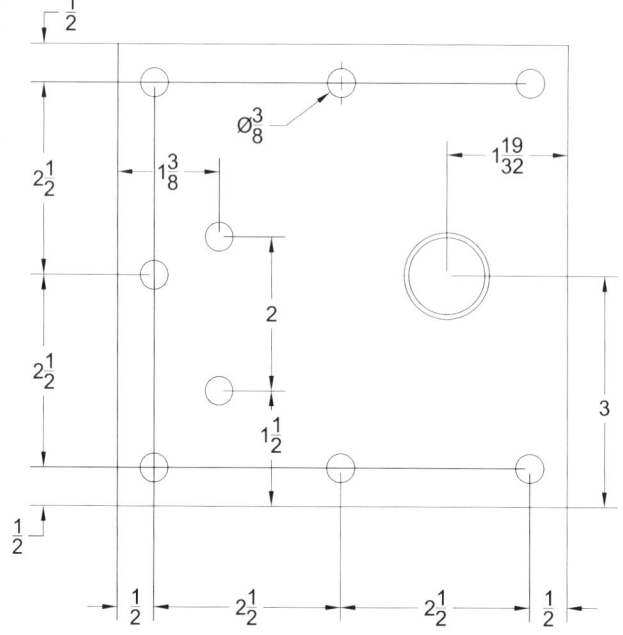

Figure 9.44

Step 2 - Drill the X Bearing Block

Use a 3/8" drill bit to create the smaller holes shown in Figure 9.45. The larger hole is used to hold the bearing. Start by using a 1-1/8" Forstner bit to drill a pocket 9/32" deep. Then, using a 1" Forstner bit, drill the rest of the way through.

When drilling the 9/32" pocket, it's important that you don't drill too deep. You can always go back and add to the pocket as needed. The goal is to have the bearing slightly exposed outside the pocket. If the pocket is too deep, the bearing will wiggle back and forth and result in excessive backlash.

Once the blocks are complete, label them "X Bearing Block Right" and "X Bearing Block Left".

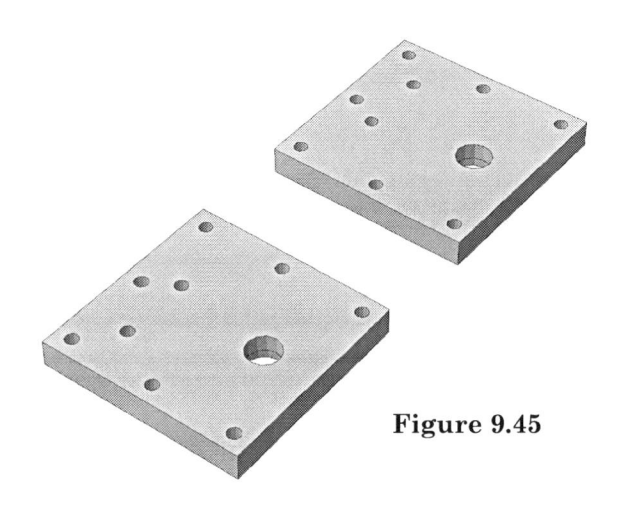

Figure 9.45

Step 3 - Layout the X Bearing Mounts

Take two of the 6" x 6" x 3/4" blocks and layout the holes as shown in Figure 9.46. The large notch can be larger than the dimensions shown, but not smaller. You can also make it a square notch if you like. This slot is to give you access to the 1/2" shaft collars for adjustment.

Once cut, label one of these "X Bearing Mount Right" and the other "X Bearing Mount Left".

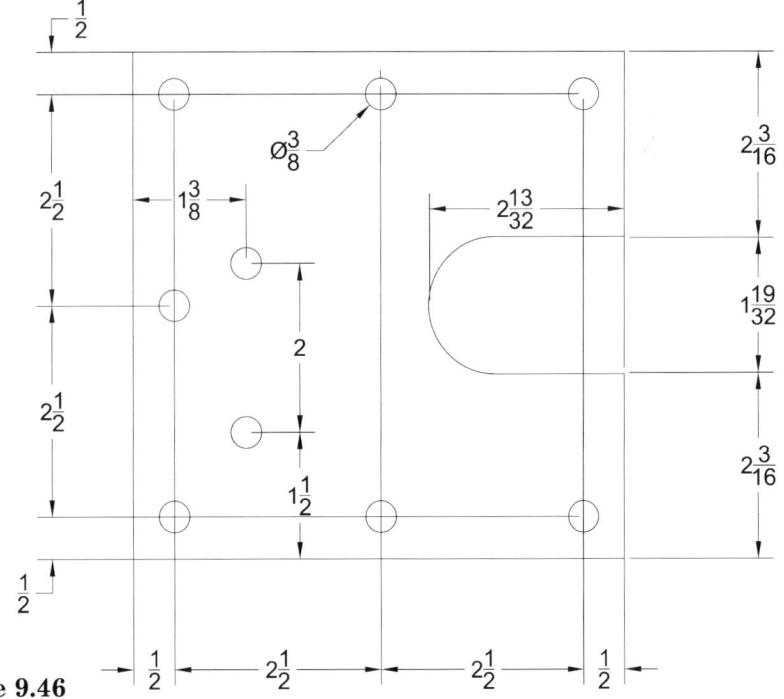

Figure 9.46

Building the KRMx01 CNC **127**

Step 4 - Drill the X Bearing Mounts

As before, drill the smaller holes shown in Figure 9.47 with a 3/8" drill bit. Use a jigsaw, band saw, or scroll saw to cut the slot. Remember that you need two of these. They are the same layout and you will simply flip one of them to use on the opposite side of the beam.

Once the blocks are complete, label one of them "X Bearing Mount Right" and the other "X Bearing Mount Left".

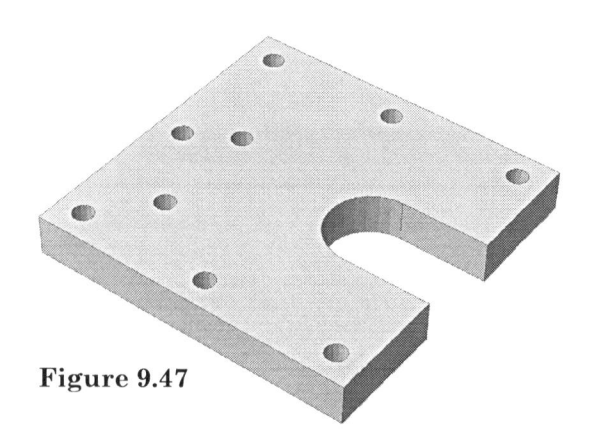

Figure 9.47

Step 5 - Layout the X Bearing Stops

Take two of the 6" x 6" x 1/8" blocks and layout the holes as shown in Figure 9.48. Make sure you use the 1/8" blocks you cut out of the hardboard.

Once cut label one of these "X Bearing Mount Stop Left" and the other "X Bearing Mount Stop Right"

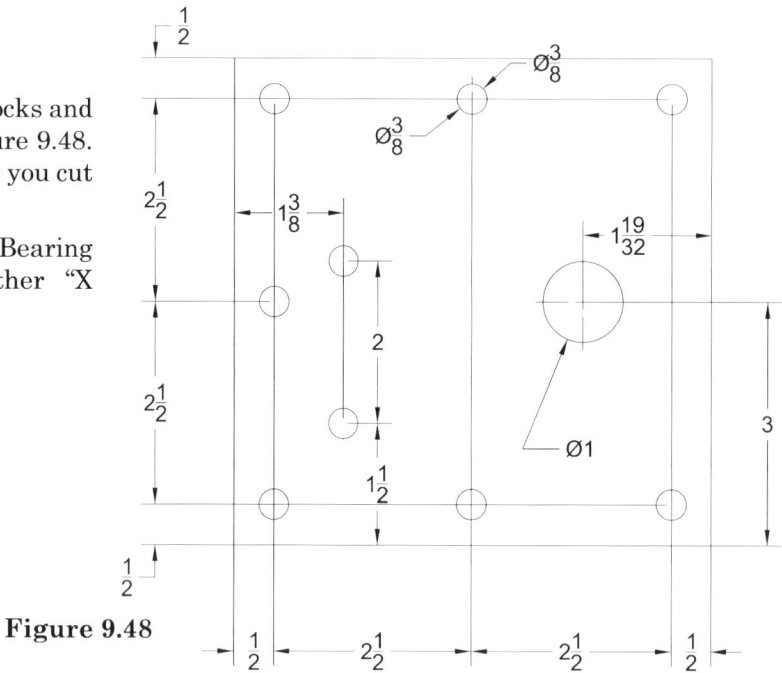

Figure 9.48

Step 6 - Drill the X Bearing Stops

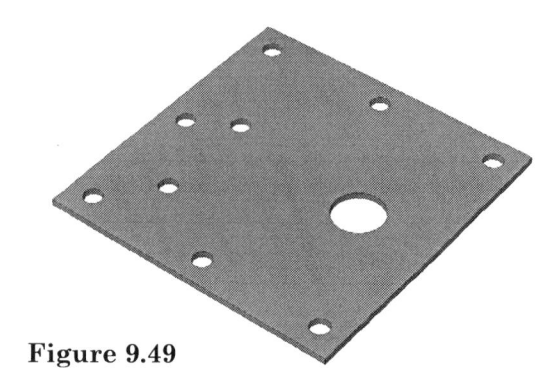

Drill the smaller holes shown in Figure 9.49 with a 3/8" drill bit. Use a 1" Forstner bit to drill the larger hole.

Figure 9.49

Step 7 - Layout the X Motor Mount

Take one 6" x 6" x 3/4" block and mark the holes indicated in Figure 9.50. The large hole is to allow a NEMA 23 motor to fit. It can be slightly larger, but not smaller. The slot is to allow access to the motor coupler. The smaller 7/32" holes will be used to mount the motor in a later chapter.

Figure 9.50

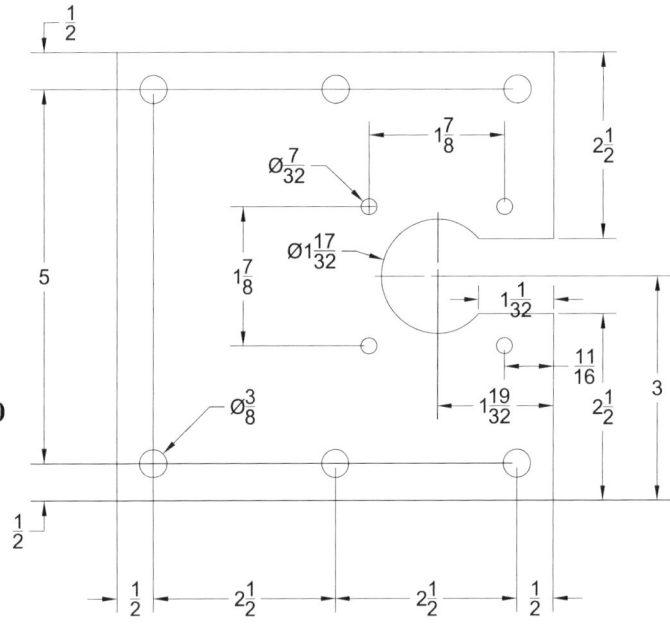

Step 8 - Drill the X Motor Mount

Drill the outside holes shown in Figure 9.51 with a 3/8" drill bit. Drill the four smaller holes with a 7/32" bit. Use a jigsaw, band saw, or scroll saw to cut the slot.

In a later chapter you will use this block to mount your X axis stepper motor.

Once the block is complete, label it "X Motor Mount"

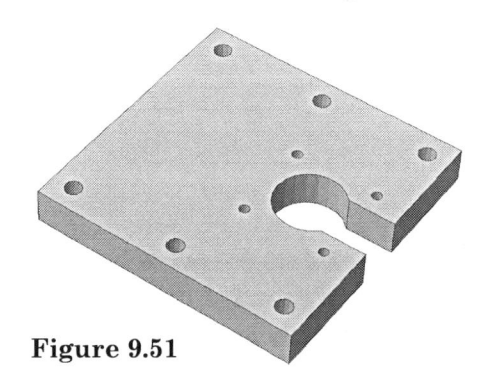

Figure 9.51

Step 9 - Layout the X Bearing Brackets

Take the two pieces of 1" x 1" x 6" steel angle and mark the five holes shown in Figure 9.52. Mark each of these "Upper X Bracket".

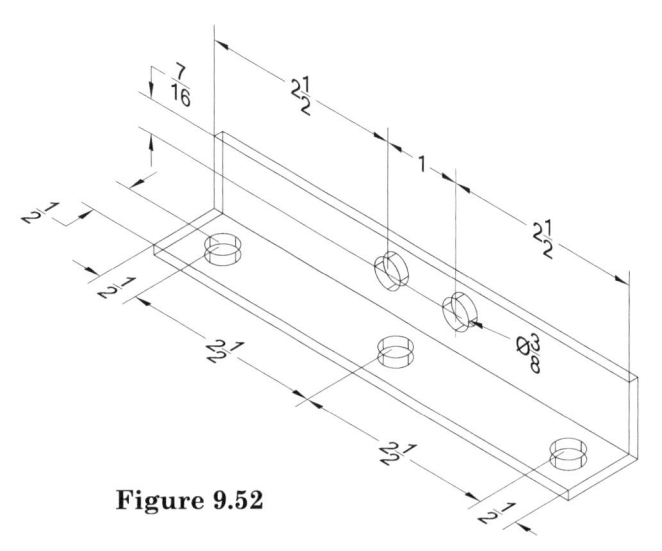

Figure 9.52

Building the KRMx01 CNC **129**

Take two of the 1" x 1" x 4" steel angles you cut earlier in the chapter and mark each with the markings shown in Figure 9.53. They are mirrored copies of each other.

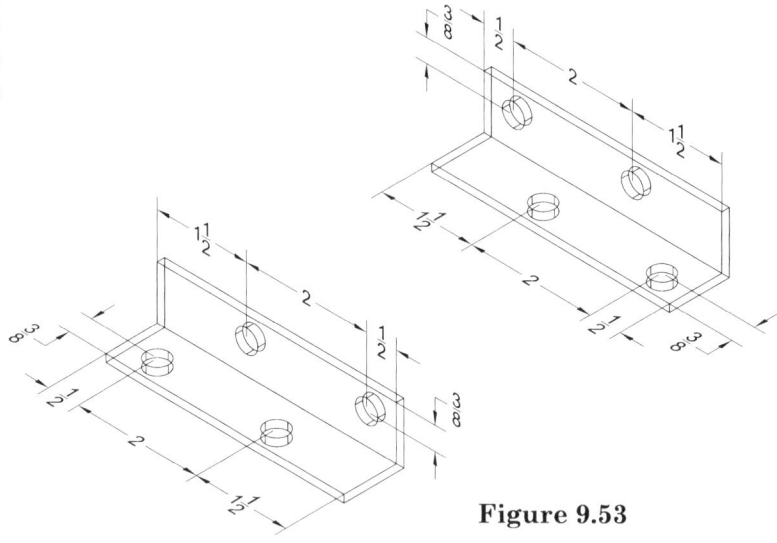

Figure 9.53

Step 10 - Drill the X Bearing Brackets

Using the techniques from previous chapters ,dent and drill the five, 3/8" holes into each of the 1" x 1" X 6" pieces that you marked in the last step. These are the upper brackets and one of each will be used to attach the block assemblies to the X-beam extrusion. The finished brackets should look like the ones shown in Figure 9.54.

Figure 9.54

Now take the 1" x 1" x 4" pieces of steel angle, dent, and drill the four, 3/8" holes into each as shown in Figure 9.55. The bracket shown on the bottom is to be used on the left bearing assembly, so mark it "X Lower Bracket Left", and mark the other "X Lower Bracket Right".

The finished brackets should look like the ones shown in Figure 9.55.

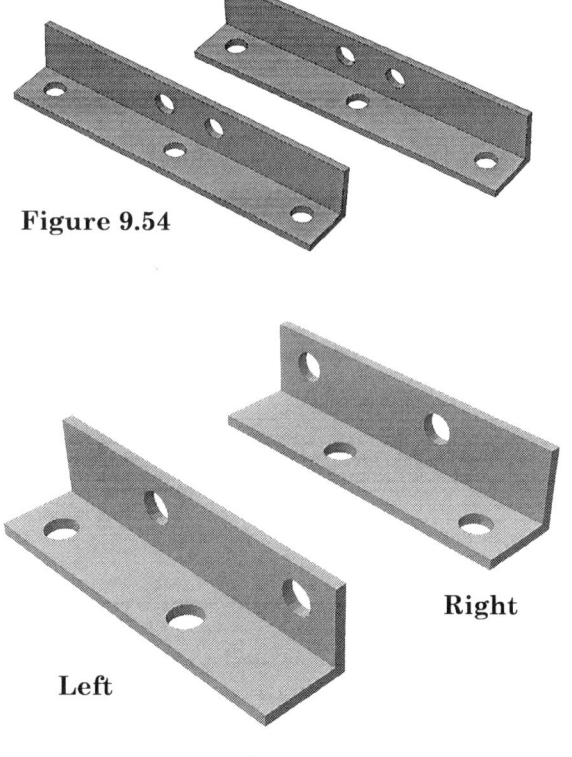

Right

Left

Figure 9.55

130   Chapter 9   Motor Mounts

Step 11 - Assemble Right Bearing Assembly

Insert a 1/2" bearing into the pocket on the bearing block. Sandwich the bearing stop block between the right bearing mount and the right bearing block as shown in Figure 9.56. Next ,insert four 1/4-20 x 2-1/2" hex bolts with washer into the lower four holes shown.

Slip a 1/4" washer, lock washer, and hex nut onto the end of each bolt. Finger tighten only.

The remaining holes will be used to attach the assembly to the bearing brackets later in the chapter.

Once the assembly is complete is should look like the one shown in Figure 9.57. Using a piece of tape mark it, "Right Bearing Assembly".

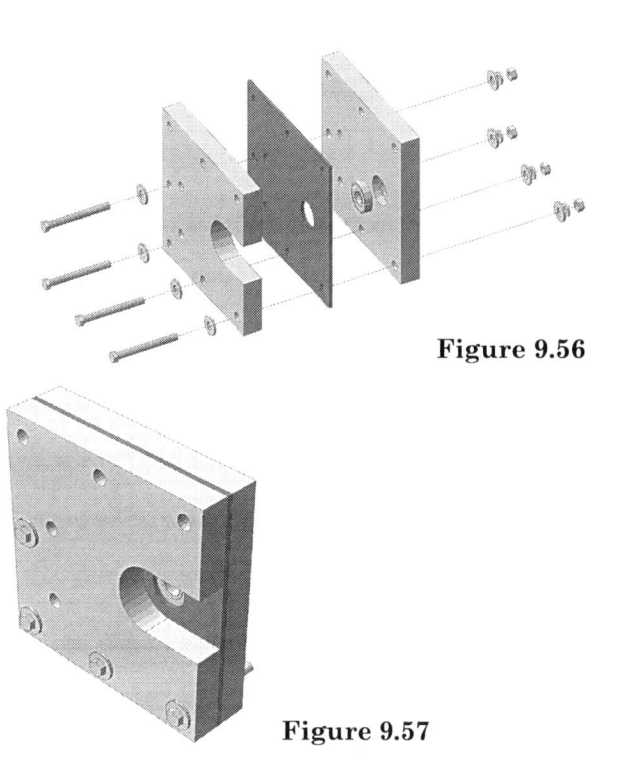

Figure 9.56

Figure 9.57

Step 12 - Assemble Left Bearing Assembly

Insert a 1/2" bearing into the pocket on the bearing block. Sandwich the bearing stop block between the left bearing mount and the left bearing block as shown in Figure 9.58. Next, insert four 1/4-20 x 4-1/2" hex bolts with washer into the lower four holes shown.

Slip a 1/4" washer and hex nut onto the end of each bolt. Finger tighten only.

Note that lock washers are not used. In a later chapter you will be adding the motor block. This is why you are using longer bolts.

The remaining holes will be used to attach the assembly to the bearing brackets later in the chapter.

Once the assembly is complete is should look like the one shown in Figure 9.59. Using a piece of tape mark it, "Left Bearing Assembly".

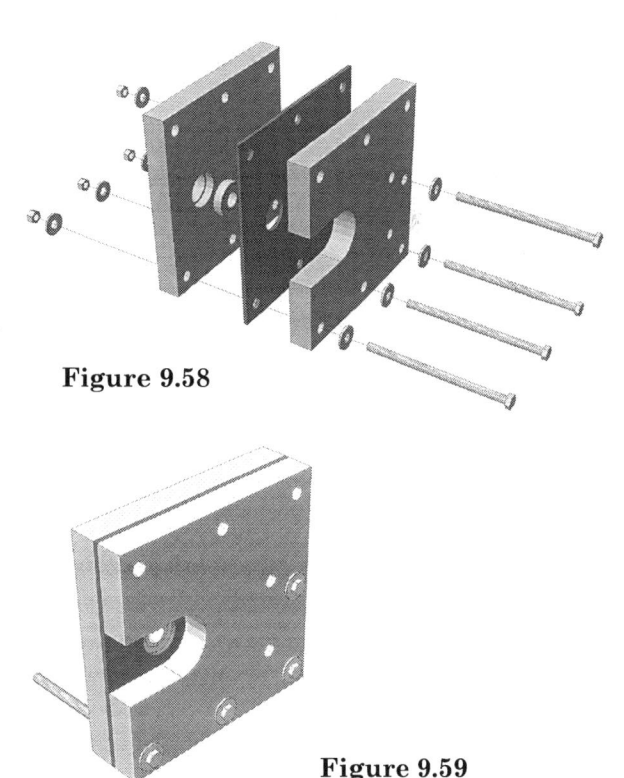

Figure 9.58

Figure 9.59

Building the KRMx01 CNC **131**

Step 13 - Attach the Right Bearing Bracket

First take seven, 1/4-20 x 5" carriage bolts and insert them into the lower (2nd from bottom) slot in the back of the X-beam as shown in Figure 9.60. These will be used later when you add a support for the dragon cable system. Move them out of the way towards the center of the beam.

Next, insert four, 1/4-20 x 3/4" carriage bolts, then attach the 6" upper bracket and the right 4" bracket as shown in Figure 9.60.

Note that the illustration is a rear view of the beam, so you are looking at the back right side of the X-beam.

Add a 1/4" washer, lock washer, and 1/4" hex nut to the bolts. The flat side of the brackets should be flush with the edge of the beam.

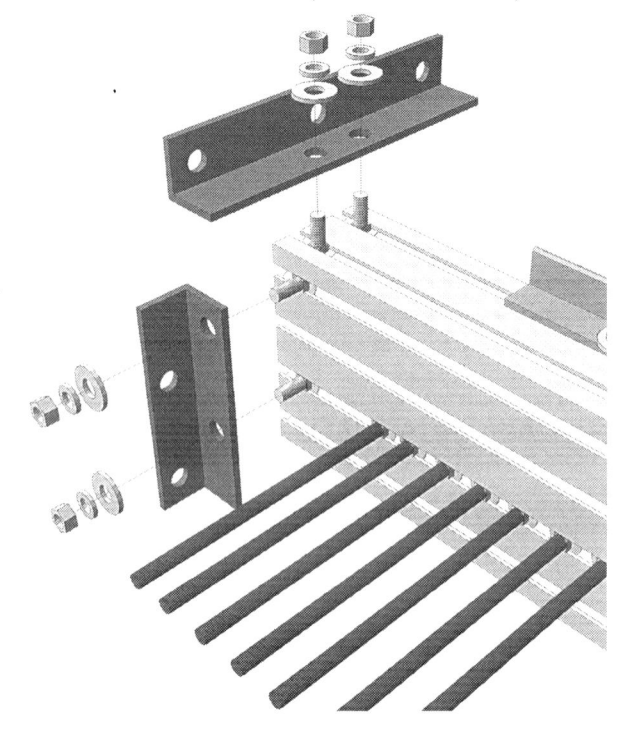

Figure 9.60

Step 14 - Attach the Left Bearing Bracket

First insert two, 1/4-20 x 3/4" carriage bolts into the top rear slot as shown in Figure 9.61. These can be used later to add a homing switch upgrade. Move them out of the way towards the center of the beam for now. Add a washer, lock washer, and a hex nut and tighten to keep them from rattling.

Next, insert four, 1/4-20 x 3/4" carriage bolts, then attach the 6" upper bracket and the left 4" bracket as shown in Figure 9.61.

Note that illustration is a rear view of the beam, so you are looking at the back left side of the X-beam.

Add a 1/4" washer, lock washer, and 1/4" hex nut to the bolts. The flat side of the brackets should be flush with the edge of the beam.

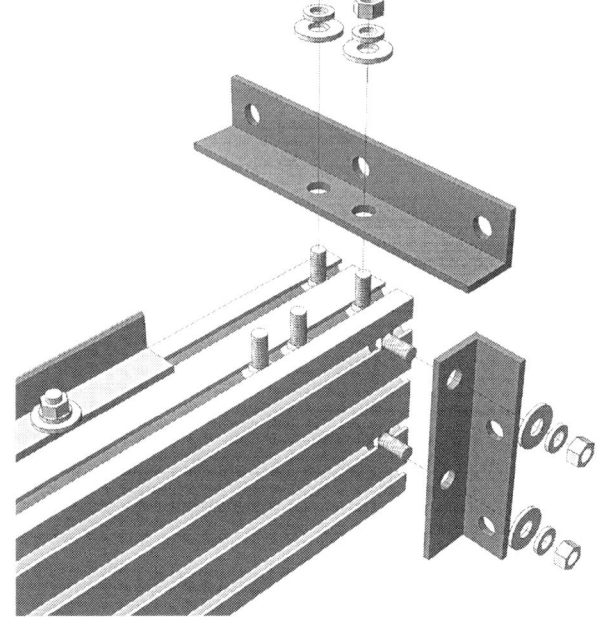

Figure 9.61

Step 15 - Attach the Right Assembly

Note the view shown in Figure 9.62 is from the right rear of the X-beam. (Right, standing in front of the machine)

Holding the right bearing assembly against the brackets, insert five, 1/4-20 x 2-1/2" hex bolts with washers into the five holes in the brackets, as shown in Figure 9.62. Add a 1/4" washer, lock washer, and hex nut. Finger tighten only.

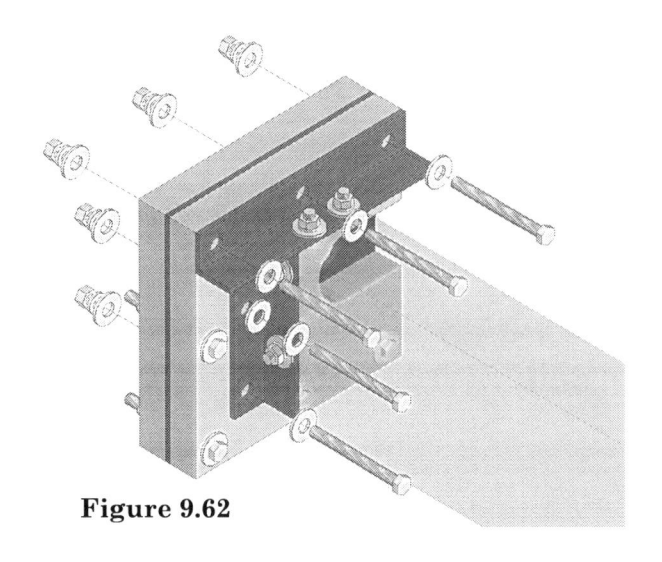

Figure 9.62

Step 16 - Attach the Left Assembly

Note the view shown in Figure 9.63 is from the left rear of the X-beam. (Left, standing in front of the machine)

Holding the right bearing assembly against the brackets, insert five, 1/4-20 x 4-1/2" hex bolts with washers into the five holes in the brackets, as shown in Figure 9.63.

Add a 1/4" washer and hex nut (no lock washers) .Finger tighten only.

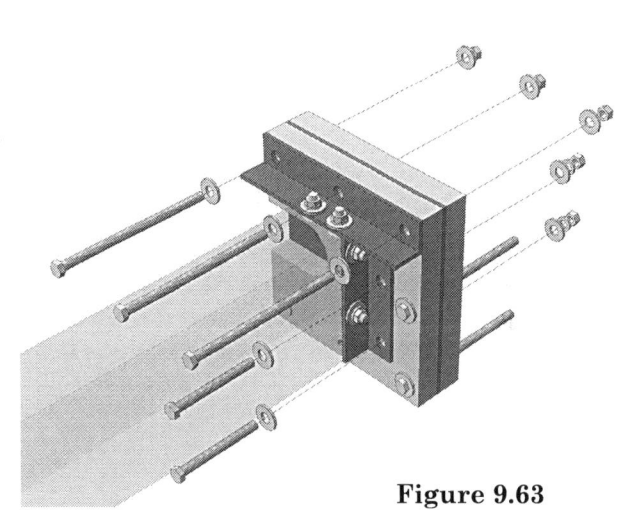

Figure 9.63

Adjustments

Tighten the 3/4" bracket bolts with a 7/16" socket wrench. The rest of the bearing bolts should be finger tightened only. You will tighten things up later once you get your ACME screws installed.

If you want to you may add the 12, 1/4-20 x 4-1/2" hex bolts to the Y bearing blocks now. Place a 1/4" washer on the bolts first then insert them into the six holes in each of the rear blocks, as shown in Figure 9.64.

Add a 1/4" washer and 1/4-20 hex nut to each bolt to hold it in place. Finger tighten only. These will be used later to mount your motors.

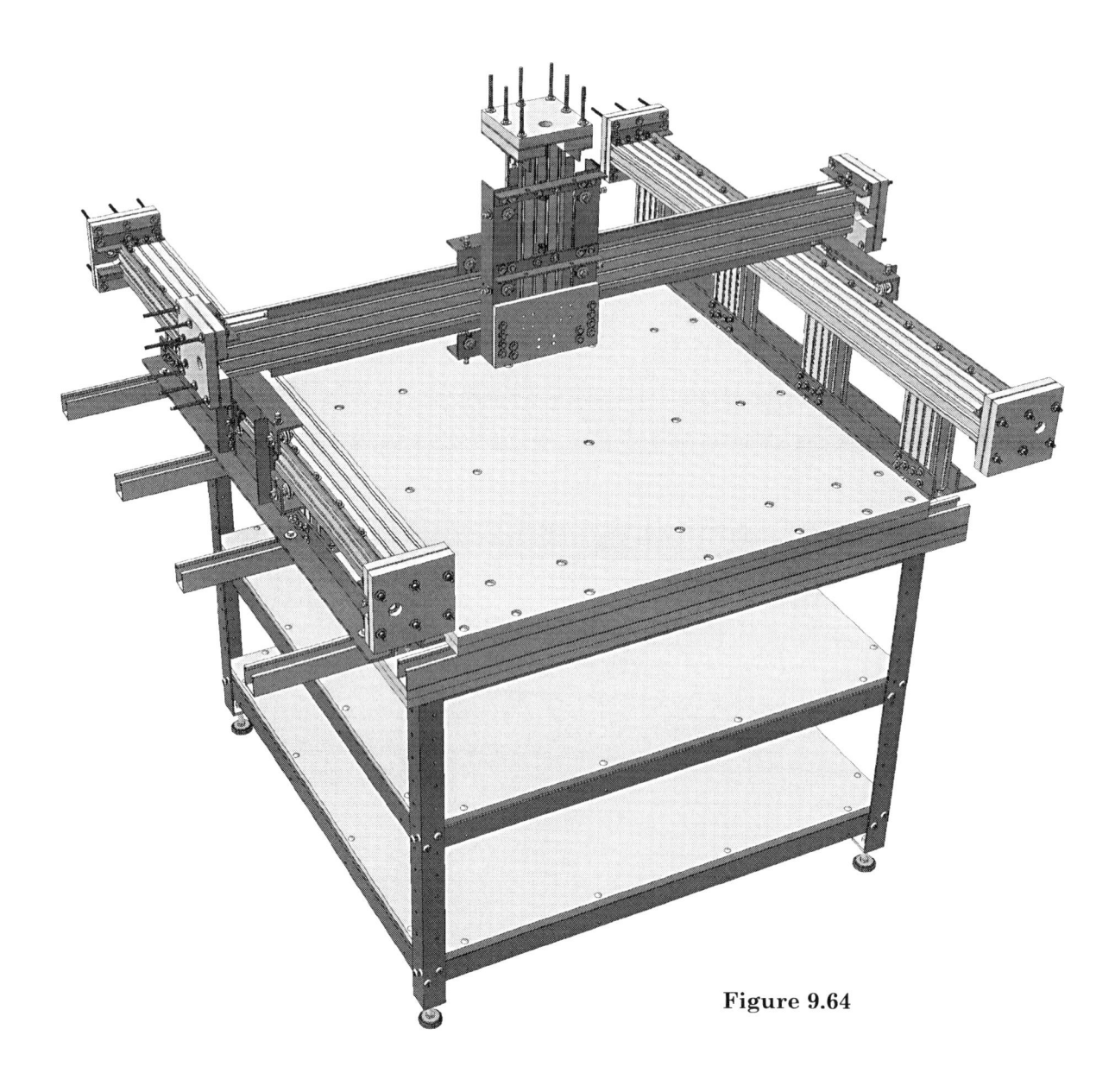

Figure 9.64

Chapter 10

Installing the ACME Screws

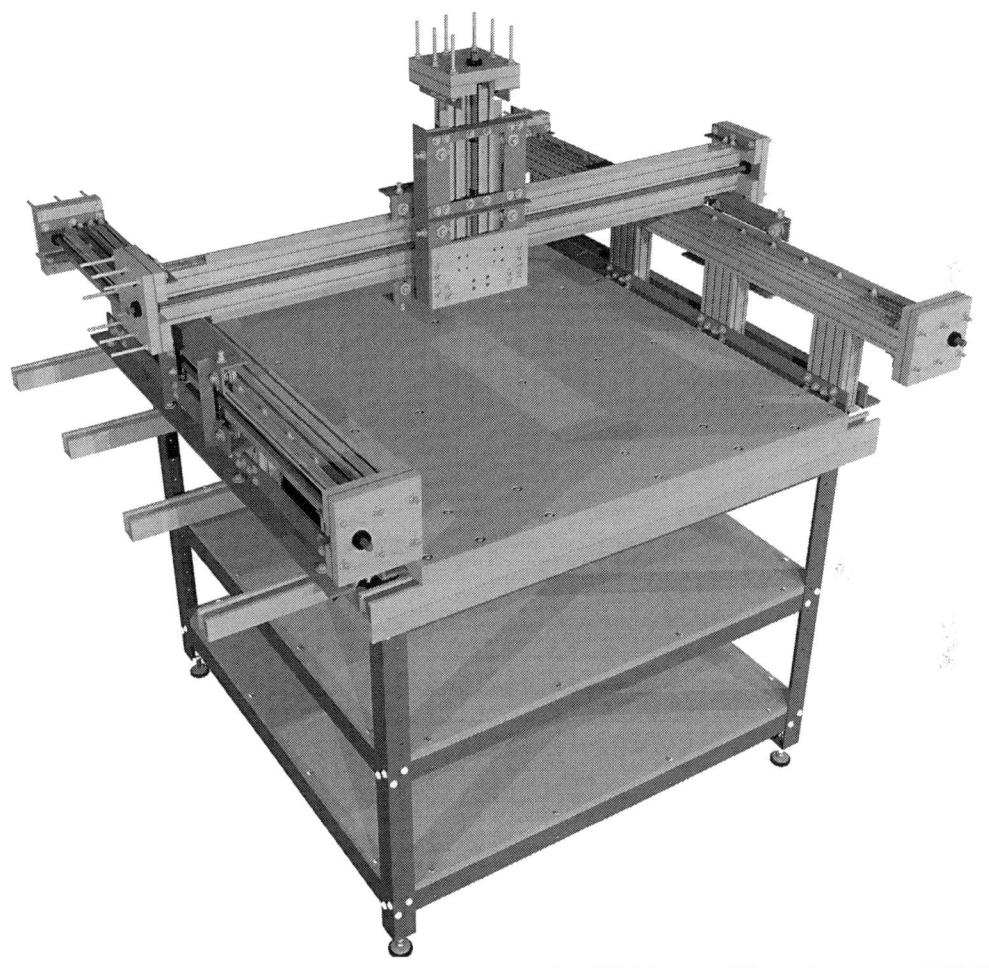

To transfer power from the stepper motors the KRMx01 utilizes five start ACME lead screws. These lead screws allow you to quickly move the carriages without excessive whip or vibration. Please note that through this chapter the term ACME rod , lead screw and ACME screw, all refer to the same thing.

Tools Needed For This Chapter

- 9/64" Allen wrench
- Reciprocating saw

Components Needed For This Chapter

- 3, 1/2-10 5 Start ACME lead screws 61-3/8"
- 1, 1/2-10 5 Start ACME lead screws 18-1/2"
- 70, 1/2" Machine bushings (OD must be less then 1")
- 14, 1/2" Shaft collar

The machine bushings used are Speeco Part #17505100. They are also available from the tractor supply company part # 1833812.

The shaft collars must be the clamping type. They are available from McMASTER-CARR Part # 6435K14. They are also available from "CNC Router Parts"

Chapter Estimates
Cost: $240
Time: One Day

Prerequisites

You need three, 1/2-10 5 Start ACME screws 61-3/8" in length. You will need to cut these from three, 72" lead screws. In addition you will need a 1/2-10 5 Start 18-1/2" long ACME screw, which will be cut from a 36" lead screw.

McMASTER-CARR sells these ACME screws. Two types are available:

Plain
- 72" # 99030A704
- 36" # 99030A304

Black Oxide
- 72" # 98940A020
- 36" # 98940A627

To cut the ACME screws to length, use a reciprocal saw with a metal cutting blade. Do not use metal to clamp the screws or you may damage them. Use some scrap MDF or other wood product to clamp them as shown in Figure 10.1. Be sure to de-bur the cut edge with a rotary tool or a metal file, or you may damage the ACME nuts.

Figure 10.1

Building the KRMx01 CNC **137**

Step 1 - Attach the Z Axis Lead Screw

Start by attaching one of the 1/2" shaft collars to the 18-1/2" ACME lead screw. It should be 1/2" from the end as shown in Figure 10.2. It's best that this end be the cut end of the lead screw; this leaves the uncut end to be inserted into the ACME nuts. Tighten this collar.

Next, take the clean end of the ACME screw and slip on seven machine bushings, then insert the screw through the top of the Z bearing assembly, as shown in Figure 10.3. Insert another three, machine bushings, and finally one of the 1/2" shaft collars.

Holding the loose shaft collar and busings, screw the ACME rod into the top ACME nut as shown in Figure 10.3. Once the ACME rod has made contact with the ACME nut, you can release the collars and bushings.

Twist the ACME screw until it is through the upper ACME nut and makes contact with the lower ACME nut. Continue twisting until about 6" of the ACME screw protrudes through the lower ACME nut. At this point you can rest the carriage on the upper shaft collar.

Note that if you attached a Z-carriage stop bolt earlier you should remove it now.

Important

While the illustration shows the machine bushings and lower collar placement well bellow the notch in the bearing mount block, this is for illustration only. The bushings and collar must always remain within the bounds of the notch or the screw will not fit properly.

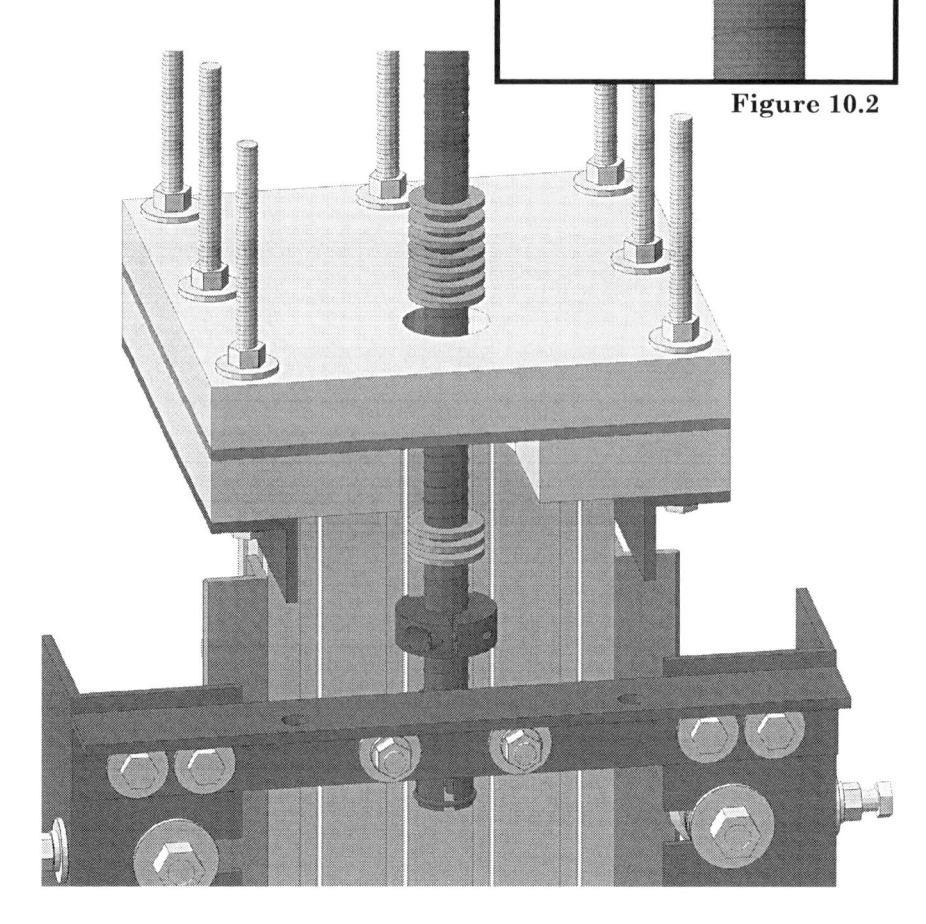

Figure 10.2

Figure 10.3

Step 2 - Position and Tighten the Bearing Collar

Pinch the two shaft collars together firmly squeezing the machine bushings between them, and tighten the lower shaft collar with the 9/64" Allen wrench. There should be no play between the two collars. The tightened collars should look like those shown in Figure 10.4.

At this point the Z bearing block assembly should still be slightly loose with a little play.

Step 3 - Attach the X Axis Lead Screw

Start by attaching one of the 1/2" shaft collars to one of the 61-3/8" ACME lead screws. It should be 1/2" from the end as shown in Figure 10.6. As mentioned before, it's best that this end be the cut end of the ACME screw. This leaves the uncut end to be inserted into the ACME nuts. Tighten this collar.

Position the X-carriage all the way to the right side of the CNC. Next take the clean end of the ACME screw and slip on seven, machine bushings then insert the screw through the left bearing assembly on the X axis, as shown here. Stop inserting when the tip is barely extruding the inside of the bearing stop block and insert another three machine bushings. Slide the screw a little more and slip on another 1/2" shaft collar.

Continue sliding the lead screw until it comes in contact with the ACME nut on the left side of the X-carriage, as shown in Figure 10.7.

Figure 10.4

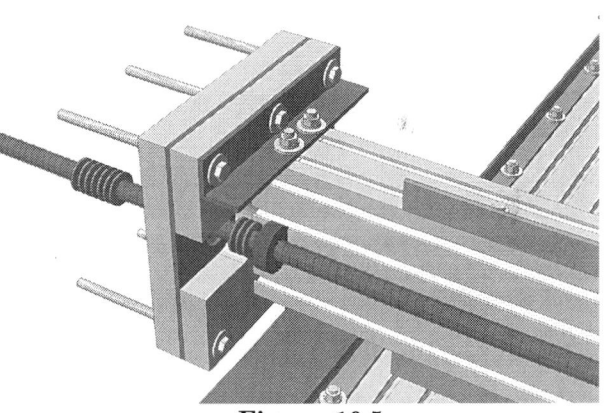

Figure 10.5

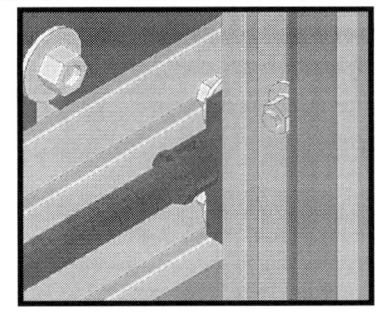

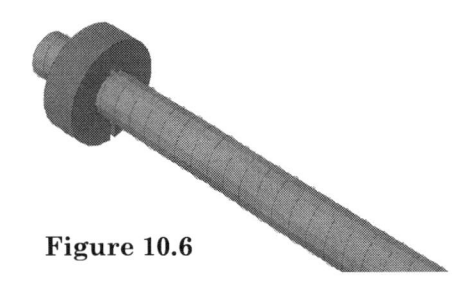

Figure 10.7

Figure 10.6

Building the KRMx01 CNC   **139**

Twist the ACME screw until it reaches the right ACME nut and then the slot on the right bearing assembly. With the lead screw just barely protruding into the slot, slip on 1/2" collar and three machine bushings.

Continue to twist the lead screw until it protrudes through the right bearing assembly and add seven more machine bushings and a 1/2" collar, as shown in Figure 10.8.

Tip

Inserting the machine bushings on the right side can be difficult because the 1/2" collar leaves very little room. Feel free to remove the five bolts attached to the brackets to slide the block off. Once removed, slip on the 1/2" collar and three machine bushings. Then reattach the right bearing assembly.

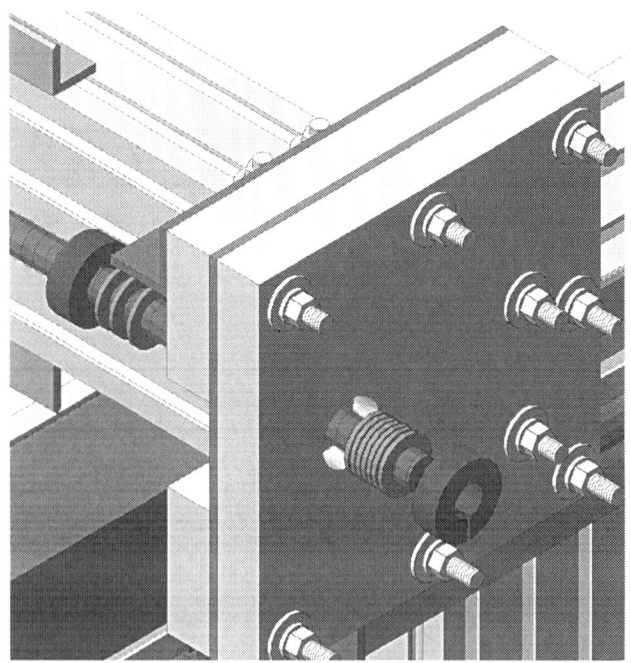

Figure 10.8

Step 4 - Position and Tighten the Bearing Collars

On the left assembly, pinch the two shaft collars together, firmly squeezing the machine bushings between them, and tighten the inside shaft collar with the 9/64" Allen wrench. There should be no play between the two collars. Do the same on the right assembly.

At this point, both the X bearing block assemblies should still be slightly loose with a little play. They should look like the assemblies shown in Figures 10.9 and 10.10.

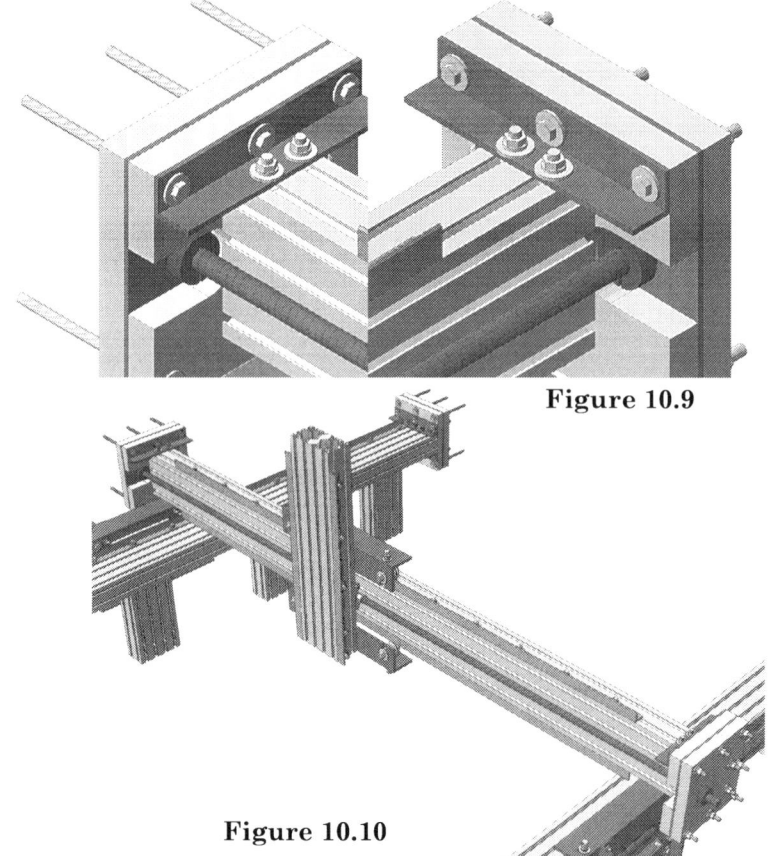

Figure 10.9

Figure 10.10

Step 5 - Attach the Y Axis Lead Screws

You can start with the left or right side Y axis. The figures show the right side. Start by attaching one of the 1/2" shaft collars to one of the 61-3/8" ACME lead screws. It should be 1/2" from the end, as shown in Figure 10.11. As mentioned before, it's best that this end be the cut end of the lead screw. This leaves the uncut end to be inserted into the ACME nuts. Tighten this collar.

You will be inserting the ACME screw from the rear of the machine. If you don't have enough space to do this then you will have to insert it from the front.

Position the Y-carriages all the way to the front of the CNC. Move them to the rear if inserting the ACME screw from the front.

Next take the clean end of the ACME screw and slip on seven machine bushings, then insert the screw through the rear (or front) bearing assembly on the Y axis, as shown in Figure 10.12. Stop inserting when the tip is barely extruding the inside of the bearing stop block and insert another three machine bushings. Slide the screw a little more and slip on the other 1/2" shaft collar.

Continue sliding the lead screw until it comes in contact with the ACME nut on the rear (or front) of the Y-carriage, as shown in Figure 10.13.

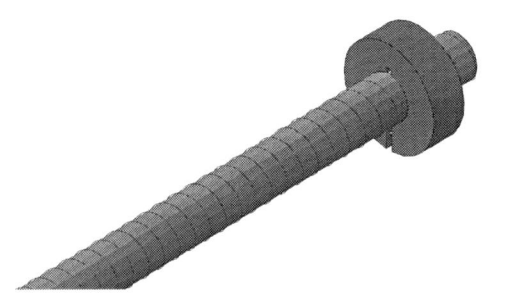

Figure 10.11

Figure 10.12

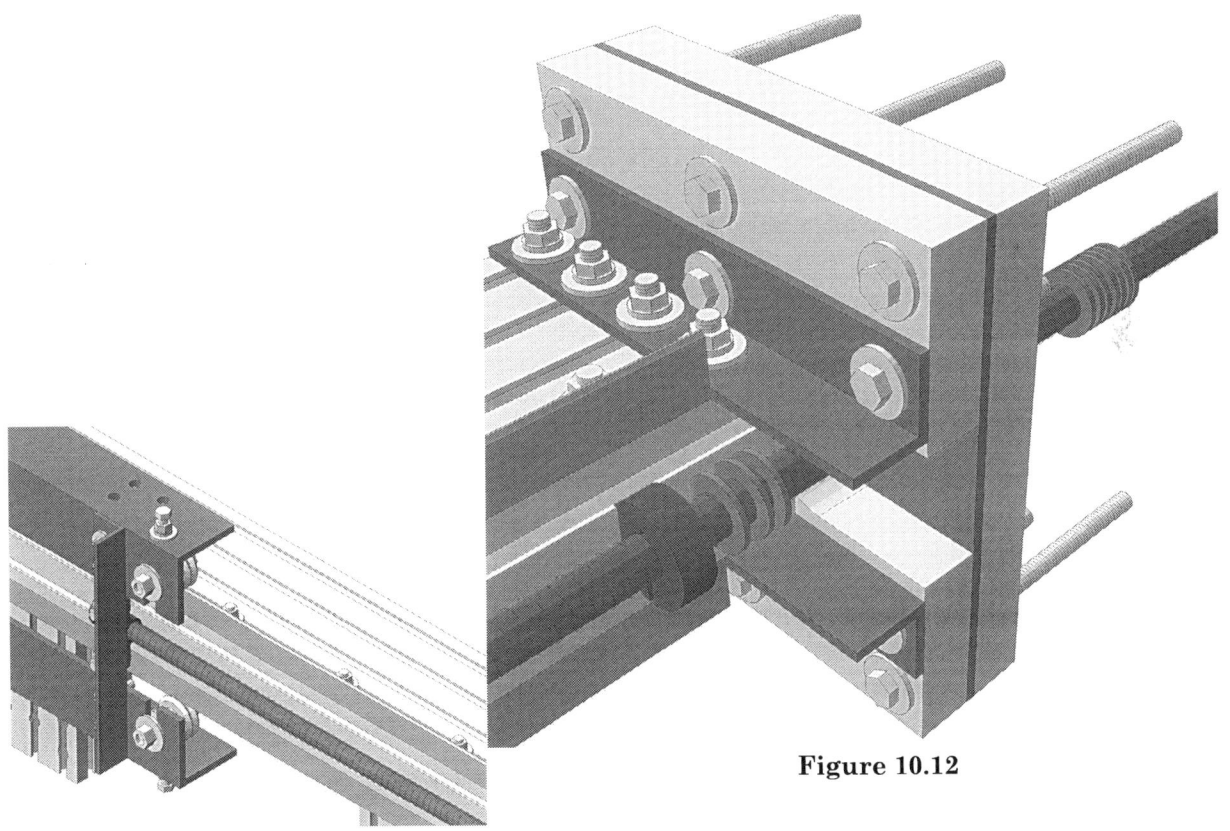

Figure 10.13

Building the KRMx01 CNC **141**

Continue screwing the ACME screw until it reaches the front (or rear) ACME nut and then the slot on the front (or rear) bearing assembly. With the lead screw just barely protruding into the notch of the block, slip on a 1/2" collar and three machine bushings. Note that Figure 10.14 shows the stop collar inserted well outside of the notch. This is only for illustration purposes. The stop collar and three bushings will only fit the ACME screw while they are positioned in the notch.

Continue to screw the lead screw until it protrudes through the front (or rear) bearing assembly and add seven more machine bushings and a 1/2" collar, as shown in Figure 10.14..

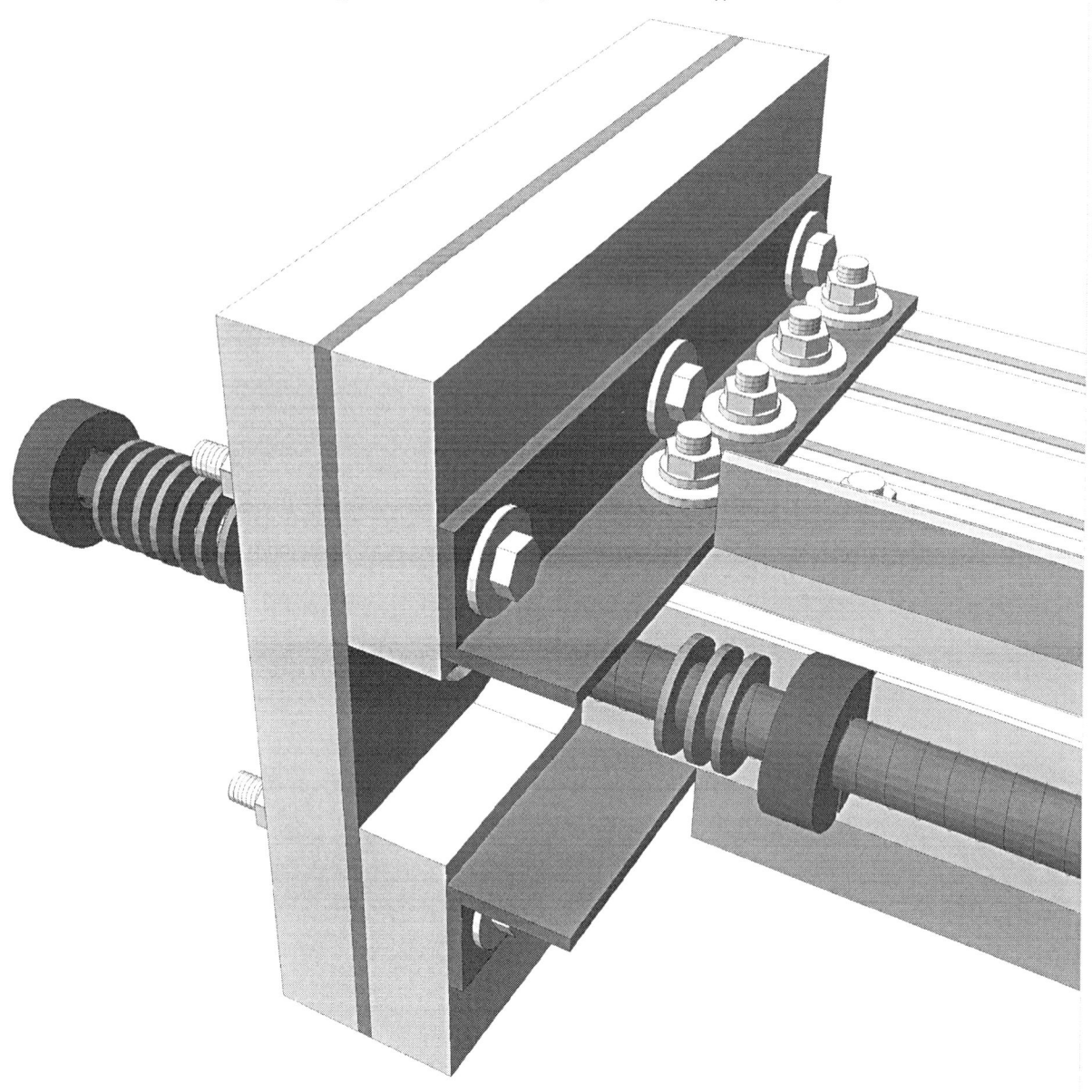

Figure 10.14

142   *Chapter 10*   Installing the ACME Screws

Step 6 - Position and Tighten the Bearing Collars

On the rear assembly, pinch the two shaft collars together, firmly squeezing the machine bushings between them, and tighten the inside shaft collar with the 9/64" Allen wrench. There should be no play between the two collars. Do the same on the front assembly. All collars should be tight and there should be no play when you mover the Y ACME screw with your hand. Repeat the process on the left side Y axis.

At this point all the Y bearing assemblies should still be slightly loose with a little play. They should look like the assemblies shown in Figures 10.15 and 10.16.

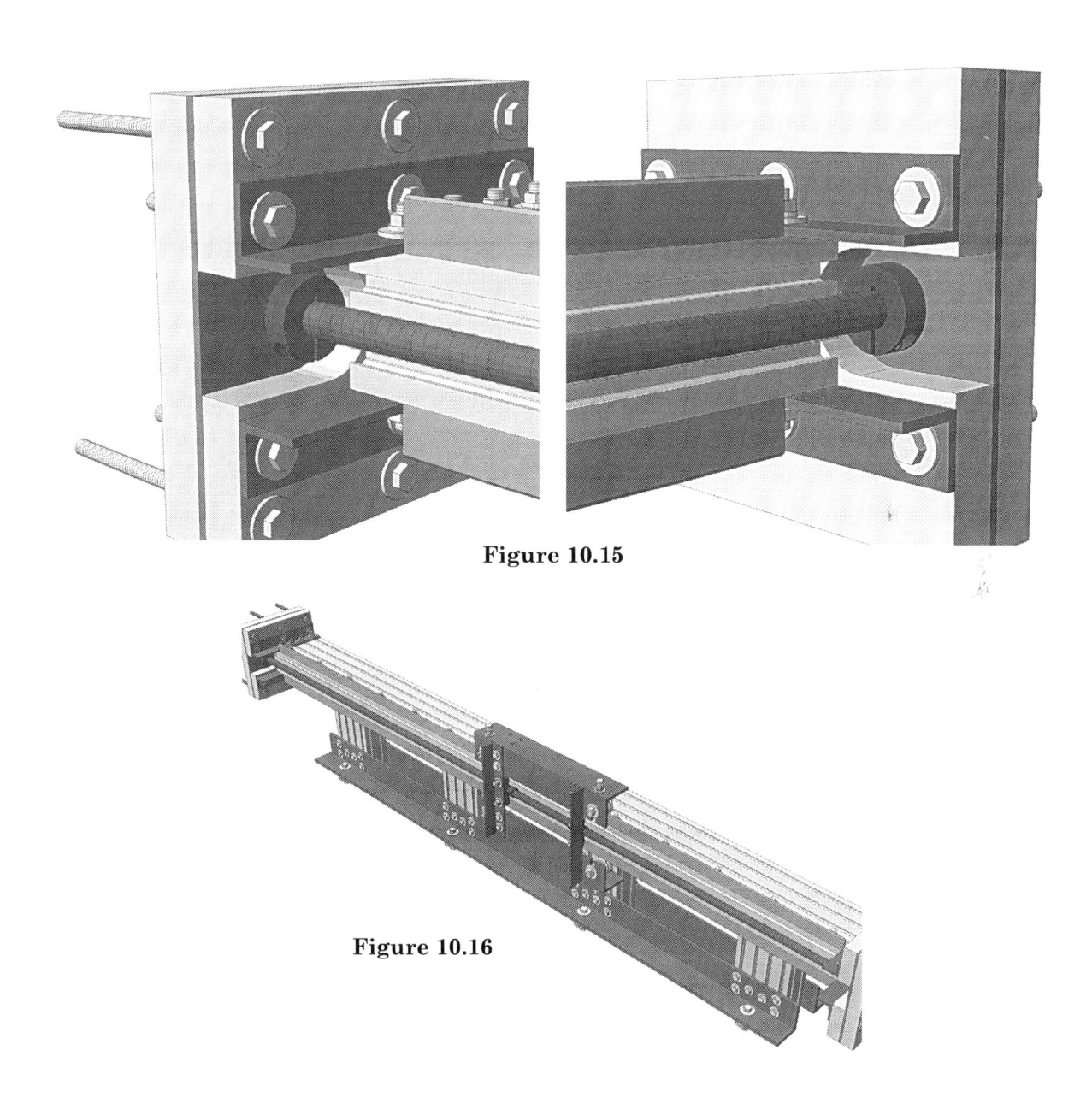

Figure 10.15

Figure 10.16

Building the KRMx01 CNC

Adjustments

All bearing assemblies should have some play in them. The lead ACME nuts should also be a loose. Later, once you have your motors and controller attached, you will move each axis into position before tightening the bearing assemblies and ACME nuts.

Keep in mind if you want to move the Y axis at this point you need to twist both front collars at the same time and in the same direction. You may want to keep the Y axis near the front of the CNC for the time being.

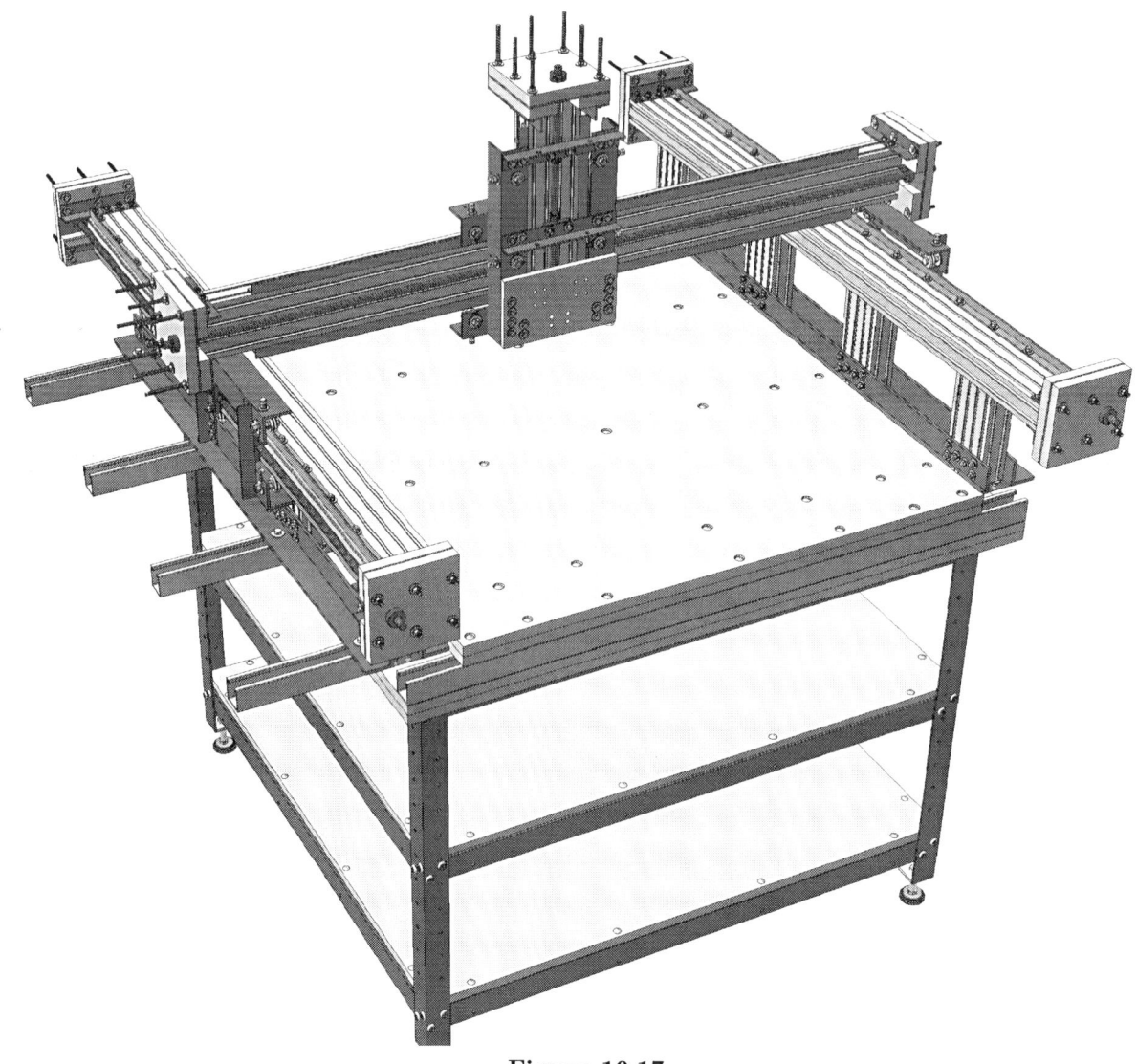

Figure 10.17

Chapter 11

KRMx01 Electronics

The next logical step in the construction of the KRMx01 would be the mounting of the motors to the CNC machine. However, once the motors are installed it is difficult to move the carriages without some sort of electrical control.

In this chapter you will hookup just enough electronics for you to control of the stepper motors. Usually, having the motors available disconnected from the CNC works best for this initial hookup and configuration.

The wiring aspect of building your own CNC can be a little daunting, therefore the approach here will be very structured and as simple as possible. Instead of jumping into advanced topics like probe hookup and motor control, you are going to start with the basics.

You will wire your power supply to the G540 controller using the simplest possible configuration. Just enough hookup and control, to gain control over the stepper motors.

Tools Needed For This Chapter

- Phillips screwdriver
- 5/32" Drill bit
- Portable drill or drill press
- Wire cutters
- Wire stripers

You will need two Phillips screwdrivers: A normal or medium sized screwdriver and a smaller screwdriver used to tighten the G540 terminals. A screwdriver that has a shaft of about 1/8" in diameter should work.

Components Needed For This Chapter

- 1, 24" x 48" x 1/4" Hardboard
- 2, 1-1/2" Angle brackets
- 2, #6-32 x 3/8" Machine screws
- 4, #6-32 x 1/2" Machine screws
- 8, #6-32 x 3/4" Machine screws
- 28, #6 Washers
- 14, #6-32 Hex nuts
- 5, M3-0.5 x 10mm Machine screws
- 1, 6 Position terminal strip
- 1, 4 Position terminal strip
- 3 feet of 18 gauge black wire
- 1 Foot of 18 gauge red wire
- 15 Ft 16/3 Extension cord
- G540 4 Axis controller (CNCRouterParts)
- 48V Power supply (Jameco #295929)

Chapter Estimates
Cost: $447
Time: One Day

Prerequisites

You need to cut a piece of 1/4" stock to 14" x 24". This can be Baltic Birch plywood, hardboard, or plastic. Use what ever your local home center has on hand. Most home centers sell 24" x 48" panels of various materials. You can even get the home center to cut it for you.

The barrier strips used are from Radio Shack (part numbers 274-658 and 274-658). If you decide to use barrier strips from another source, you may need to change the mounting holes.

An extension cord is used to provide AC power to the 48V power supply. To prep the cord, you need to remove the female portion of the cord (the end that does not plug into the wall). Strip about 1/4" of the plastic on each of the leads. Its this exposed portion that will be attached to the power supply.

18 gauge wire was listed in the components section. Feel free to use larger wire such as 16 gauge. Anything thicker will not fit into the terminals on the G540. A good source for wire is your local home center. Auto parts centers also sell various colors of wire that would be suitable for this project. It is also important that you use only stranded wire. Stranded wire is less likely to break when handled or moved.

In this chapter you will be connecting your G540 and 48v power supply.

Tip

The electronics kit is the most expensive component in the KRM0x1 project. In reality, it is multiple components and as such they can be purchases separately. CNC Router Parts sell the same components as individual items. For this chapter you need only the G540 controller and the 48V power supply.

It's cheaper in the long run to purchase the complete kit. However, if you are budgeting your build, purchasing the items as needed may be a better option.

If you decide to purchase the complete electronics kit, be sure to order it with one 20' cable and three 12' cables.

Step 1 - Drill Controller Mounting Board

To mount the G540 controller, 48V power supply, and two barrier strips, you need to drill 17, 5/32" holes in the positions shown in Figure 11.1.

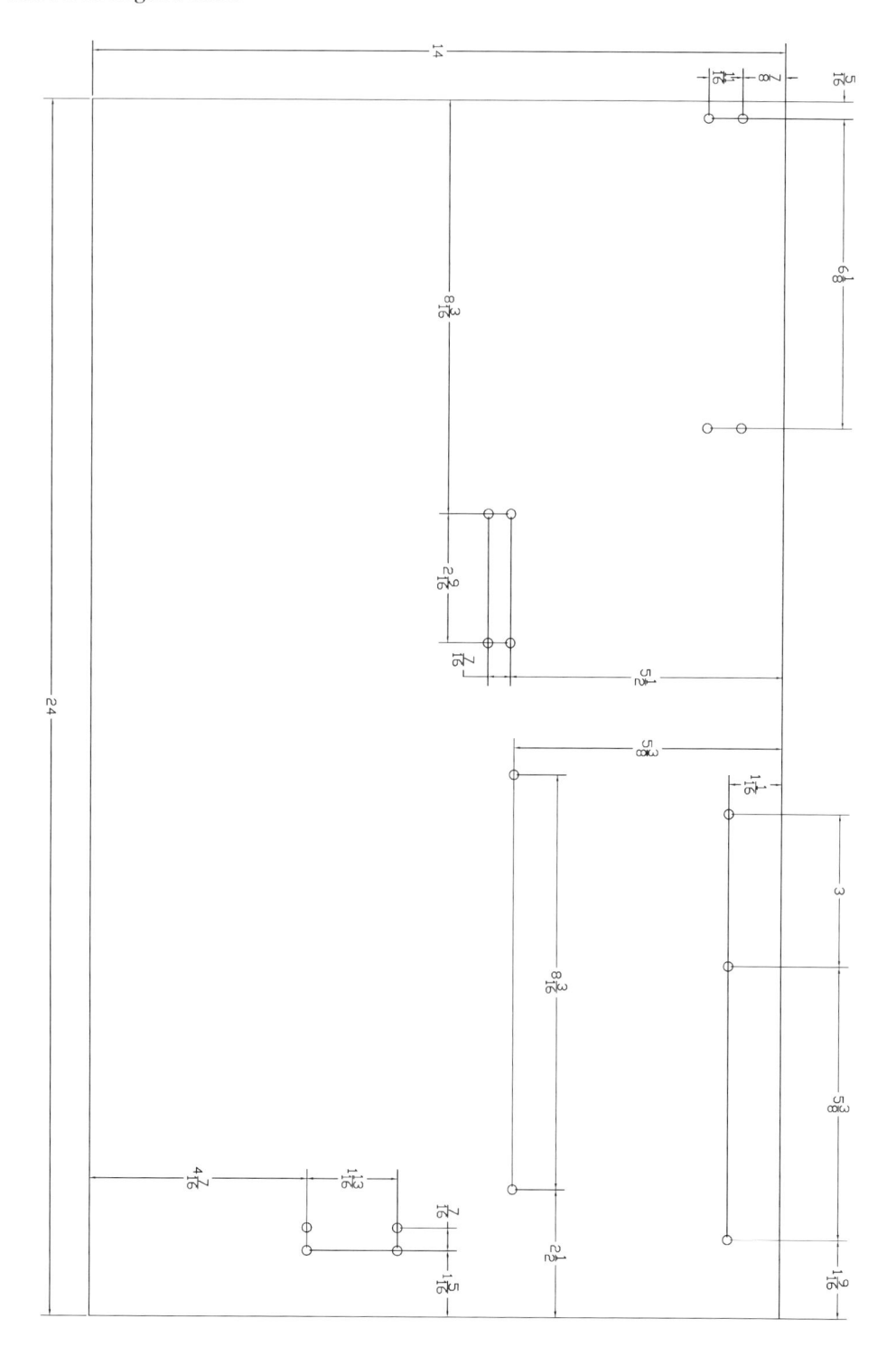

Figure 11.1

Step 2 - Mount the G540

Use #6-32 x 3/8" machine screws and attach one of the 1-1/2" brackets to the G540 controller. Do this by inserting the machine screw into a washer and then through the bottom hole in the controller face as shown in Figure 11.2. Slip the bracket onto the screw then add another washer and finally a #6 hex nut. The brackets should be flush with the bottom of the G540. Repeat with the other bracket.

Using the drawing in Figure 11.4 as a guide, set the controller and bracket assembly over the four holes in the upper right hand side of the mounting board.

From the bottom of the mounting board insert four #6-32 x 1/2" machine screws with washers through the four holes and brackets.

From the top of the brackets add a washer and a #6-32 hex nut as shown in Figure 11.3.

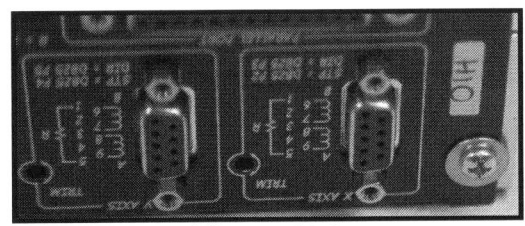

Figure 11.2

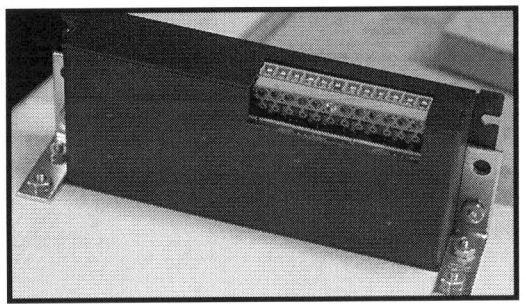

Figure 11.3

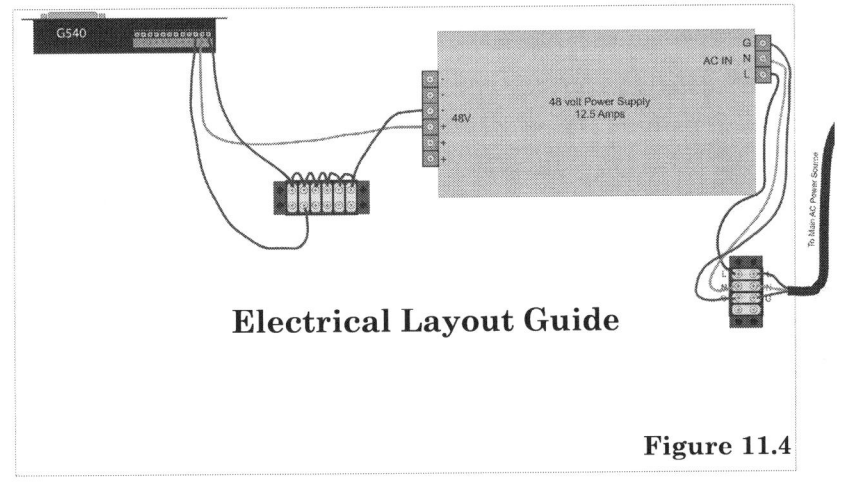

Electrical Layout Guide

Figure 11.4

Step 3 - Mount the Power Supply

The 48 volt x 12.5 Amp power supply has five, 3mm threaded holes in the bottom. You will need five, M3-.5 x 10mm machine screws.

Using the layout guide on the previous page, place a #6 washer on each M3 screw and insert it from the underside of the mounting board into one of the holes in the upper right hand corner. Set the power supply down on the board and screw the screws into the mating holes.

Its probably best to mount a single screw into one of the corners of the power supply to hold things in place. Then proceed with each screw leaving them just a little loose until all are in place. Once in place, tighten all screws.

Figure 11.5

Building the KRMx01 CNC **149**

Step 4 - Mount the Barrier Strips

You will need two barrier strips: 4 terminal and a 6 terminal strip like the ones shown in Figure 11.6.

To mount the strips refer to the layout guide in Figure 11.4. Start by placing a #6 washer on a #6-32 x 3/4" machine screw. Insert it up through the bottom of the mounting board then through a mating hole in the strip. Add a washer and #6 hex nut and tighten as shown in Figure 11.7.

Figure 11.6

Figure 11.7

Step 5 - Connect Negative Voltage Source

Connect one of the negative leads on the power supply (marked -) to all the terminals in the top row of the indicated terminal strip. Then connect one of the top terminals to position 12 on the G540 controller, as shown in Figure 11.8.

Note that this terminal strip now becomes the source for most of your negative connections in the future.

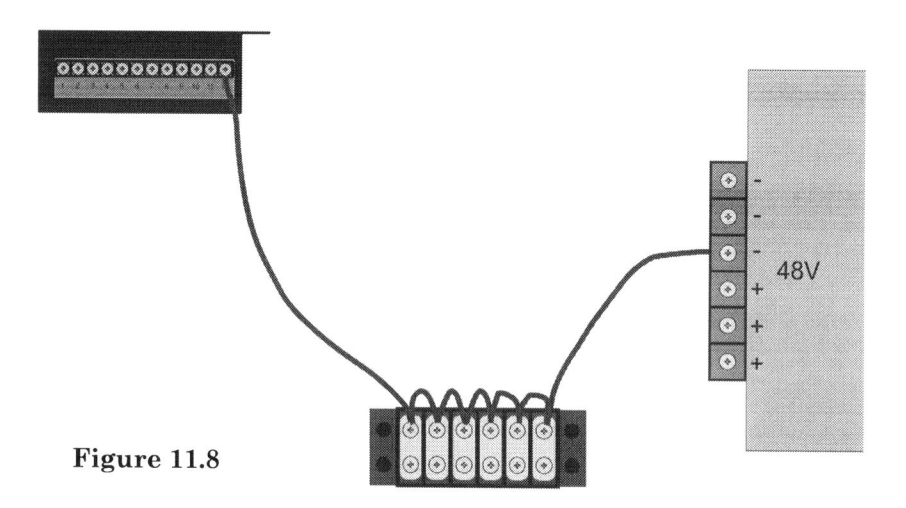

Figure 11.8

Tip

You can daisy chain the wire by stripping a couple inches from the middle of the wire. Or you can do the run shown with a single bare wire.

Step 6 - Connect Positive Voltage Source

Using a piece of 18 gauge red wire, connect one of the positive terminals (marked +) on the power supply directly to position 11 on the G540, as shown in Figure 11.9.

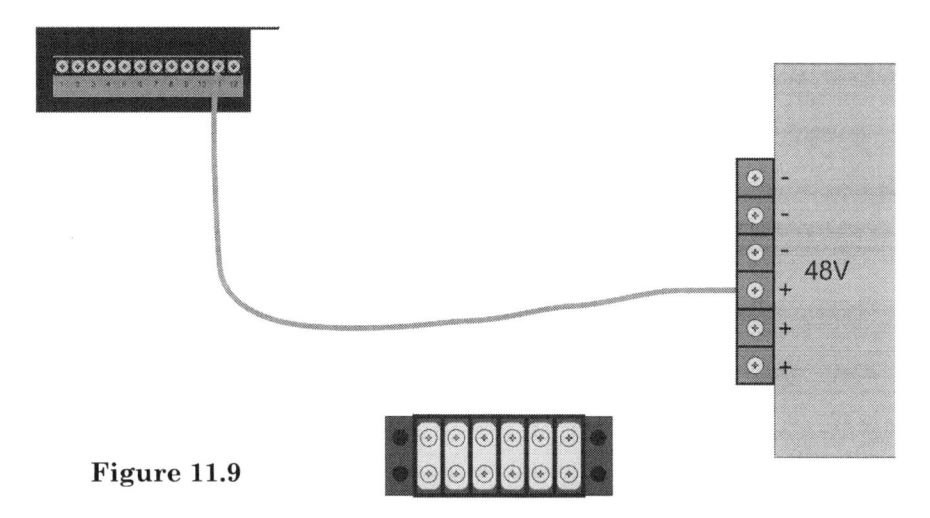

Figure 11.9

Step 7 - Bypass the EStop on the Controller

Using a piece of 18 gauge black wire, connect position 10 on the G540 to one of the negative terminals on the barrier strip as shown in Figure 11.10.

Note that this effectively bypasses the *Emergency Stop* supported by the controller. The Estop upgrade will be covered in book 2 of the KRMx01 series

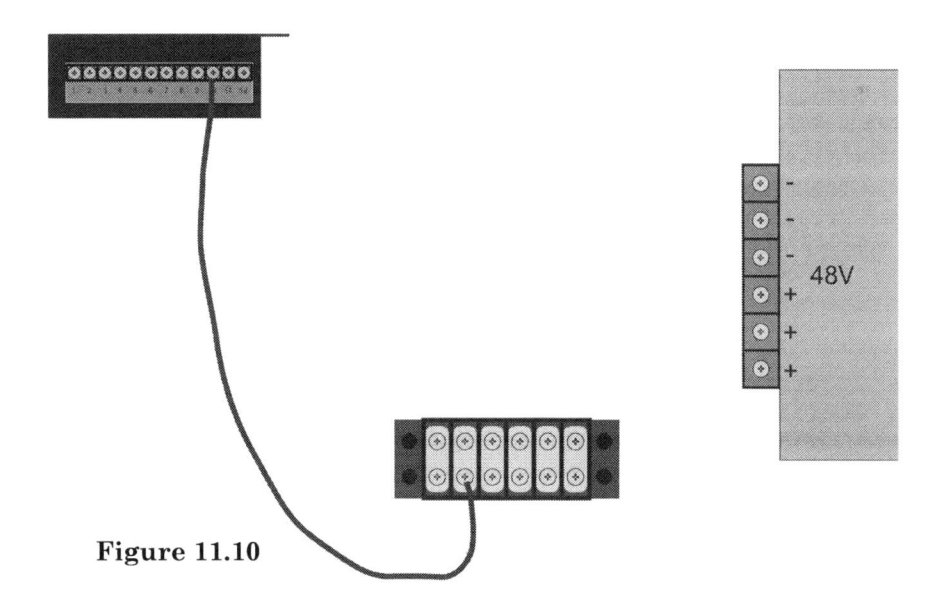

Figure 11.10

Building the KRMx01 CNC

Step 8 - Connect the Power Supply to the AC Terminal Strip

Using 18 gauge wire connect the terminal labeled L on the power supply to the first terminal on the barrier strip shown in Figure 11.11.

Using 18 gauge wire connect the terminal labeled N on the power supply to the second terminal on the barrier strip.

Using 18 gauge wire connect the terminal labeled G on the power supply to the third terminal on the barrier strip.

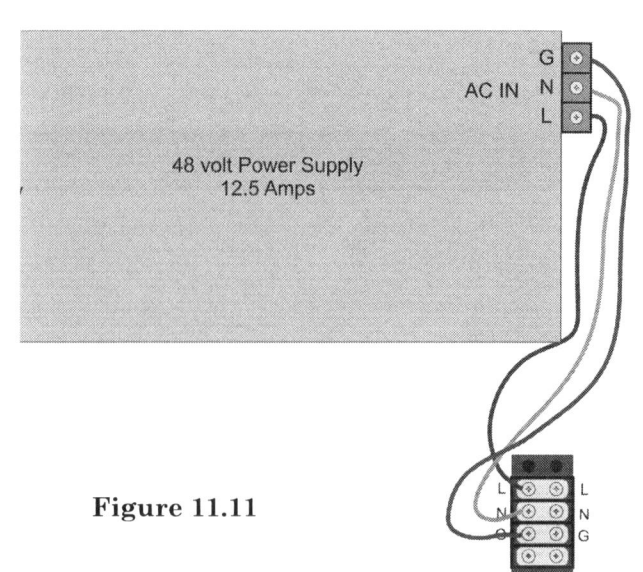

Figure 11.11

Step 9 - Connect the Power Cable to the AC Terminal Strip

Using the prepared cord connect the black lead to the first terminal shown in Figure 11.12. The white lead should be connected to the second terminal. The green lead should be connected to the third terminal.

Important!

If you purchase a 16/3 extension cord and the colors on the individual wires are not black, white, and green, you will need to use a Ohm meter to determine the ground wire. To locate the neutral wire (N) place the ground terminal down and facing you, the neutral terminal with be the one on the right.

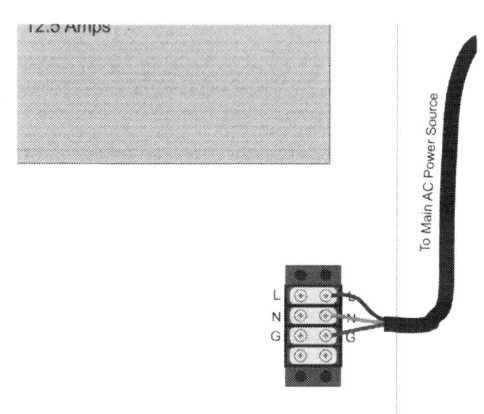

Figure 11.12

Tip

While not absolutely necessary, it is recommended you put some sort of strain relief on the cable. You can purchase small cable clamps like the ones shown in Figure 11.13. They come in various sizes; for the cord used in this chapter, a 3/8" would probably work best.

It is useful to have several sizes of these on hand, and 1/4", 3/8", and 1/2" are what you will use the most for projects like the CNC.

To use one of these on your main power cord, place it on the cord near the edge of the mounting board and drill a hole through the clamp's hole into the board. A #6-32 x 3/4" machine screw and nut will secure it.

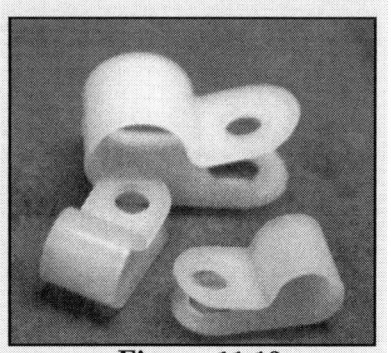

Figure 11.13

Step 10 - Double Check the AC Connections

Starting at the power supply, follow the wire connected to the terminal labeled G. Follow it to the strip, then to the cord. This should be the green wire.

Starting at the power supply, follow the wire connected to the terminal labeled N. Follow it to the strip, then to the cord. This should be the white wire.

Starting at the power supply, follow the wire connected to the terminal labeled L. Follow it to the strip, then to the cord. This should be the black wire.

Figure 11.14

Step 11 - Smoke Test

You might be asking why we call this the smoke test. In essence, if you have hooked something up wrong, it is very likely you will burn it up. Go back and double check your wiring a third time.

Visit the www.geckodrive.com web site for manuals on the G540. I recommend reading and understanding these before proceeding with this step.

Before applying AC power to the power supply be sure that the charge pump switch is in the "ON" position as shown in Figure 11.15.

Important!!

The AC cord is connected to the AC terminal strip and then to the terminals on the power supply. Consider these connections extremely dangerous. If you touch them while the cord is plugged into an AC source *you will get shocked*.

Plug the power cord into an AC outlet. The red fault light should immediately glow red. If it does not, quickly remove the AC power from the cord by disconnecting it from the outlet, then go back and check your connections.

If it does glow red, all is good and you are ready to proceed to the next chapter. Remove the power and continue.

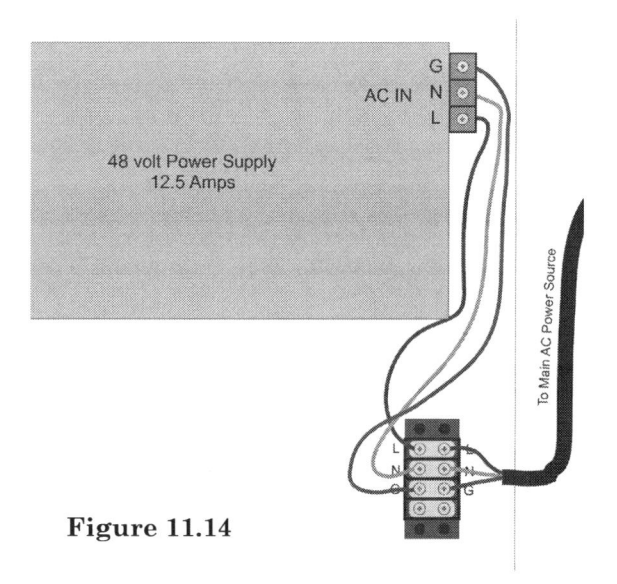

Figure 11.15

Figure 11.16

Building the KRMx01 CNC   **153**

Conclusion

While this basic electronic hookup is the minimal that can be used to operate you CNC, without cabling to the motors and computer it is still not operational. At this point, after all the effort you have put into the construction you are likely anxious to at least see something move under power. Be patient, you are very close, and you will be connecting the cables soon.

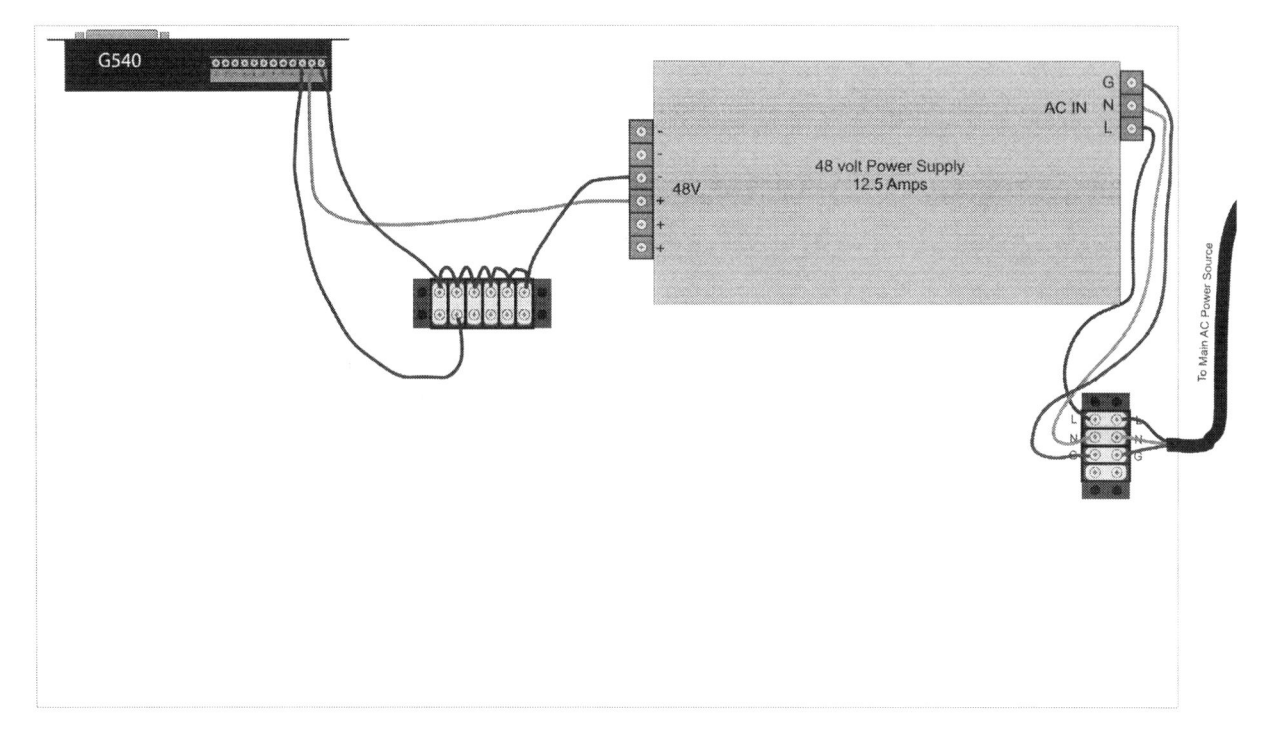

Figure 11.17

Chapter 12

Mach 3

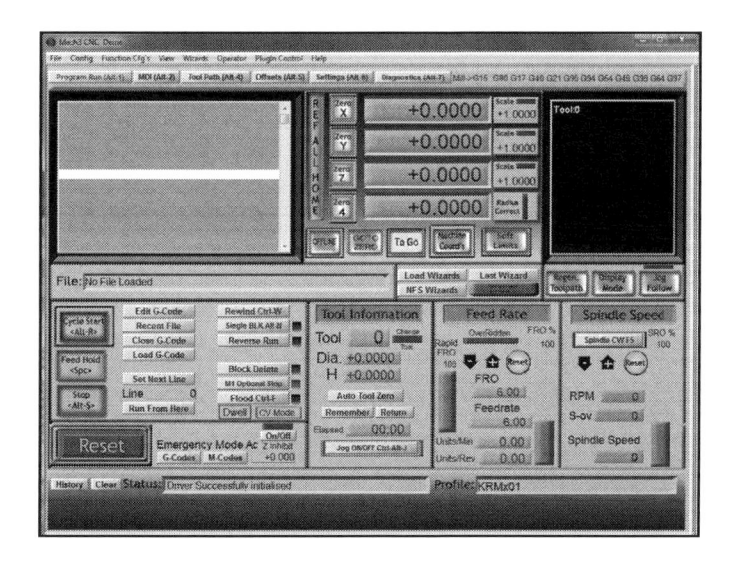

The controller software is the key software component in the operation of your KRMx01 CNC. Its proper installation and configuration is crucial to the success of this project. For this reason, a complete chapter has been devoted to its installation and configuration.

Components Needed For This Chapter

- Mach 3 software (demo)
- Fully operational PC with parallel port
- Parallel cable
- 4, Stepper motors
- PC with a 32-bit version of Windows installed
- Wired G540 controller and power supply

Chapter Estimates
Cost: $221

Time: Half Day

Prerequisites
Before going any further, the PC you plan to use must have the following:
- The PC must have a built in parallel port
- The PC must be running a 32 bit version of XP, Vista, or Windows 7
- The PC must have at least a 1 Ghz CPU
- 512MB RAM if using XP, and 2GB for Vista or Windows 7

Parallel Port

The parallel port must be built-in. You absolutely cannot use a USB to parallel port converter, as these will not work. Even add-in PCI cards are problematic and their use is not recommended. So before proceeding, make sure the PC you plan to use has a parallel port built into the motherboard.

Note that this may present a problem if purchasing a new machine, as many no longer have parallel ports.

For another option see the Tip box on the opposite page.

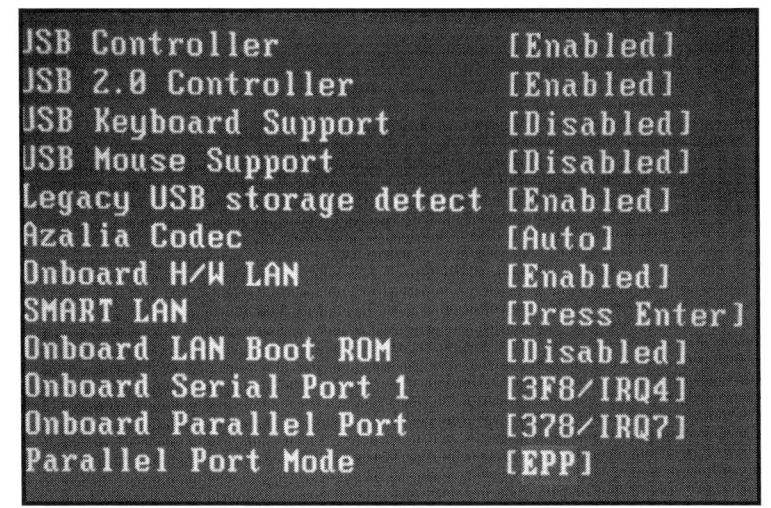

Figure 12.1

156   Chapter 12   Mach 3

EPP Mode

To further complicate things, the parallel port needs to be set to EPP mode in the BIOS. Generally this is not the default operation of most parallel ports. There is no standard in how to configure a BIOS. The screen shots shown in Figures 12.1 and 12.2, are only an example of the BIOS settings. Your machines BIOS setting will most certainly be different.

Chances are if your PC does not have these settings in its BIOS, it does not support EPP mode.

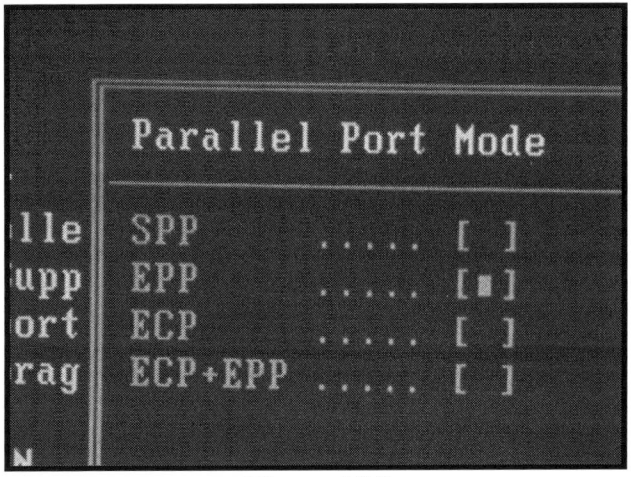

Figure 12.2

32 Bit OS

While the Mach 3 software will work on a 64 bit machine, the port driver will not. Therefore, do not use a PC with a 64 bit OS.

CPU Speed

While you can get by with only a 1 Ghz CPU, it is not recommended. The faster the machine the smoother and faster your CNC will operate. For this reason, the minimum recommended CPU speed is 2 Ghz.

Laptop Machines

Since most laptops don't have parallel ports, this pretty much eliminates their use.

Mach 3 Software

Mach 3 can be downloaded and installed for free. It can be configured and even operated in demo mode. However, you will need to purchase a licence in order to properly operate your CNC.

Tip

If you don't have a PC with a parallel port, and you don't intend on purchasing one, you still have options. There is a device called the SmoothStepper that will connect between your PC's USB port and the parallel connector on the G540 controler. There are a few differences in setup as well as limitations that may effect upgrades to your machine.

For more information visit the Kronos Robotics web site at:

http://www.kronosrobotics.com/krmx01/

Step 1 - Download the Software

Mach 3 is a product of ArtSoft. It is available for download at:

http://machsupport.com/

Once installed the software runs in demo mode until a license file is purchased and installed. Demo mode is suitable for the installation and the configuration of the software, but it does limit the number of GCode commands to 500 which is unsuitable for anything but very simple operations.

Proceed to the download site and download the latest version. The actual version used in this book is version R3.043.022

The downloaded file will have its name based on the current version of the software. In this case, the name is "Mach3Version3.043.022.exe"

Step 2 - Initiate the Installation

Once the Mach 3 install file has been downloaded, you need only double click the file to start the install process. Once started, you will be presented with a welcome screen like the one shown in Figure 12.3. This welcome screen will indicate the version of the software you plan to install. Click the Next button to proceed to the next form.

Figure 12.3

Step 3 - Agree to License

Next you will be presented with a license agreement. Read the agreement, then select the "I agree " option and click the Next Button as shown in Figure 12.4.

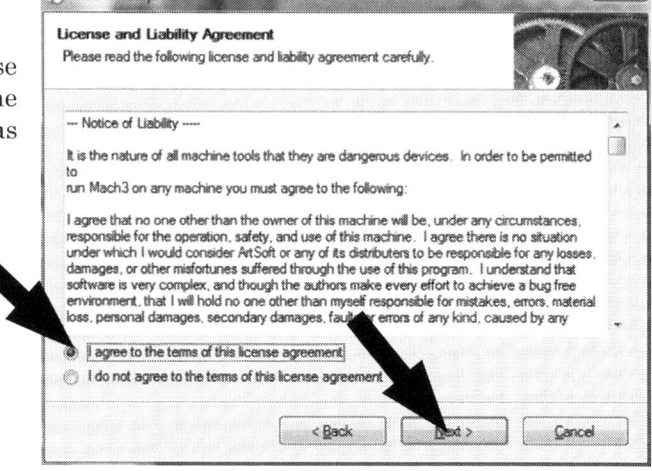

Figure 12.4

158 *Chapter 12*   Mach 3

Step 4 - Select the Install Directory

The install software will pick the "C:\Mach3" directory as a default. While you may choose any directory you wish, it is recommended that you keep the default directory as this is the directory the book will refer to when adding or changing configuration files. Click the Next button to continue, as shown in Figure 12.5.

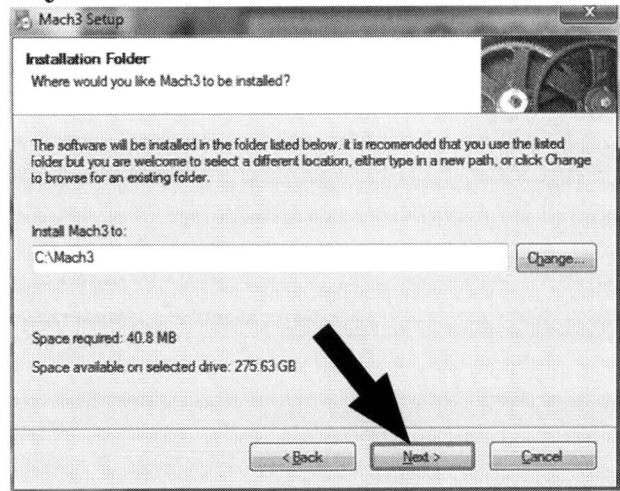

Figure 12.5

Step 5 - Select Packages

It is recommended that you use the default packages, as you will utilize them when you perform upgrades to the KRMx01 CNC. Click Next to continue as shown in Figure 12.6.

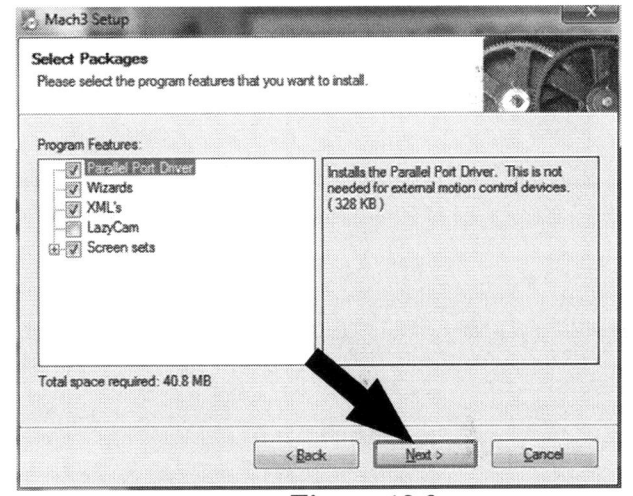

Figure 12.6

Step 6 - Create a Custom Profile

The main reason for creating a custom profile is that if you make a mistake and find it difficult to remember the settings you have changed, you can go back to the original installed configuration.

Click the Mill Profile button as shown in Figure 12.7.

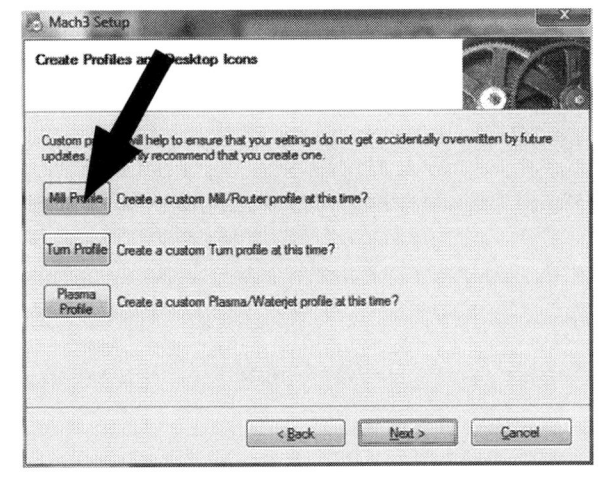

Figure 12.7

Building the KRMx01 CNC   **159**

You will be presented with a small input screen. In the field provided, type "KRMx01" and hit the OK button as shown in Figure 12.8.

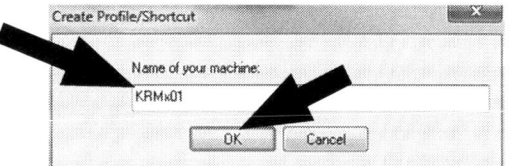

Figure 12.8

Next, you will be taken back to the profile screen. Click the Next button to continue as shown in Figure 12.9.

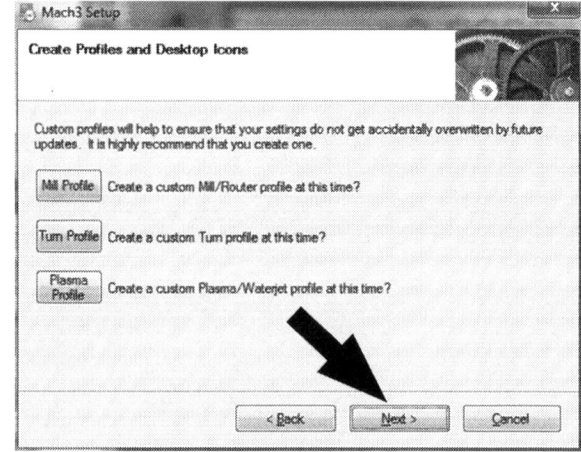

Figure 12.9

Step 7 - Start the Install Process

You will be presented with a screen that will allow you to verify all the choices you have made up to this point. Click the Next button as shown in Figure 12.10 to start the install process. In most cases this should only take a few seconds.

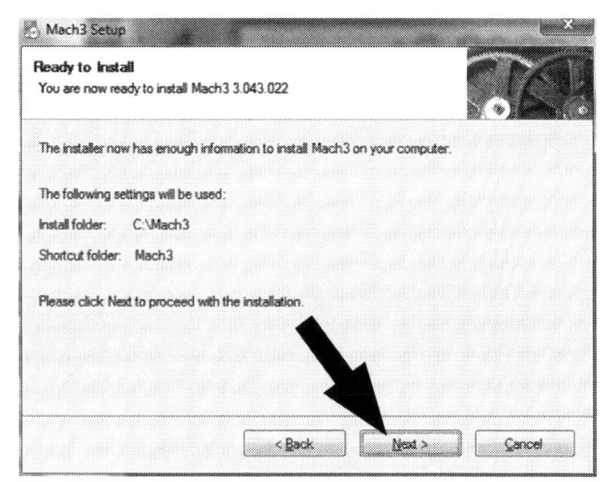

Figure 12.10

160   *Chapter 12*   Mach 3

Step 8 - Install the Port Driver

Once the main portion of Mach 3 has been installed you will be presented with the "Port Driver Installation" screen shown in Figure 12.11. Click Next to install the driver.

The port driver must be installed in order for Mach 3 to talk to your CNC. This driver bridges the gap between the actual Mach 3 software and the G540 controller.

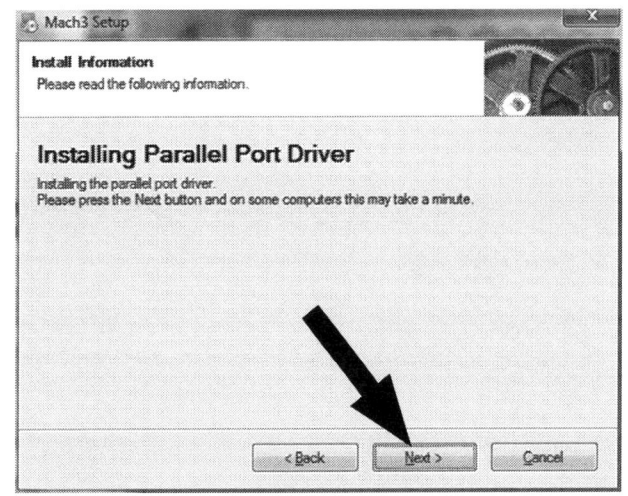

Figure 12.11

Step 9 - Reboot Machine

Once the port driver has been installed, you will need to reboot your machine. Click the Finish button shown in Figure 12.12, and the Mach 3 install software will close and reboot your machine.

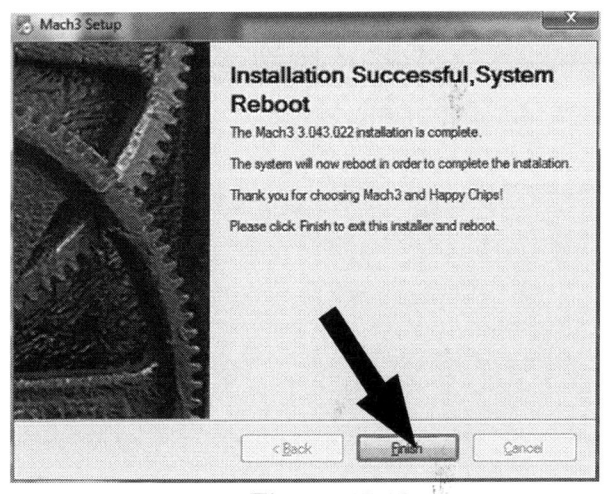

Figure 12.12

Step 10 - Start Mach 3

Once Mach 3 has been installed, it will place several icons on your desktop like the ones shown in Figure 12.13.

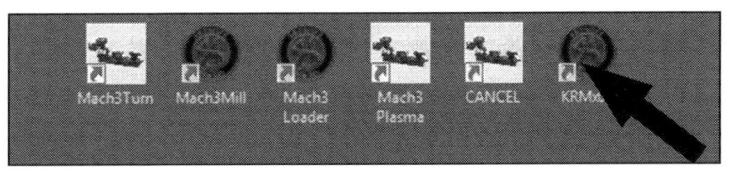

Figure 12.13

The only one you should be concerned with is the one labeled KRMx01. Move all the others into a folder and set it aside.

To start Mach 3, double click the icon labeled KRMx01. Once started, you will be presented with the legal notice shown in Figure 12.14 on the next page. Read the notice, click the "do not ask again" check box, and click the "I Agree" button to continue.

Building the KRMx01 CNC   **161**

This notice will appear each time you start Mach 3. By checking the "Please do not ask this again" check box, you will be able to override this default setting.

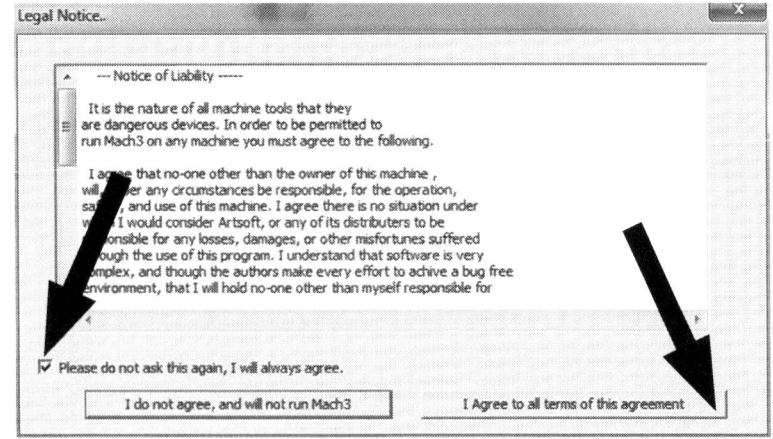

Figure 12.14

Step 11 - Configure Native Units

Mach 3 is set to millimeters as its default base unit. Throughout this book you will be using inches, so this needs to be changed. Please note that this has nothing to do with processing jobs where the GCode is in metric units. It is only for motor tuning.

From the Config menu, click on the "Select Native Units" option as shown in Figure 12.15.

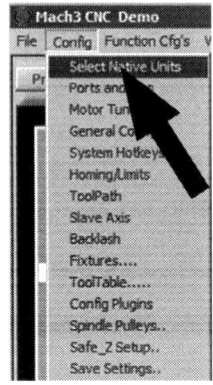

Figure 12.15

You will be presented with the dialog box shown in Figure 12.16. Read the message and click the OK button.

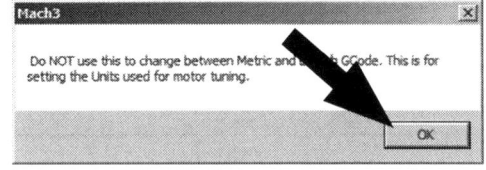

Figure 12.16

Once again you will be presented with a dialogue box. Click the Inches option and hit OK as shown in Figure 12.17

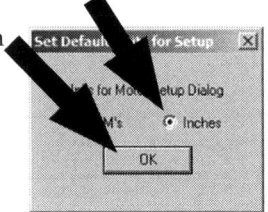

Figure 12.17

162   Chapter 12   Mach 3

Step 12 - Connect the PC

Connect a parallel port cable between the 25 pin parallel port on your PC and the 25 pin connector on the G540 controller. Apply power to the 48v power supply. At this point the G540 should be in a fault condition as indicated by the red LED.

Step 13 - Configure Charge Pump

The charge pump is used to tell the G540 that the PC is connected to the G540 and that Mach 3 is up and running. The Mach 3 driver does this by outputting a pulse on a particular pin while running. Any time the G540 does not get this pulse it will go into emergency mode and remove all power from the stepper motors.

Note that this is why you set the charge pump switch on the G540 to the ON position.

From the Config menu select the "Ports and Pins" option as shown in Figure 12.18.

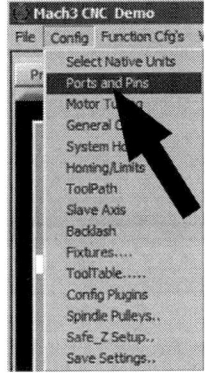

Figure 12.18

For now, you are going to keep the default settings on this tab and select the Output Signals tab shown in Figure 12.19

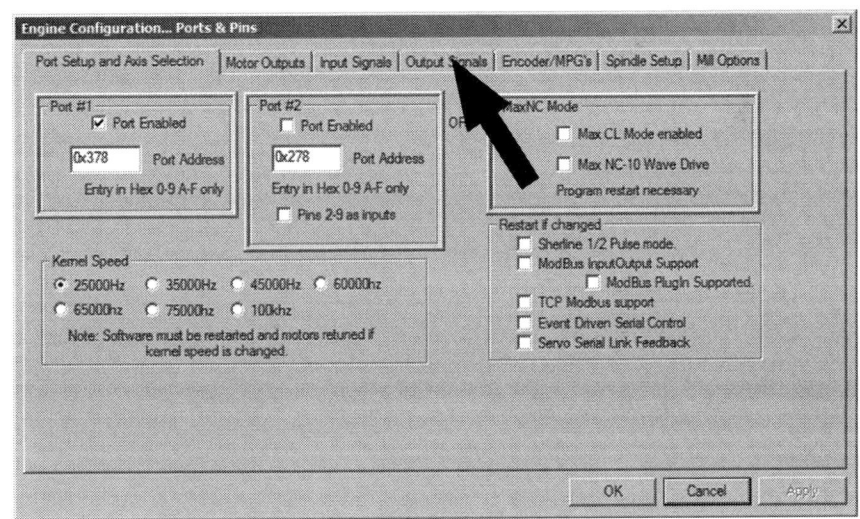

Figure 12.19

Building the KRMx01 CNC   **163**

On the Output Signals tab, slide the scroll bar down until the Charge Pump line item is shown. Click the Enabled option and set the Port # to 1 and the Pin Number to 16. Click the OK button shown in Figure 12.20 to save your settings.

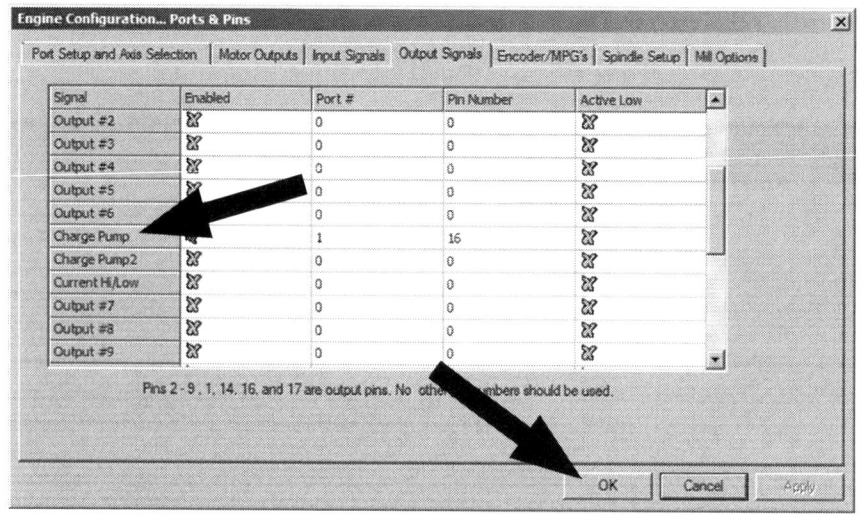

Figure 12.20

Click the OK button to continue back to the main Mach 3 screen shown in Figure 12.21.

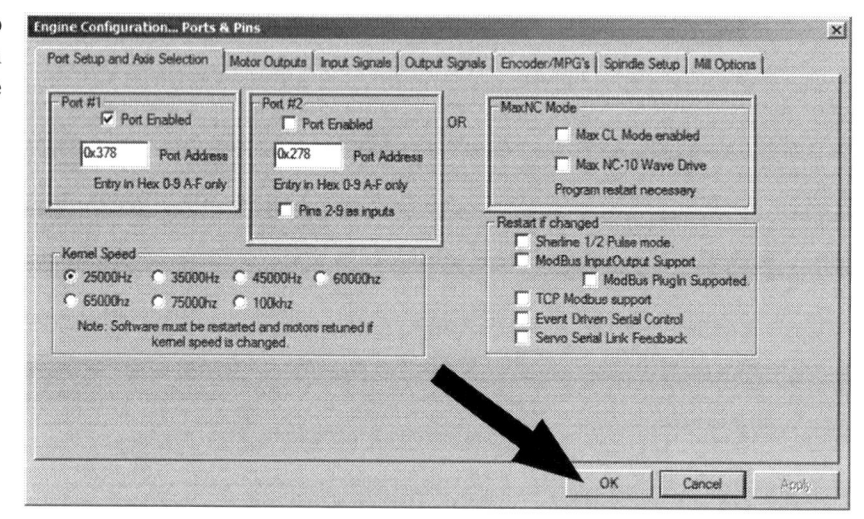

Figure 12.21

Each time you make changes in the Ports and Pins dialog, Mach 3 will automatically go into reset mode. This will require you to hit the reset button to put the software into normal run mode.

Once you hit the Reset button shown in Figure 12.22, the outer rings on the button will change to green.

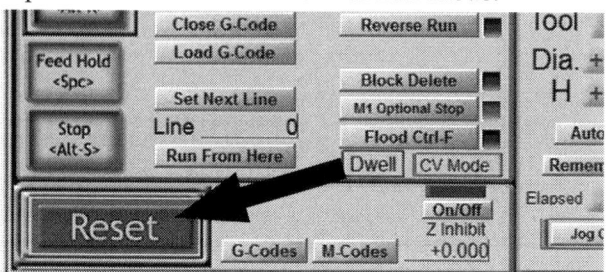

Figure 12.22

Step 14 - Configure Motor Ports

You must tell Mach 3 how the stepper motor ports are configured on the G540. Again, you do this with the "Ports and Pins" dialog.

From the Config menu, select the "Ports and Pins" option as shown in Figure 12.23.

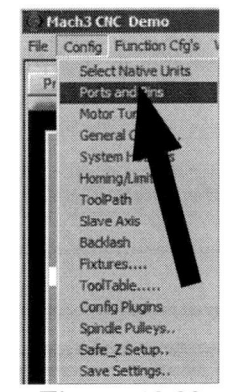

Figure 12.23

Select the Motor Outputs tab shown in Figure 12.24.

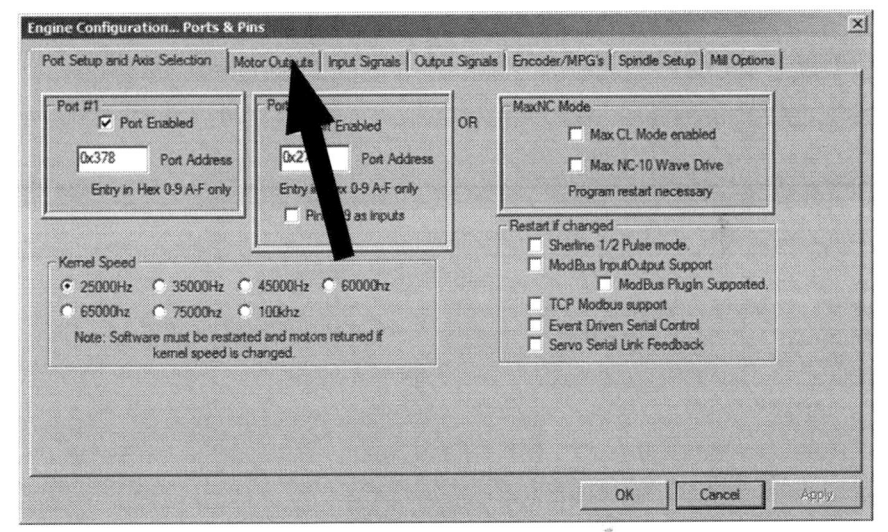

Figure 12.24

On the Motor Outputs tab, enable the X, Y, Z and A axis and set all the ports and pins, as shown in Figure 12.25. Note that the Step and Dir Low active settings should be checked, but the X axis Dir Low setting should not. Click the OK button once all settings have been changed.

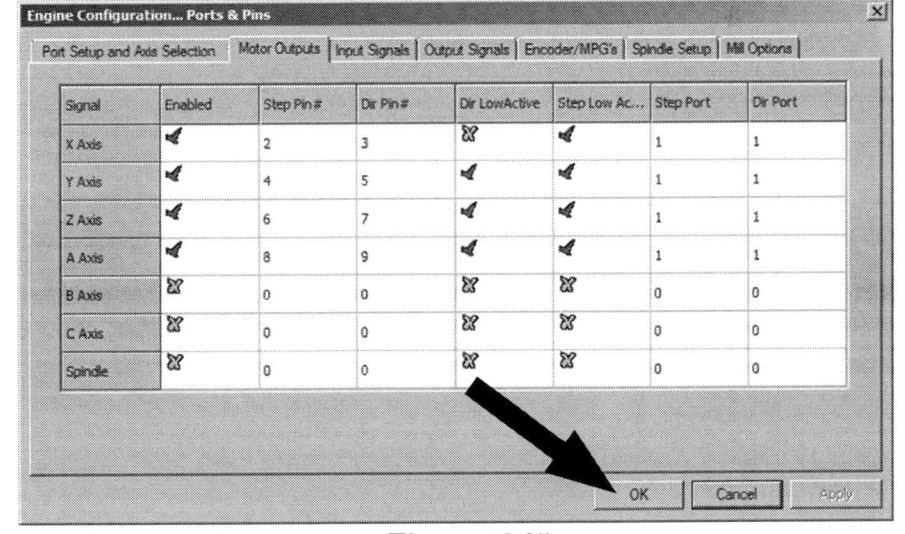

Figure 12.25

Building the KRMx01 CNC **165**

Step 15 - Connect Motors to G540 Controller

Before continuing, please note that you should never connect or disconnect a motor while power is applied to the G540. Doing so could destroy the G540. That said, the key here is to know that no power is being applied to the motor. If the G540 is in fault mode then the G540 has shut down the power to the motors. One way to remove the charge pump signal from the G540, is to shutdown the Mach3 software. *When in doubt shut down the 48v power supply.*

Remove power from the G540 and connect each of the four stepper motors to the G540.

Next, apply power and make sure that the Mach 3 software is in active (run) mode, i.e., the green bars around the reset button are on. The power light on the G540 should now be on.

At this point when on the main screen of Mach 3, you should be able to use the arrow keys to operate the X and Y motors. The page up and page down keys will operate the Z axis motor.

Step 16 - Enable the Y Slave Axis

The Y axis has two stepper motors. These are the Y axis motor and the A axis motor. In order to move the A motor, you need to tell Mach 3 that it is slaved to the Y axis.

From the Config menu select the Slave Axis option, as shown in Figure 12.26.

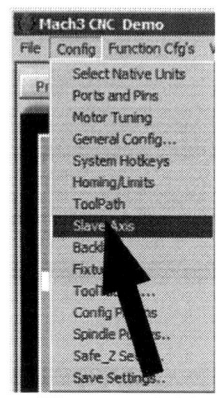

Figure 12.26

When the Slave Axis Selection dialog pops up, you need to select the A Axis option under the Y axis panel as shown in Figure 12.27. Click OK once set.

You will be prompted with a popup dialog that tells you that you must restart Mach 3. Do so and then restart the application. Now when you move the Y axis both the Y and A motors will operate.

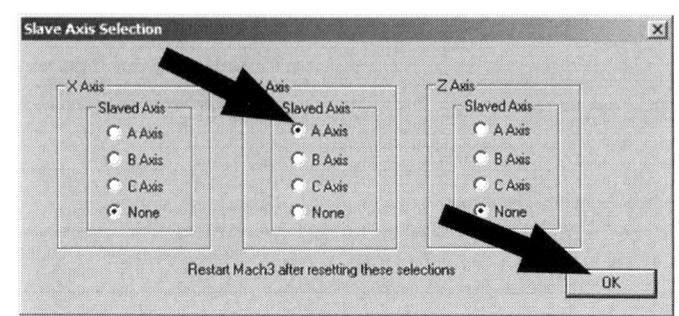

Figure 12.27

Step 17 - Tune the Motors

You need to tell Mach 3 how many steps per inch that your motor/screw/controller combination produces. Since you are using the same motor and ACME screws on all the axis the settings are all the same.

To start, bring up the Motor Tuning dialog by selecting the "Motor Tuning" option under the Config menu as shown in Figure 12.28.

Since the dialog works for all the axis, you need to load the settings for a particular axis before changing them. Do this by clicking the X Axis button shown in Figure 12.29, then enter 4000 in the Steps Per field. Since you set your units to inches earlier, this field indicates steps per inch. Next, enter 349.98 in the velocity field. This is your top speed, which in this case is 350 inches per minute. It is a good starting point, but you can increase this setting after you have broken in your machine. The next step is to enter 20 in the acceleration field. This number indicates how fast you want an axis to get to its top speed. This value is a good middle of the road staring point as it is fairly quick yet still yields a smooth transition when the CNC switches the direction of a particular axis. Keep the default settings for the other two fields.

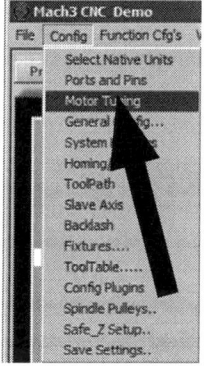

Figure 12.28

Before moving to the next axis you must first save your settings for this one. Click the Save Axis Settings button to save the settings, then proceed to the next axis by clicking the Y Axis button on the right of the screen. Repeat the procedure with the same numbers as before and click the Save Axis Settings button. Do this for all four axis. Once you complete all four, hit the OK button to return to the main screen.

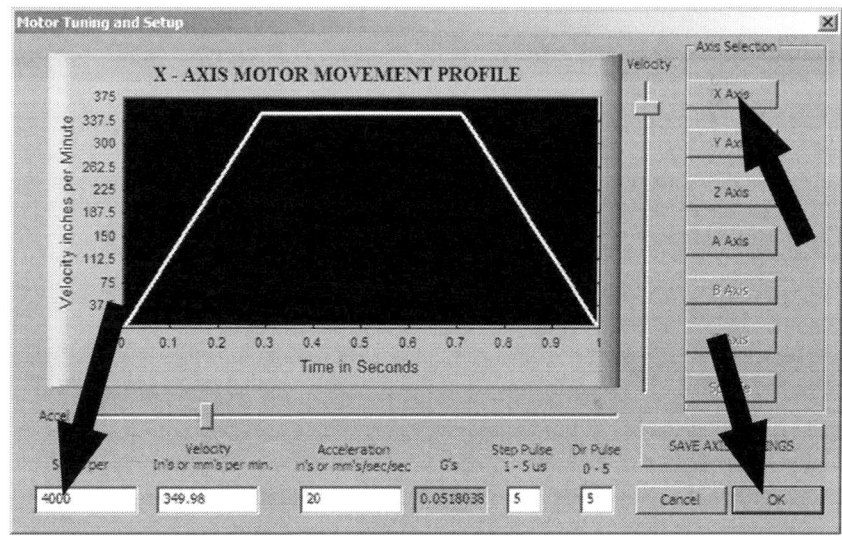

Figure 12.29

Step 18 - Map the Keyboard

You need to map the arrow keys to the axis on the KRMx01 CNC. To do this, select the "System Hotkeys" option from the Config menu as shown in Figure 12.30.

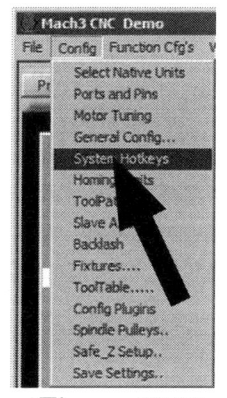

Figure 12.30

Building the KRMx01 CNC **167**

On the System Hotkeys Setup dialog shown in Figure 12.32, you will see six axis buttons marked "X++", "X--", "Y++", "Y--", "Z++", and "Z--". These are used to set the scan codes for the keys you wish to map.

Each time you hit one of these buttons, you will be presented with the SetHotKey popup dialog shown in Figure 12.31. On this popup you simply hit the appropriate key you want to map to the axis button.

The following table indicates which key is hit for each of the axis buttons.

Axis Button	Key	Axis Button	Key
X++	Right Arrow	X--	Left Arrow
Y++	Up Arrow	Y--	Down Arrow
Z++	Page Up	Z--	Page Down

Once all keys have been mapped, click the OK button to continue to the main screen.

Figure 12.31

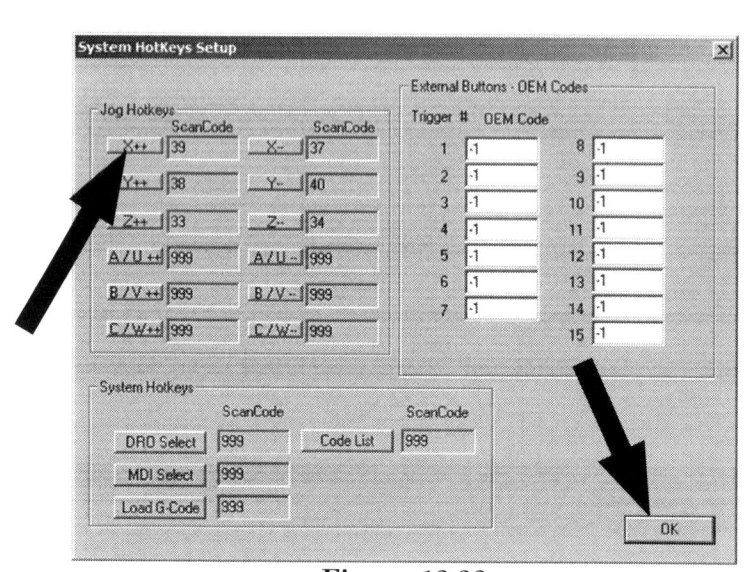

Figure 12.32

Step 19 - General Configuration

You need to make a few changes to the General Configuration dialog. Do this by selecting the "General Config" option from the Config menu as shown in Figure 12.33.

Figure 12.33

168   *Chapter 12*   Mach 3

Change all the settings in the first two columns so that they read the same as those shown in Figure 12.34. The black arrows point to those items that need to be changed from the default settings, but it would be wise to check all of the settings at this time.

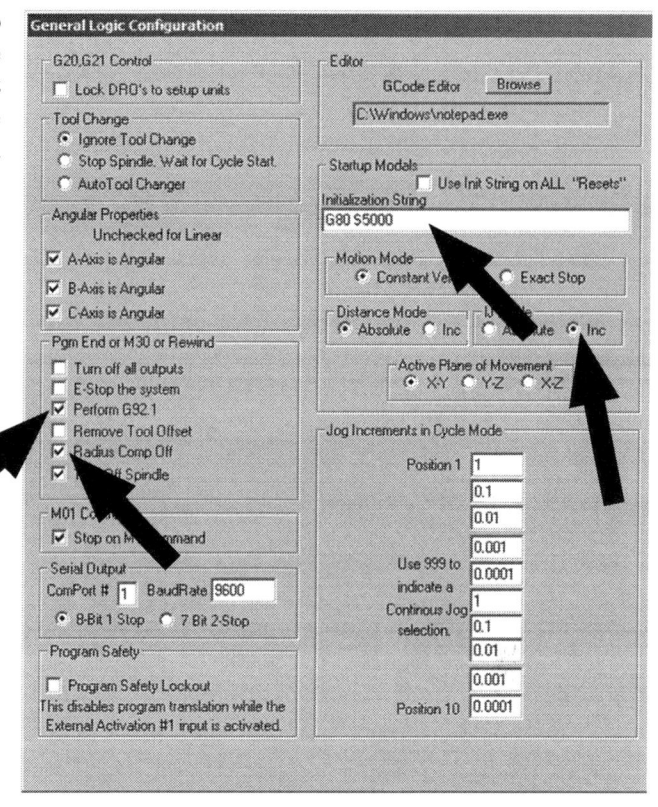

Figure 12.34

Accelerating and decelerating as you start and stop the carriages can induce a certain amount of error if not compensated for. The settings marked by the arrows in Figure 12.35 do just that. Make the changes indicated and click OK to continue to the main screen.

Note that some of the changes are for upgrades you will add in the future.

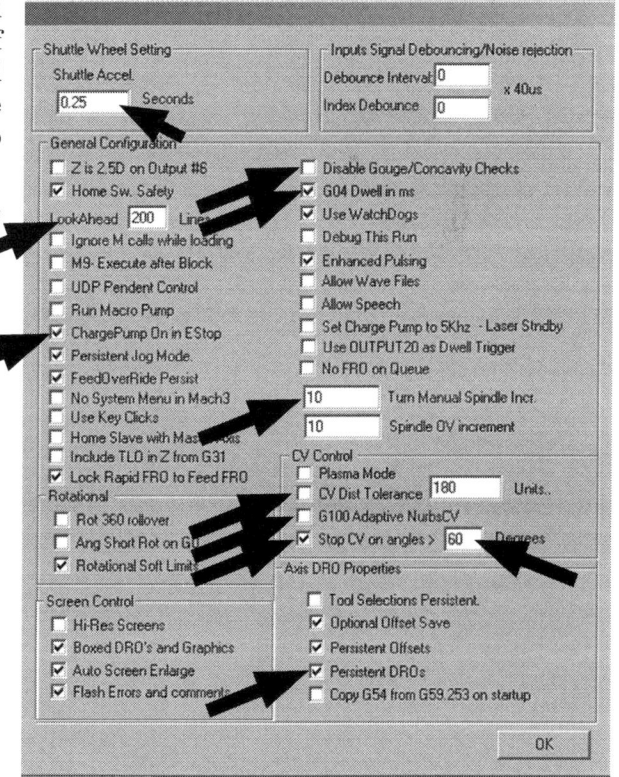

Figure 12.35

Building the KRMx01 CNC   **169**

Conclusion

Mach 3 is now configured so that you can accurately control your KRMx01 CNC. There are many upgrades you can add to the KRMx01, the most important of which is an EStop switch. Each upgrade will most likely require further configuration changes.

While this book provides a brief overview of the operation of Mach 3 as it pertains to the KRMx01 CNC, there is no way to pay it justice with a single chapter or, for that matter, a single book. The Artsoft web site has complete manuals available for download. It is recommended that you take the time to review the various configuration and operation chapters to gain a better perspective on the full extent of available system features.

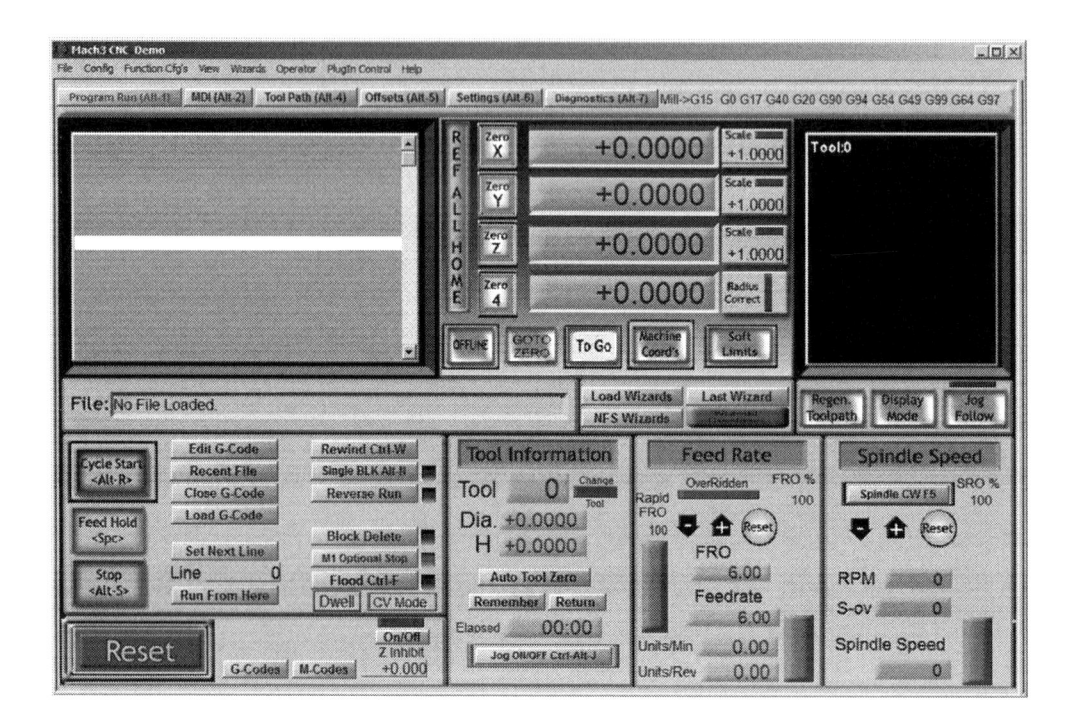

Tip

When you installed Mach 3, I had you provide a mill setting of KRMx01. When you actually start Mach 3, you should be using the KRMx01 shortcut. Doing so ensures all the configuration settings are saved to the file KRMx01.xml, which can be backed up and used to reconfigure your machine if necessary.

Chapter 13

Installing Stepper Motors

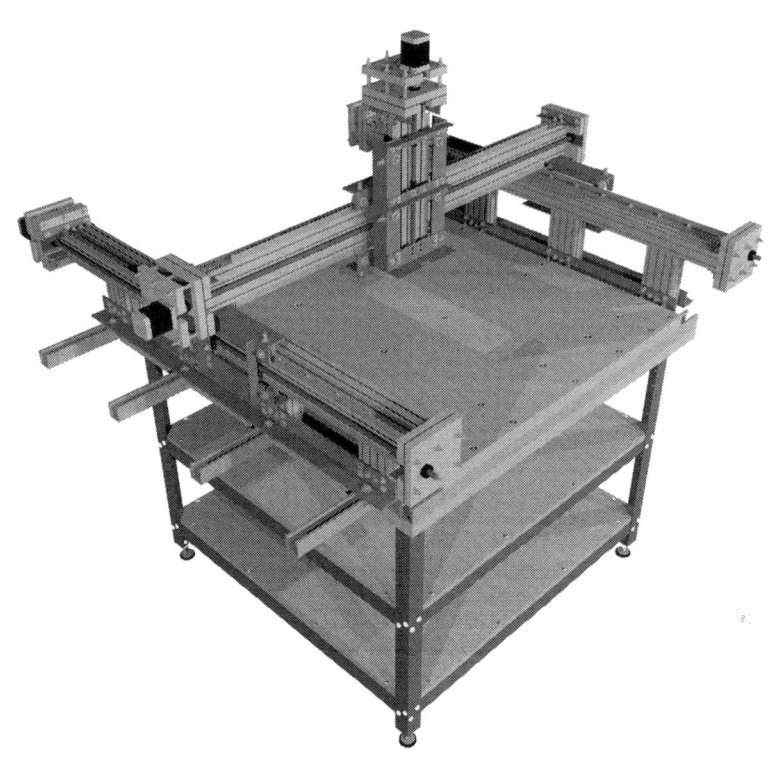

The stepper motors represent the last portion of the mechanical construction of the KRMx01 CNC. If you were to connect the motors directly up to the G540, you would be able to operate them on their own. It's now time to connect them to your CNC.

Tools Needed For This Chapter

- 7/16" Wrench
- 3/8" Wrench
- 5/64" Allen wrench (used to adjust set screws on shaft coupler)
- 3/32" Allen wrench (used to adjust clamp screws on shaft coupler)

Components Needed For This Chapter

- 4, Zero backlash helical shaft couplers (see text)
- 4, Stepper motors
- 26, 1/4-20 x 7/8" Standoffs (rod couplings)
- 26, 1/4-20 Hex nuts
- 56, 1/4" Washers
- 26, 1/4" Split lock washers
- 16, #10-24 x 1-1/4" Machine screws
- 16, #10-24 Hex nuts
- 16, #10 Washers

Chapter Estimates

Cost: $138
Time: One day

Prerequisites

The stepper motors you purchased in the previous chapter will be installed in this chapter.

In addition, you will need to order four shaft couplers, which are available from CNC Router Parts. These shaft couplers tie the 1/4" shaft on the motors to the 1/2" lead screw.

Important!

It is recommended that you add a drop of thread lock to each of the screws in the couplers. They have a tendency to work loose if you don't.

Step 1 - Attach Shaft Coupler

The shaft coupler has a 1/4" hole on one end and a 1/2" hole on the other. Use a 5/64" Allen wrench and loosen the small set screw on both ends of the coupler. Insert the end with the 1/4" opening onto the stepper motor shaft, as shown in Figure 13.1. Make sure the side with the set screw is mated with the flat portion of the stepper motor shaft. The idea is to have the end of the set screw resting on the flat area.

The coupler should be about 1/16" from the motor base as shown in Figure 13.2. In other words, you want a 1/6" gap between the shaft coupler and motor body.

Use the 5/64" Allen wrench and tighten the set screw. Using a 3/32 Allen wrench, tighten the clamp screw closest to the motor.

Repeat with all four motors.

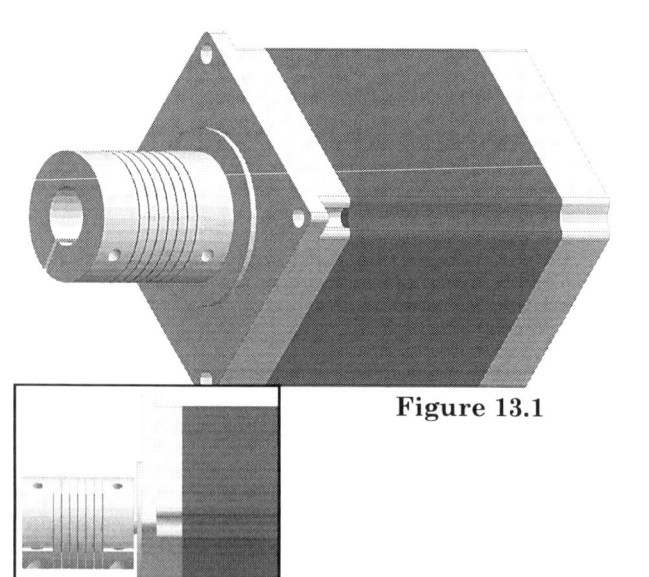

Figure 13.1

Figure 13.2

Step 2 - Attach Motor to Motor Mount Block

Insert four #10-24 x 1-1/4" machine screws into the mounting holes on the stepper motor and then insert the motor and screws into the motor mount block as shown in Figure 13.3. Slip on a #10 washer and #10-24 hex nut as shown. If you want you may also add a #10 lock washer to the screw before adding the hex nut.

Tighten all nuts with a 3/8" wrench.

Figure 13.3

The cable protruding from the motor should be oriented away from the slot in the motor mount.

Repeat with all four motor mounts.

Once completed, the motor assembly should look like the one illustrated in Figure 13.4. Note that the two Y motor mounts only have six mounting holes.

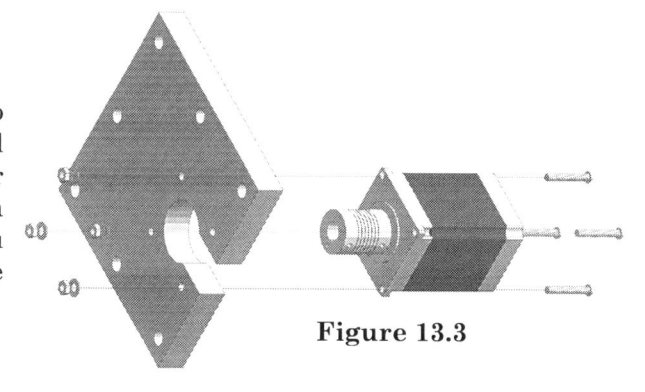

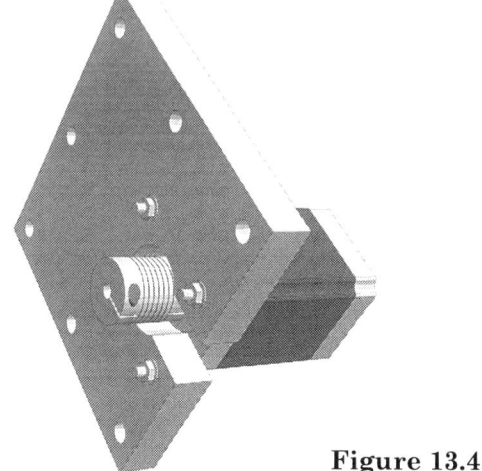

Figure 13.4

Step 3 - Attach Motor Assembly to Z Axis

First, make sure the nuts on the main bearing assembly are firm but not tight. Then add seven 1/4-20 x 7/8" standoffs. Screw them finger tight only. Add a 1/4" washer, then slip the motor assembly over the seven bolts as in Figure 13.5. The shaft coupler should fit over the protruding ACME screw. If the coupler will not slip over the ACME screw, it's possible the clamp screw or setscrew nearest the end of the ACME screw, may need to be loosened.

Once in place, add a 1/4" washer, lock washer and 1/4-20 hex nut. Finger tighten. Tighten both the clamp screw and set screw on the shaft coupler.

The completed Z assembly should look like the one shown in Figure 13.6.

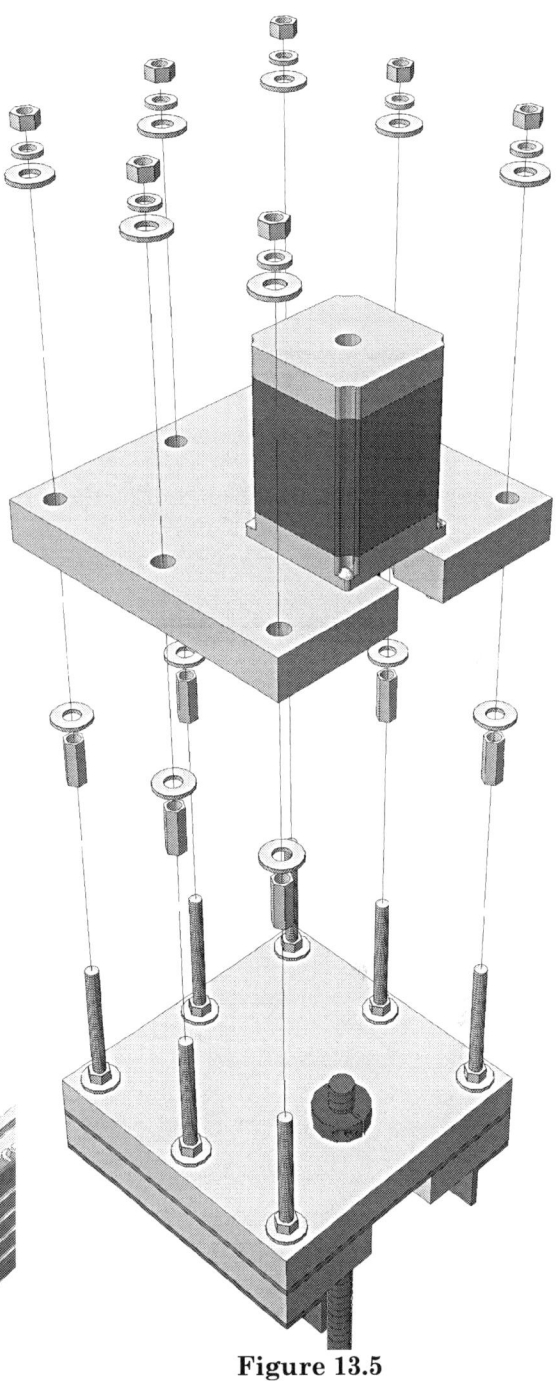

Figure 13.5

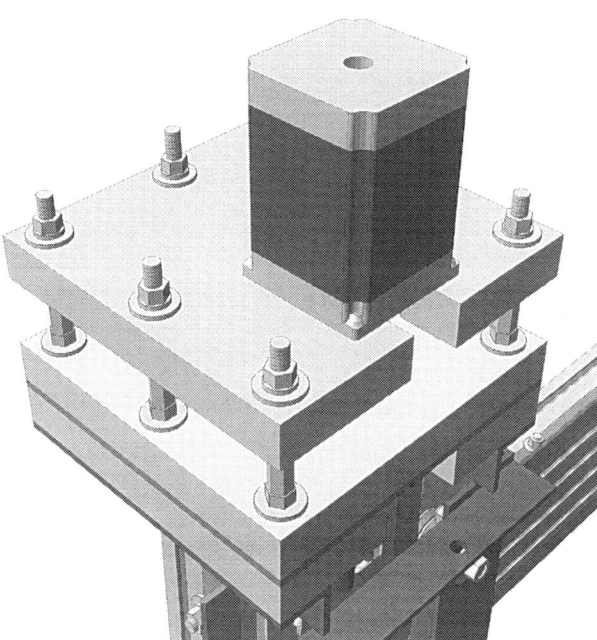

Figure 13.6

Building the KRMx01 CNC **175**

Step 4 - Attach Motor Assembly to X Axis

Again, make sure the nuts on the main bearing assembly are firm but not tight. Then add seven 1/4-20 x 7/8" standoffs. Screw them finger tight only. Add a 1/4" washer then slip the motor assembly over the seven bolts, as shown in Figure 13.7. The shaft coupler should fit over the protruding ACME screw.

Once in place, add a 1/4" washer, lock washer, and 1/4-20 hex nut. Finger tighten. Tighten both the clamp screw and set screw on the shaft coupler.

The completed X assembly should look like the one shown in Figure 13.8.

Figure 13.7

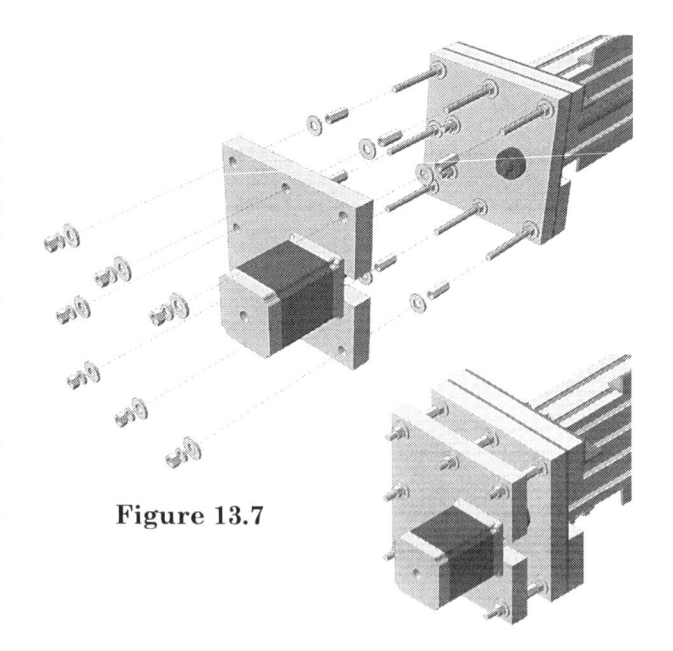

Figure 13.8

Step 5 - Attach Motor Assemblies to Y Axis

If you have not added the 12, 1/4-20 x 4-1/2" hex bolts to the rear blocks do it now.

Make sure the nuts on the main bearing assembly are firm but not tight. Then add six 1/4-20 x 7/8" standoffs. Screw them finger tight only. Add a 1/4" washer then slip the motor assembly over the six bolts, as shown in Figure 13.9. The shaft coupler should fit over the protruding ACME screw.

Once in place add a 1/4" washer, lock washer and 1/4-20 hex nut. Finger tighten. Tighten both the clamp screw and set screw on the shaft coupler.

The completed Y assembly should look like the one shown in Figure 13.10.

You will need to repeat the process for both Y axis bearings. The orientation of the slot and shaft will be reversed.

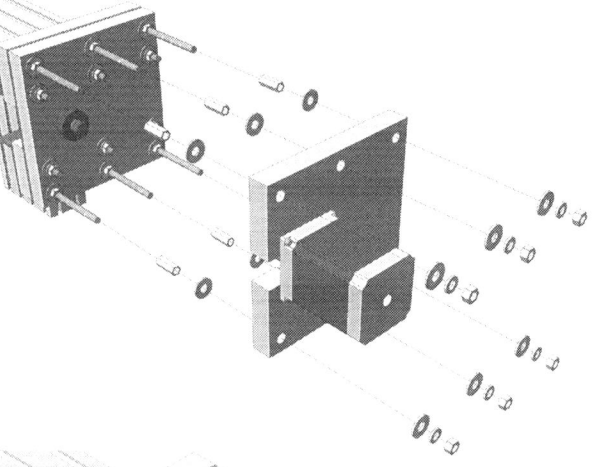

Figure 13.9

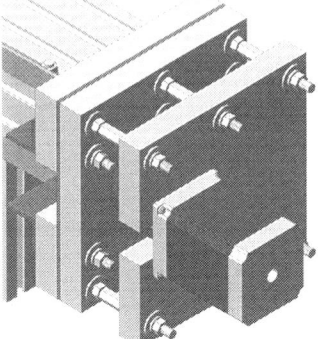

Figure 13.10

Step 6 - Recheck All Clamp and Set Screws

It is important that all the set screws and clamp screws be tight on the shaft couplers. If they are loose, they will fly out and will have to be replaced.

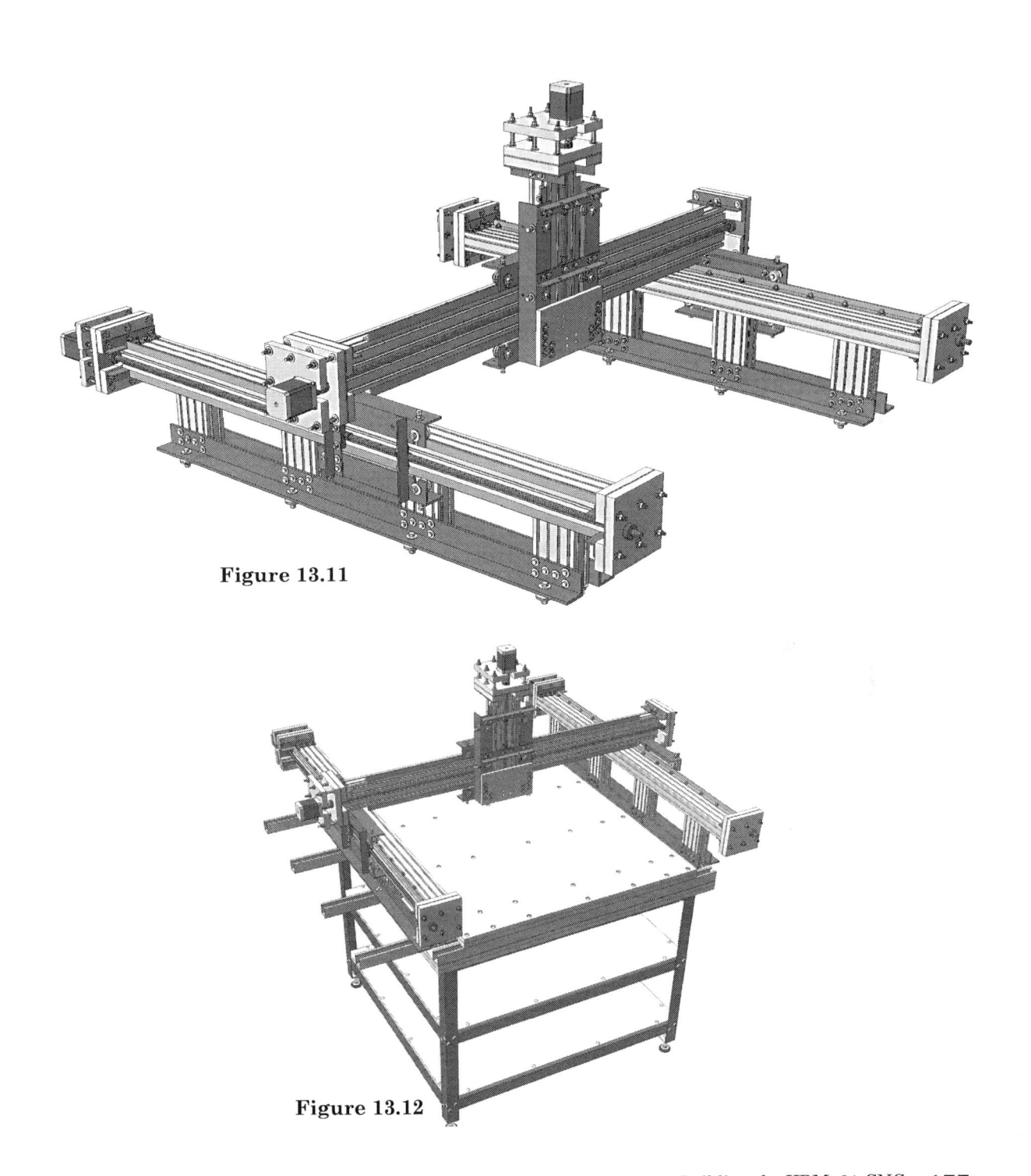

Figure 13.11

Figure 13.12

Adjustments

You still have not tightened your bearing assemblies. The main reason for this is that you need to move the carriages back and forth a few times, which would be too difficult without the CNC connected to our PC. Rest assured, you will do this in a later chapter.

There is one thing you need to look out for at this point in the construction. The shaft coupler has tiny slits or helical cuts. These are provided to give the shaft some flexibility. This flexibility greatly smooths the transfer of power from the stepper motor to the ACME screw. The problem is that the helical cuts can also add backlash under load unless certain precautions are taken.

When attaching the motor assembly to the bearing assembly, you want the slits to be as compressed as much as possible. You also don't want the motor assembly so tight that you put undo pressure on the motor bearings.

There are two ways to adjust the amount the slits are collapsed. The first is by adding an additional washer between the standoff and the motor mount. The second is by simply readjusting the shaft coupler on the motor shaft..

In the configuration shown in Figure 13.13, the slits are almost closed, this is the proper configuration. By having these slightes gaps in the slits you will not have any excesive stress on the motors internal bearings.

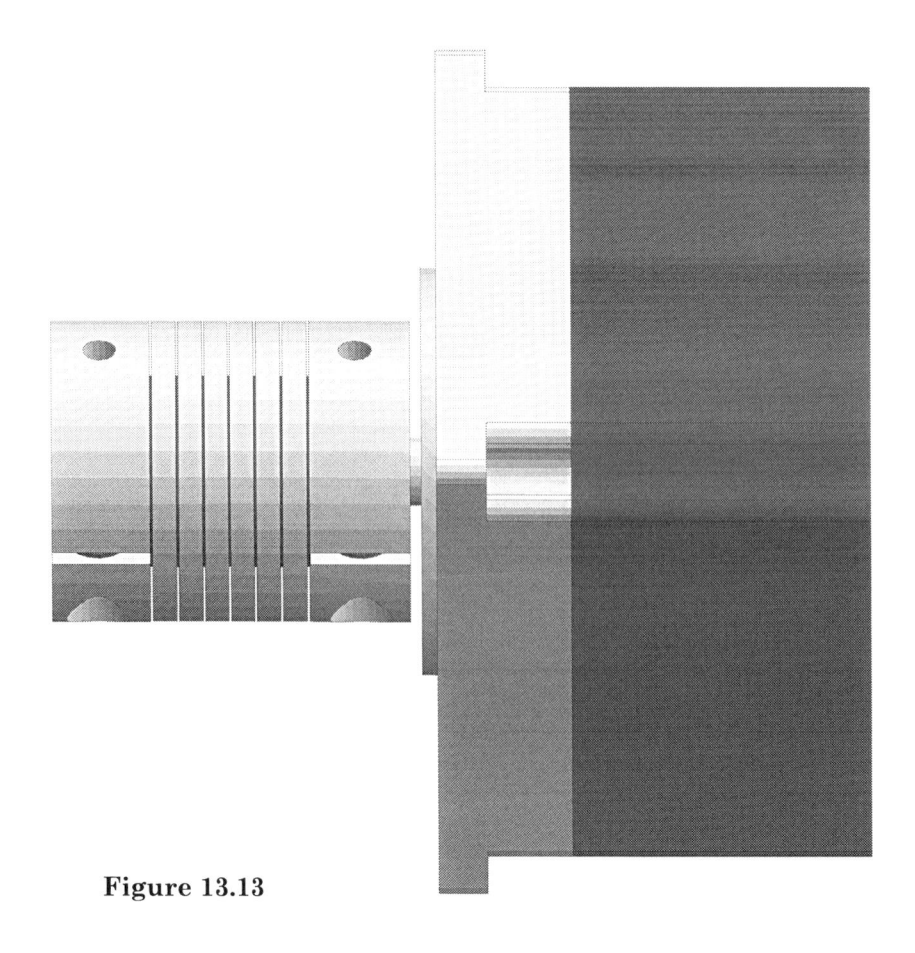

Figure 13.13

Chapter 14

Cable Hookup

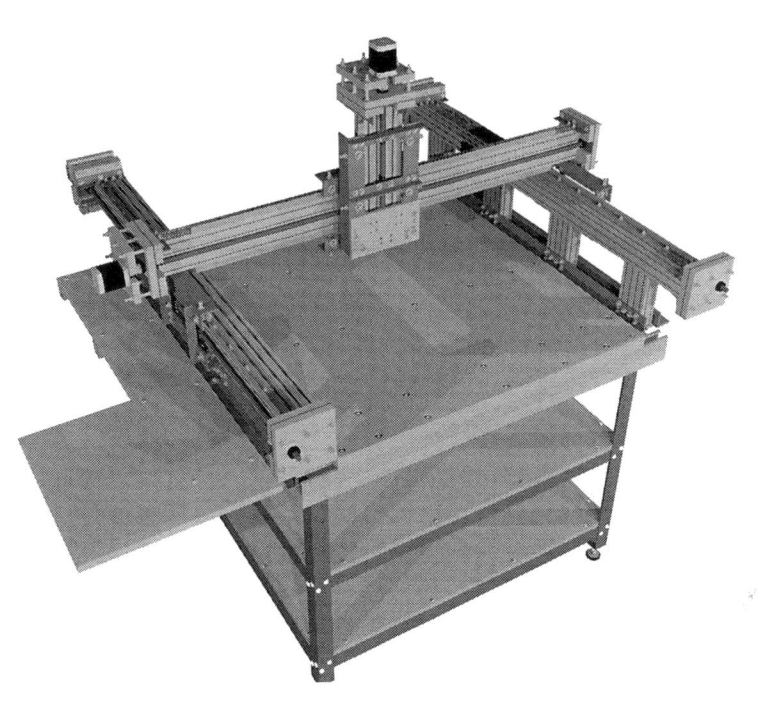

A good cabling system will allow your CNC to operate reliably and without undo downtime.

The cable types have been broken down into the following three categories:

- Internal Cables
- External Cables
- Moving Cables

All three categories have various difficulties that must be overcome to create a reliable and easy to maintain cabling system.

Tools Needed For This Chapter

- 7/16" Wrench
- Power drill
- 1/4" Drill bit
- Saw (see text)

Components Needed For This Chapter

- 1 20' Motor cable
- 3 12' Motor cables
- 6 3-1/2"x 1/4" Rubber bands (#64)
- 2 Hook and loop straps
- 1 24" x 48" x 3/4 Particle board panel
- 8 1/4-20 x 3" Carriage bolts
- 8 1/4-20 Hex nuts
- 8 1/4" Washers
- 8 1/4" Split lock washers
- 8 3/8" Washers
- 4 String tags

Chapter Estimates

Cost: $91
Time : Half Day

Prerequisites

You will need a piece of 24" x 48" x 3/4" particle board cut down to 20" x 48". Your home center should be able to do this for you at no charge. You will be cutting a section out of this piece and can do this with just about any saw; jig saw, circular saw, band saw, or scroll saw. Even a reciprocating saw can be used.

The three cable categories are reviewed in more detail below.

Internal Cable

This cable is simply a cable or wire that connects from one point on the CNC to another point on the CNC. An example of this would be a limit switch connected to the G540 controller. The two cables connecting your Y axis stepper motors to the G540 controller are also internal cables.

There are two areas of concern for internal cables. First, you must make sure they are securely tied down so they don't work themselves loose or even worse, get snagged by the CNC's movable components. The second concern is that you properly label your cables so that you can easily identify and trouble shoot problems as they arise. An effective and inexpensive way to identify cables is with string tags like the ones shown in Figure 14.1.

Figure 14.1

External Cable

This cable is similar to the internal cable except that it runs from a connection on the CNC to an external device. The main power cable is a good example of this. You might even consider your dust collection hose an external cable.

The external cable has the same concerns as the internal cable but adds an additional hazard. For example, an exposed cable may get snagged as someone walks by the CNC. For this reason, these cables should be covered with mats or taped to the floor. Another option is to run them overhead.

Moving Cable

These are cables that run the length of the X and Y axis and are connected directly to, or run through, an X or Y-carriage. Because the axis moves, the cables can easily get caught or even pinched. While there are a multitude of ways to handle the problems associated with moving cables, the most effective way is with a special cable holder called an Energy Chain or an E-Chain, like the one shown in Figure 14.2. The E-Chain is a lot like a very large bicycle chain with a couple of exceptions. It is hinged in such a way that it won't sag into itself and it also has a large cavity so that you can easily fit all your cables inside. Some even have special properties so that they can be opened or unzipped to make it easy to add or remove cables once they have been installed. When using an E-Chain, you normally connect one end of the chain to your carriage and the other end to your table.

The predominate manufacturer of E-Chain is a company called Igus. The problem is that an E-Chain purchased directly from Igus or one of its distributors can be prohibitively expensive. As a result, there is a big surplus market for E-Chains and it can be difficult to accurately source one that does not require special considerations. For this reason, it is recommended you go a different route. The second book in the KRMx01 series includes an upgrade project called Dragon Cable.

Figure 14.2

Dragon Cable

The original Dragon Cable was designed and cut with a laser and looked like the cable shown in Figure 14.3. The Dragon Cable upgrade project in the second book has been totally redesigned so that it can be cut with your KRMx01.

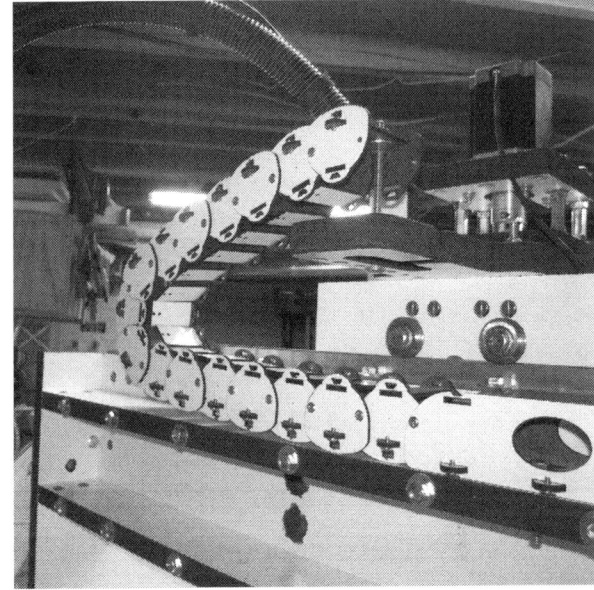

Figure 14.3

Chicken or the Egg?

Making your own E-Chain poses a slight dilemma. You need an E-Chain in order to use your CNC and you need your CNC to make an E-Chain. What do we do?

It's simple; you need to handle your cables in a less than optimal manner so you can get your machine in an operational state. Don't panic; it's not as bad as it sounds.

The goal for this chapter is to get your motors hooked up to your G540 controller in such a way that you can use your CNC without snagging a cable during operation.

One of the first things you are going to do in this chapter is to add the side table shown in Figure 14.4. This will solve two problems: first, it will cover the struts that tend to snag cables during operation; and second, it will provide a temporary support location for your electronics mounting board. Later, this table will also provide a place to hold your computer monitor and keyboard.

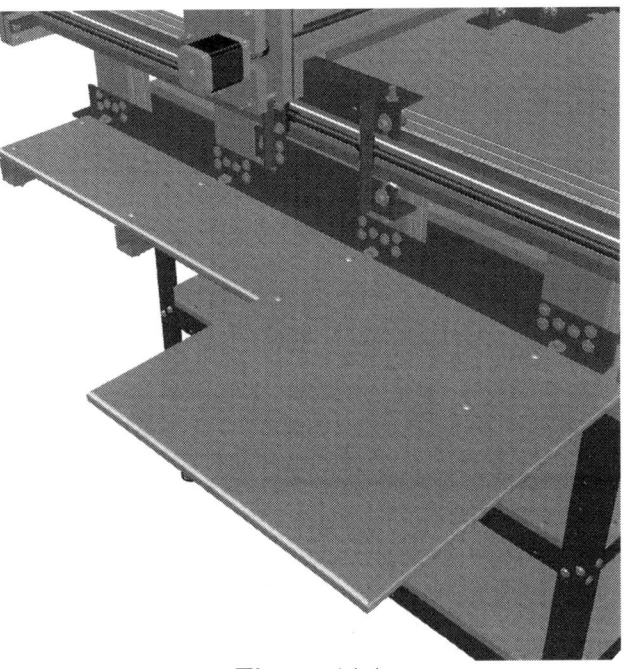

Figure 14.4

Step 1 - Cut Side Table

Take the 20" x 48" x 3/4" piece of particle board and cut the section shown in Figure 14.5.

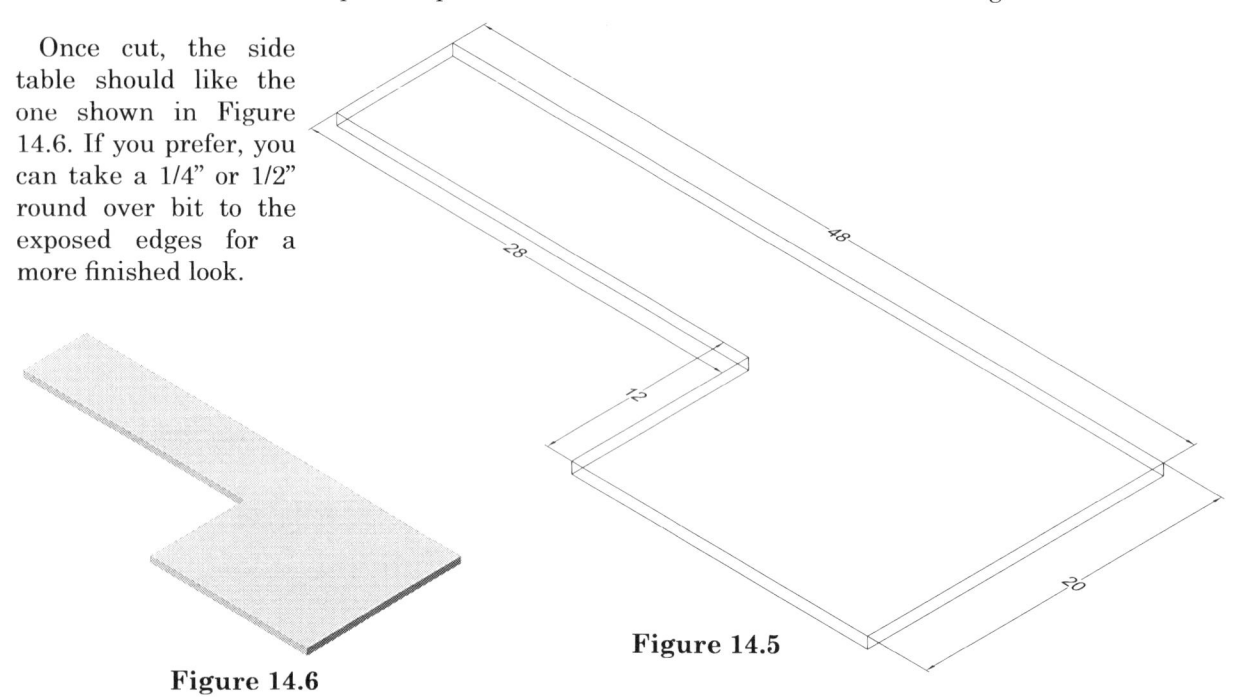

Once cut, the side table should like the one shown in Figure 14.6. If you prefer, you can take a 1/4" or 1/2" round over bit to the exposed edges for a more finished look.

Figure 14.5

Figure 14.6

Step 2 - Put the Table in Place

Place the side table on the four struts as shown in Figure 14.7. The front edge of the side table should be flush with the front of the CNC table, and the side edge should be up against the steel angle.

Use a small clamp near the back to hold the side table in place.

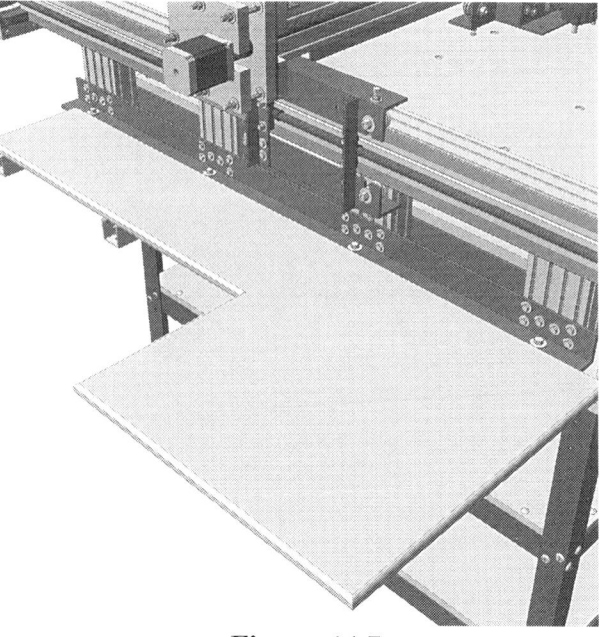

Figure 14.7

Step 3 - Drill Mounting Holes

From the under side of the table, take a 1/4" drill bit, and drill holes through the center of the indicated slots, and up through the table, as shown in Figure 14.8.

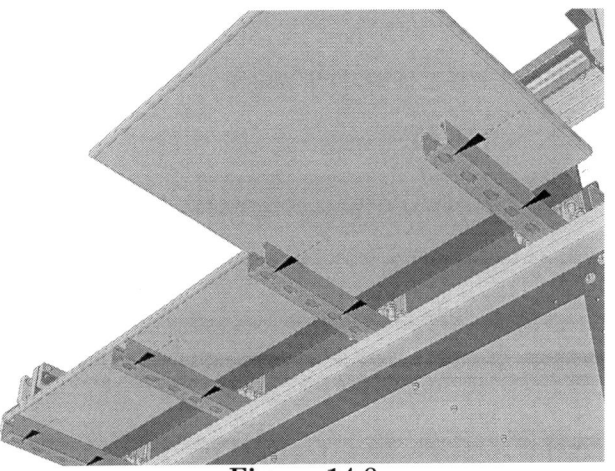

Figure 14.8

Step 4 - Install Table Mounting Bolts

Insert eight 1/4-20 x 3" carriage bolts into the eight holes you just drilled, as shown in Figure 14.9.

From the bottom insert a 3/8" washer, 1/4" washer, 1/4" lock washer and 1/4-20 hex nut as shown in Figure 14.10. Tighten with a 7/16" wrench.

Figure 14.9

Figure 14.10

Building the KRMx01 CNC **185**

Step 5 - Create Two Cable Hangers

Take three #64 rubber bands and tie them together as shown in Figure 14.11. Then add a hook and loop strap to the end. You will need two of these.

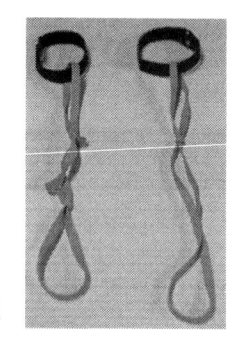

Figure 14.11

Step 6 - Hang the Cable Hangers

Hang the first hanger at dead center of the CNC machine as shown in Figure 14.12. The hook and loop strap should be about 12" from the top of the Z axis stepper motor.

The second hanger should be about 33" to the left of the first, and should hang the same distance.

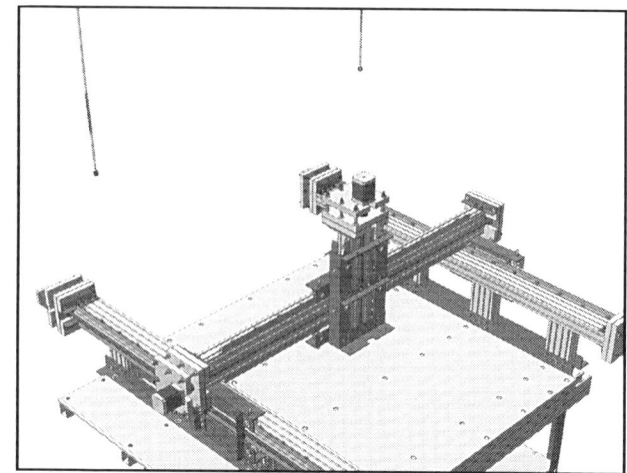

Figure 14.12

Step 7 - Connect the Z Axis Cable

Connect the female end of the 20' motor cable to the Z axis connector on the stepper motor, as shown in Figure 14.13.

Figure 14.13

Step 8 - Hang the Z Axis Cable

Run the Z axis cable through the hook and loop straps at the end of each of the cable hangers as shown in Figure 14.14. For now, let the end hang free and use a string tag to label the male end of the cable "Z Axis."

Figure 14.14

Step 9 - Connect X Axis Cable

Connect the female end of the 12' motor cable to the X axis connector on the stepper motor as shown in Figure 14.15.

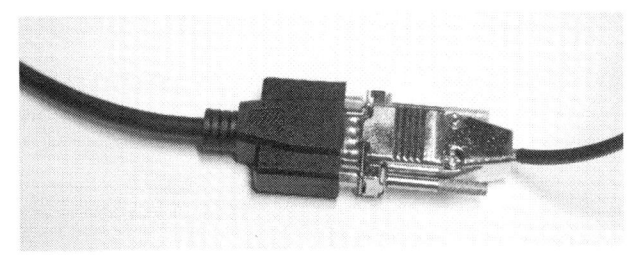

Figure 14.15

Step 10 - Hang the X Axis Cable

Run the X axis cable through the hook and loop strap at the end of the left hanger as shown in Figure 14.16. For now, let the end hang free and use a string tag to label the male end of the cable "X Axis."

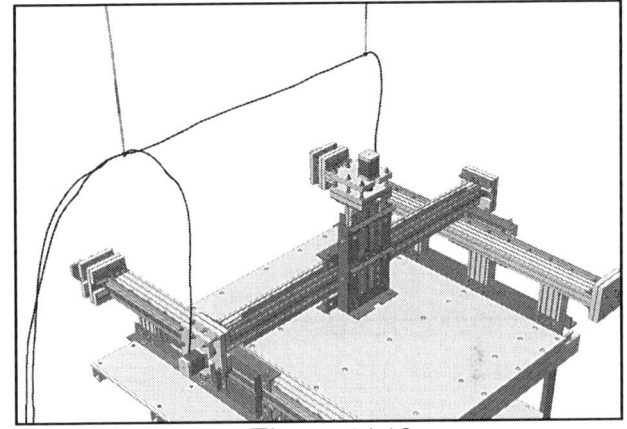

Figure 14.16

Step 11 - Connect Y Axis Cable

Connect the female end of the 12' motor cable to the Y axis connector on the stepper motor. The Y axis motor is the right hand beam (from the rear), as shown in Figure 14.17.

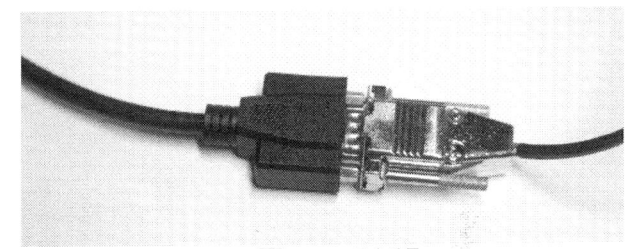

Figure 14.17

Step 12 - Run the Y Axis Cable

Run the Y axis cable as shown in Figure 14.18. Use a string tag to label the male end of the cable "Y Axis."

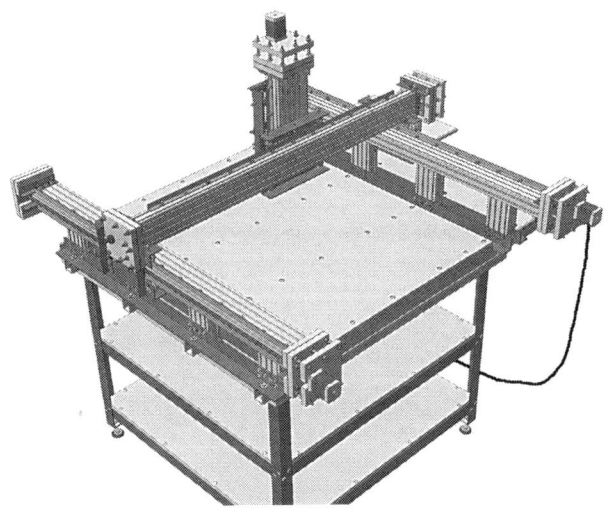

Figure 14.18

Building the KRMx01 CNC

Step 13 - Connect the A Axis Cable

Connect the female end of the 12' motor cable to the A axis connector on the stepper motor, as shown in Figure 14.19. The A axis motor is on the left hand beam (from the rear). The A axis is slaved off of the Y axis, so whenever you move the Y axis, the A axis will move in exactly the same way.

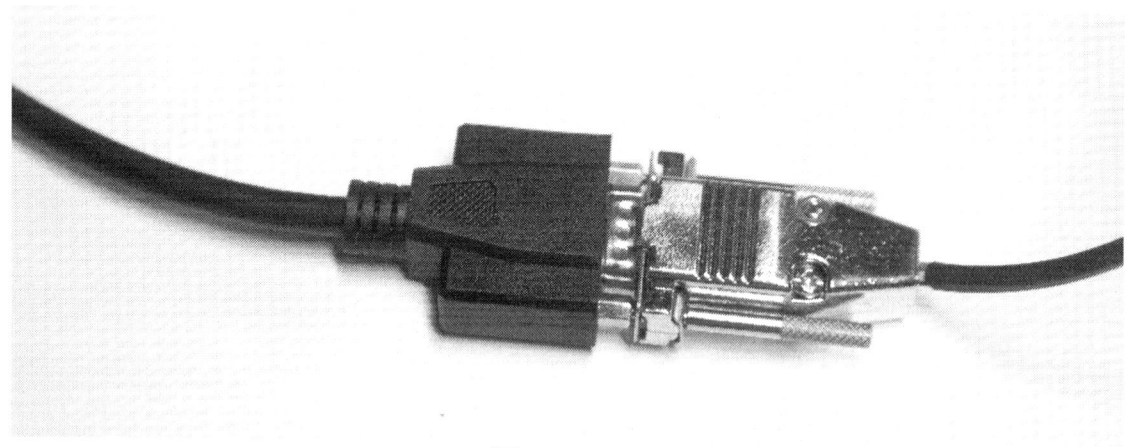

Figure 14.19

Step 14 - Run the A Axis Cable

Run the A axis cable as shown in Figure 14.20. Use a string tag to label the male end of the cable "A Axis."

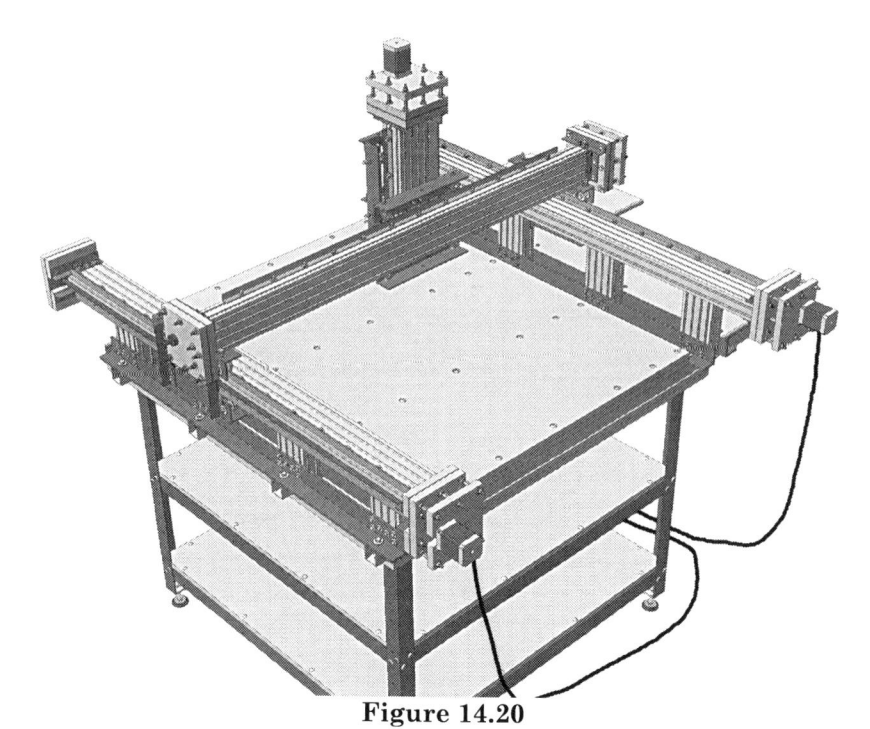

Figure 14.20

Step 15 - Setup Location of Computer and Electronics

You need to pick a location for your computer, monitor, keyboard, and electronics mounting board. This should be easy since you have a side table and two shelves below the CNC. The cables should reach nearly any location.

For now, your cabling is somewhat temporary so placement is not critical. You should however start thinking of where you want to put things permanently.

Recommendations

Place your monitor, keyboard and mouse on the side table. Place your PC on the left front side of the bottom shelf and place the electronics mounting board on the front right side of the bottom shelf. This will allow for some of the future upgrades that have been planned.

Step 16 - Connect Cables to Controller

Connect the four stepper motor cables to the controller as shown in Figure 14.21. Be sure to tighten the mounting screws to secure the cable to the controller.

If it is not already connected, connect the parallel port cable from the G540 to the computer.

!!Important!!

When connecting motor cables be sure the power is disconnected from the 48V power supply.

Figure 14.21

Building the KRMx01 CNC **189**

Conclusion

With the hookup of the four axis cables, you can now control your CNC. Resist the urge to test it out too much, as your motor mounts and ACME nuts have not yet been tightened.

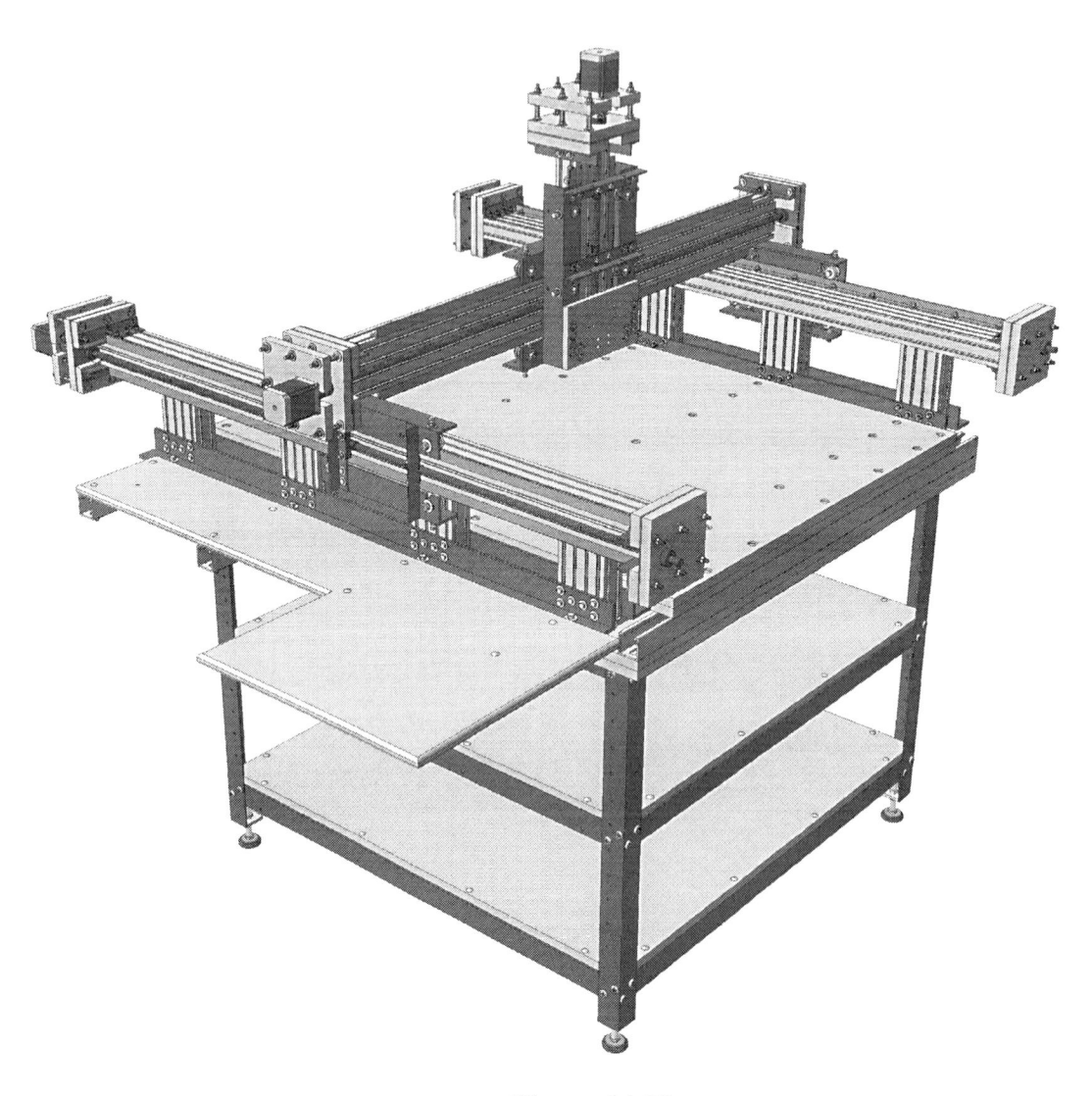

Figure 14.22

Chapter 15

Adjusting the Drive Train

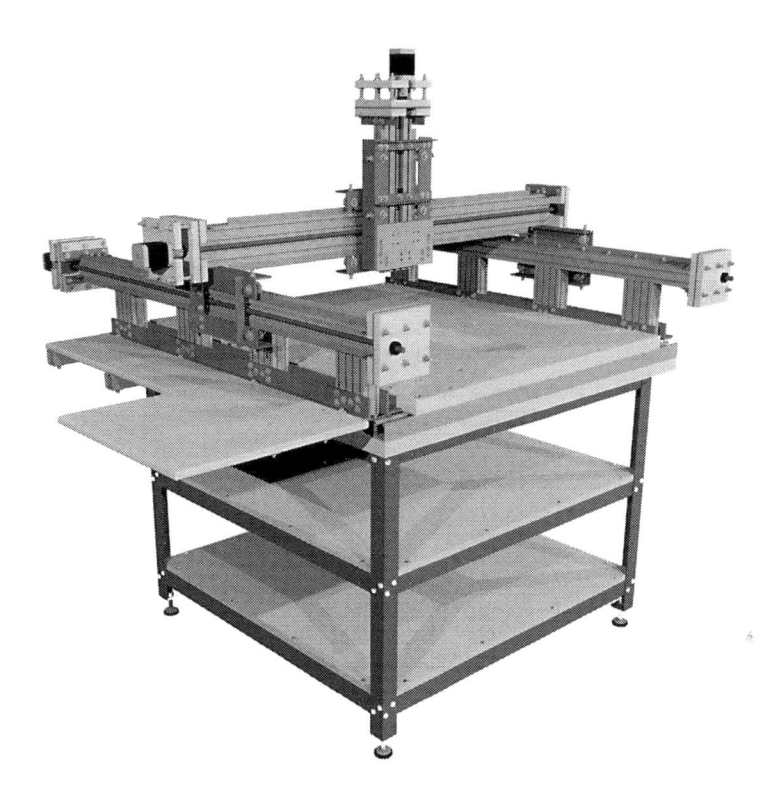

In a previous chapter, the motor mounts and ACME nuts were left loose so that they can be properly aligned. In this chapter, you will align them simply by moving a particular carriage from one end to another and adjusting in sequence.

Tools Needed For This Chapter

- 2 7/16" Wrenches or sockets
- 3/8" Wrench

Chapter Estimates
Cost: None

Time: Couple hours

Prerequisites

In order to complete this chapter, you will need your temporary cables run and connected to your PC and G540. The basic wiring of your power supply and G540 should be complete, and your parallel cable connected between the G540 and PC.

Additionally, the Mach 3 software needs to be installed and configured.

Important

Before proceeding it is important that motor mount bolts (the ones protruding through the blocks) are fairly loose. There should be enough play that you can shift the position of the complete block assembly. The same goes for the mounting bolts on the ACME nuts.

Step 1 - Power Up the Machine

With everything connected, power up your PC and CNC power supply. Do not start the Mach 3 software. At this point the fault light on the G540 controller should be glowing red. If it is not, make sure the charge pump switch is in the "ON" position.

Step 2 - Start Mach 3

Start Mach 3 by double clicking the KRMx01 shortcut icon shown in Figure 15.1. During the startup process you should hear your stepper motors click as they are provided power by the G540 controller. The fault light on the G540 should go out and the green power light should be glowing, as shown in Figure 15.2.

Figure 15.1

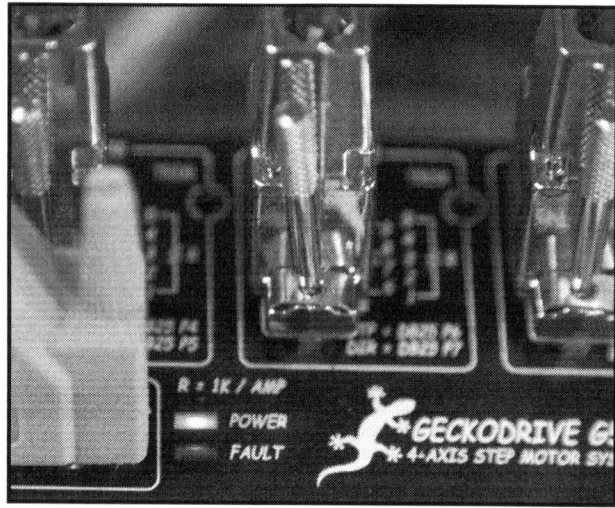

Figure 15.2

Step 3 - Set the Jog Speed

Starting out, you want to take things a little slow and so you should lower the jog speed. Jogging is what it is called when you move one of the CNC axis by some sort of external control, which in this case is the arrow keys on your PC keyboard.

To adjust the jog settings, use the jog fly-out, which is toggled by hitting the "TAB" key on your keyboard.

Activate it by hitting the "TAB" key. Change the "Slow Jog Rate" field to 30, as show in Figure 15.3, then close the fly-out by hitting the "TAB" key once again.

TIP

While most of the settings that you change in Mach 3 will automatically be saved, a few of them will exist only in your current session of Mach 3. As soon as you close the application they will be forgotten. The jog settings is one of these such settings. To keep them from session to session, select the "Save Settings" option in the Config menu, as shown in Figure 15.4.

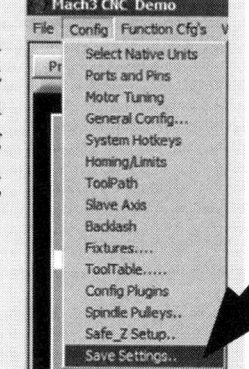

Figure 15.3

Figure 15.4

194   Chapter 15   Adjusting the Drive Train

Step 4 - Position the Z Axis

If you have not done so, place Mach 3 in run mode by clicking the "Reset" button on the main screen. The outside border on the button should be glowing green, as shown in Figure 15.5.

Figure 15.5

If by chance the soft limits option has been turned on, you will need to turn it off now. Do this by hitting the "Soft Limits" button shown in Figure 15.6. When soft limits is on, the button will have a green border. The border will be black when off.

The Page-Up and Page-Down keys control the Z axis jog. Press and hold the Page-Up key for about a second. The Z-carriage should move upward about an inch.

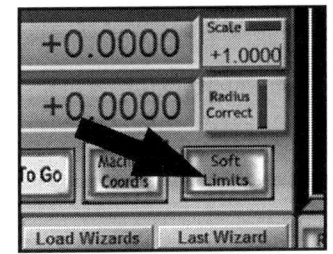

Figure 15.6

If it does not move, go back and review the electronics and configuration chapters. It may not move because the carriage is already at its top most position. If so, you will hear the stepper motor clicking as it stalls. This is normal.

Move the Z-carriage all the way to its top position. When moving the carriage try to keep it from hitting the end and stalling the motors. While this will not damage the KRMx01, it will put stress on the lead screws and force you to make more frequent adjustments. In addition, any time the stepper motor stalls or loses a step you will need to re-home the CNC, which will be covered in a later chapter. So for now, raise the Z axis so that it's within an inch or so of the top- most position, as shown in Figure 15.7.

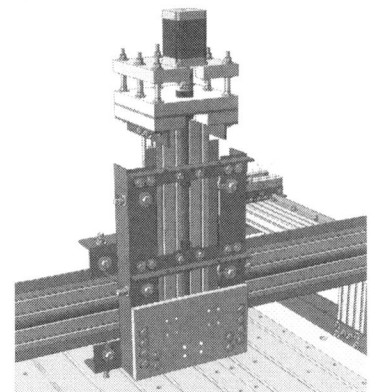

Figure 15.7

Step 5 - Tighten the Z Axis Motor Mount

Tighten the seven motor mount bolts shown in Figure 15.8. Do this by first tightening all the inner hex nuts with a 7/16" wrench, then tighten all the standoffs with a 3/8" wrench. Finally tighten all the outside hex nuts with a 7/16" socket or wrench.

At this point, the motor should be firmly in place. If you try and move it or the mount, it should not move at all. Grab the ACME screw and try to rock it up and down. It should not move, but if it does then the 1/2" shaft collars need to be tightened.

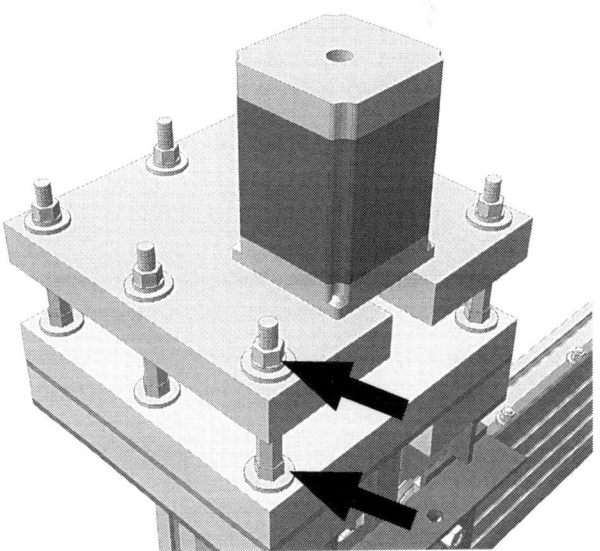

Figure 15.8

Building the KRMx01 CNC

Step 6 - Move the X Axis to the Right

Use the right arrow key to move the X carriage all the way to the right as shown in Figure 15.9. Tighten the nine hex nuts on the bearing mount using a 7/16 wrench. If the X-carriage does not move, go back and review the previous chapters, particularly the configuration settings.

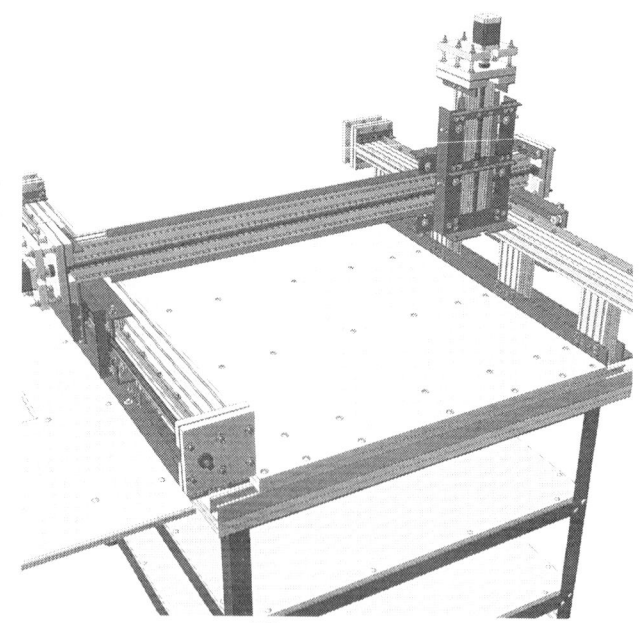

Figure 15.9

Step 7 - Move the X Axis to the Left

Use the left arrow key to move the X-carriage all the way to the left as shown in Figure 15.10. First, you need to tighten the two internal hex nuts protruding through the steel angle connected to the back face of the X-beam. Next, tighten the seven internal hex nuts with a 7/16" wrench. Following the hex nuts, tighten the seven internal standoffs with a 3/8" wrench. Finally tighten the seven outside hex nuts with a 7/16" wrench.

At this point, the motor should be firmly in place and if you try to move it or the mount, it should not move at all. Grab the ACME screw and try to rock it left and right. It should not move, but if it does then the 1/2" shaft collars need to be tightened.

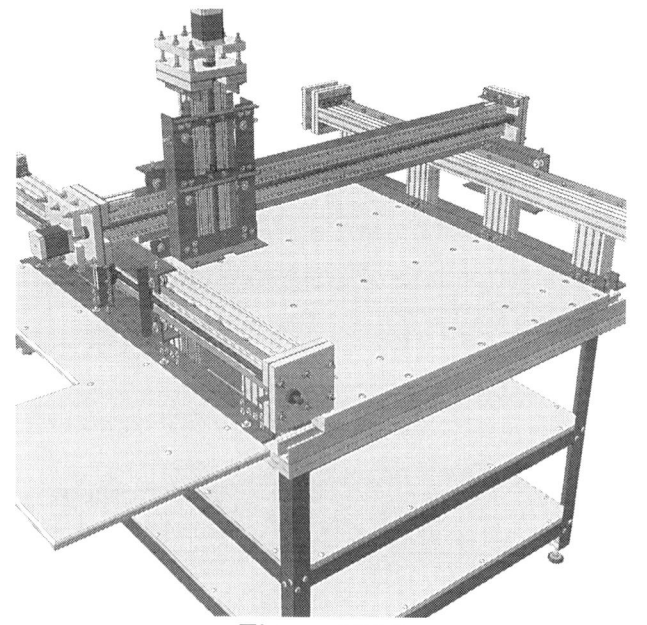

Figure 15.10

Step 8 - Move the Y Axis to the Front

Hold down the down arrow for about one second. Both sides of the Y axis should move forward about one inch. If they do not, you need to go back and review the last few chapters. It is important that both sides of the Y axis move exactly the same amount when moved forward or backward.

Use the down arrow key to move the Y-carriages all the way to the front as shown in Figure 15.11. Tighten the 6 hex nuts on the bearing mount using a 7/16 wrench.

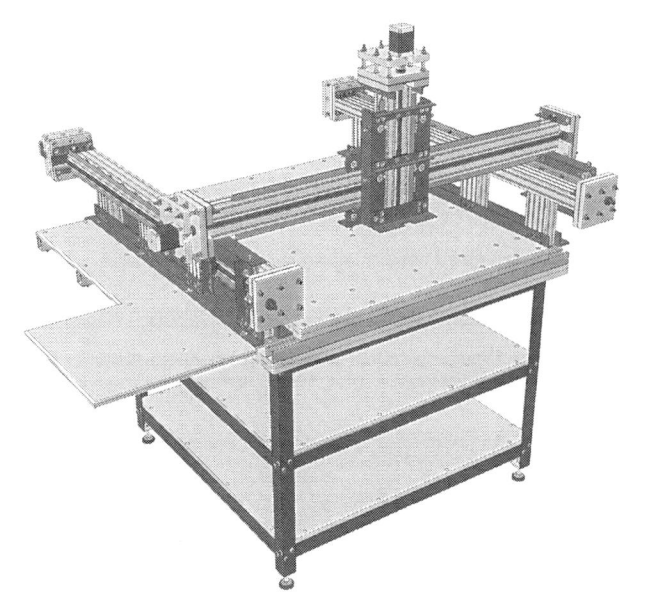

Figure 15.11

Step 9 - Move the Y Axis to the Rear

Use the up arrow key to move the Y-carriages all the way to the rear, as shown in Figure 15.12. Tighten the six internal hex nuts protruding through the two steel angle connected to the Y-beam. Tighten the six internal hex nuts connecting the two bearing blocks. Next, tighten the six standoffs. Finally, tighten the 6 hex nuts on the outside of the motor mount.

At this point, both motors should be firmly in place and if you try to move it or the mount, it should not move at all. Grab each of the ACME screws and try to rock them forward and backward. They should not move, but if they do then the 1/2" shaft collars need to be tightened.

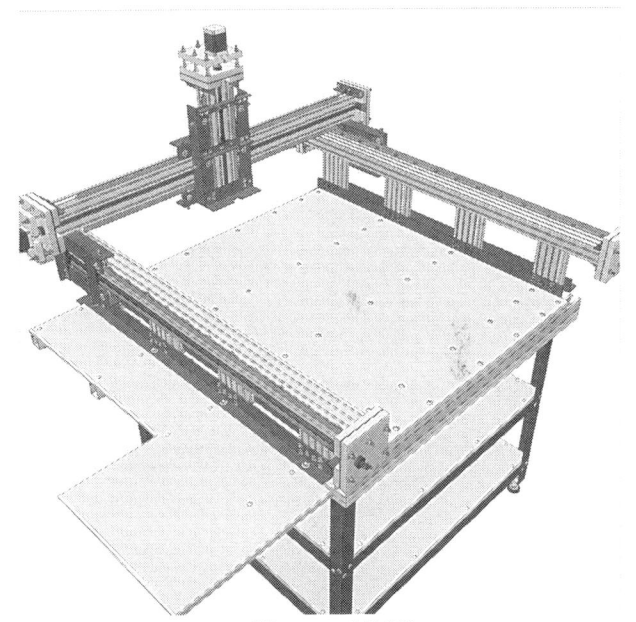

Figure 15.12

Step 10 - Tighten the two ACME Nuts on Z Axis

Using two 7/16" wrenches, tighten the four bolts on the two ACME nuts, as shown in Figure 15.13. While tightening the bolts, apply pressure to the two ACME nuts to force them apart. It is this pressure that will enable you to remove any backlash that may develop. As the ACME nuts wear a little, you may need to adjust the two nuts. To do this, loosen the bolts, apply opposing pressure, then re-tighten the bolts.

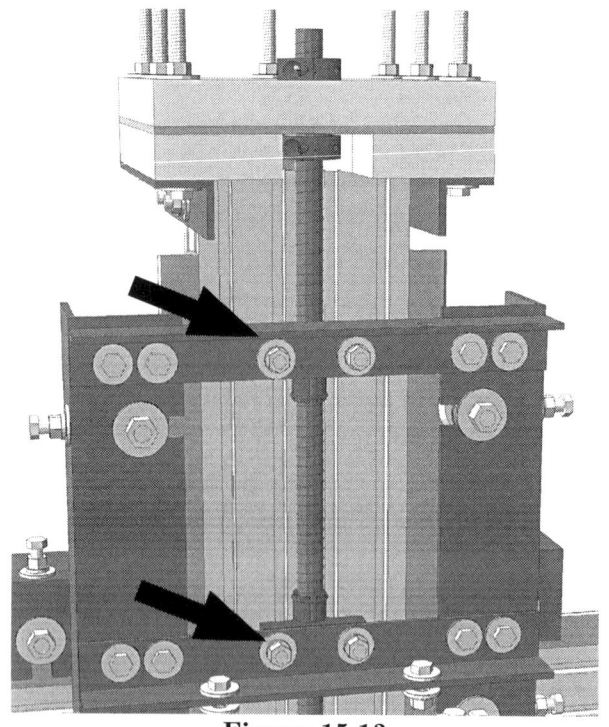

Figure 15.13

Step 11 - Tighten the two ACME Nuts on X Axis

Using a single 7/16" wrench, tighten the four nuts on the two ACME nuts, as shown in Figure 15.14. While tightening the nuts, apply pressure to the two ACME to force them apart.

Figure 15.14

198   Chapter 15   Adjusting the Drive Train

Step 12 - Tighten the four ACME Nuts on Y Axis

Using two 7/16" wrenches, tighten the four bolts on the two ACME nuts on both carriages, as shown in Figure 15.15. While tightening the bolts, apply pressure to the two ACME nuts to force them apart.

Step 13 - Final Test

Using the four arrow keys move the CNC fully to the right, then the left. Move it forwards and backwards. Change the jog rate to 50% and run the full extent of the table several times. Increase the jog rate to 60% and continue to test. The goal here is to work up to 100% slowly.

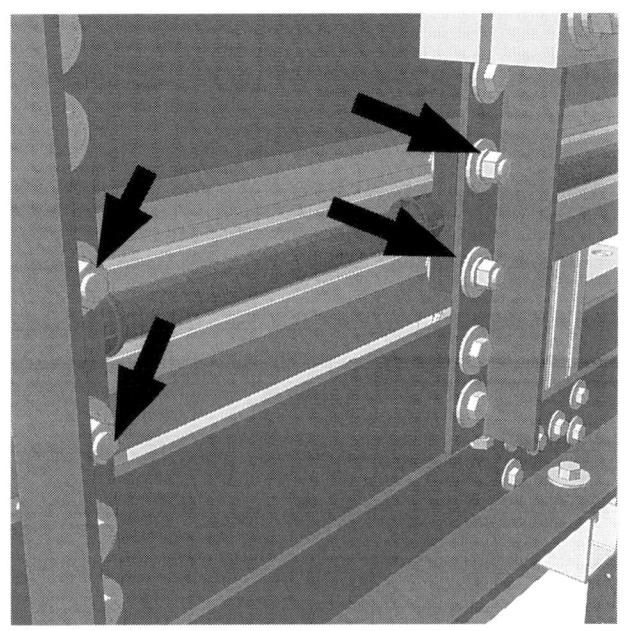

Figure 15.15

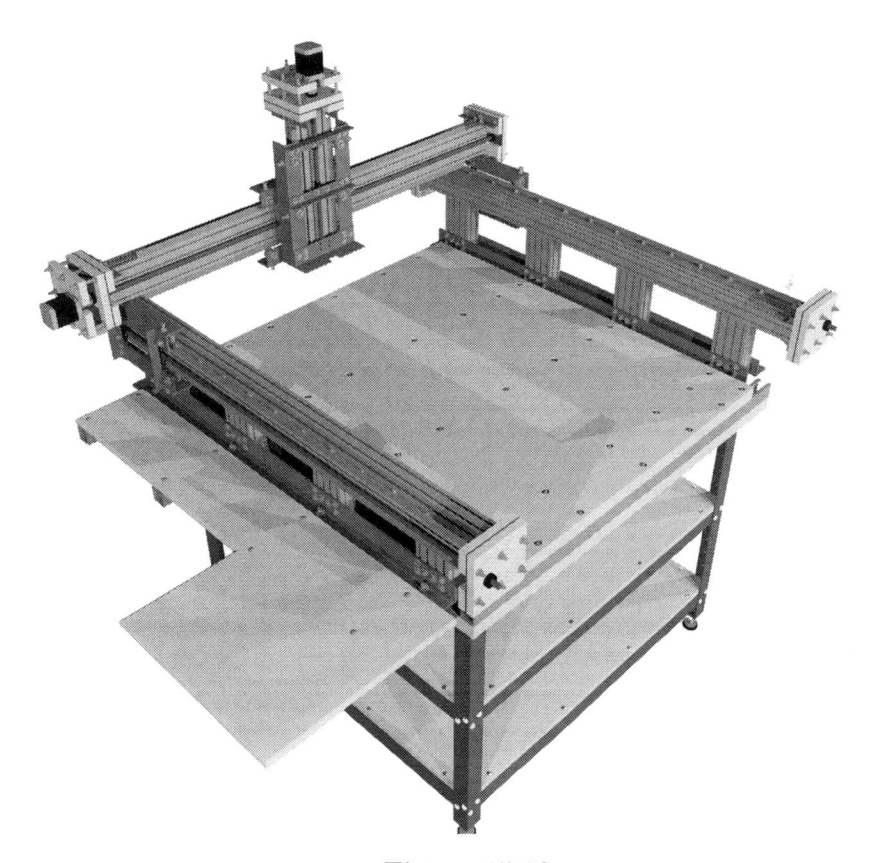

Figure 15.16

Conclusion

Your CNC is fully operational at this point. However, it is missing the router, which you will be adding in the next chapter.

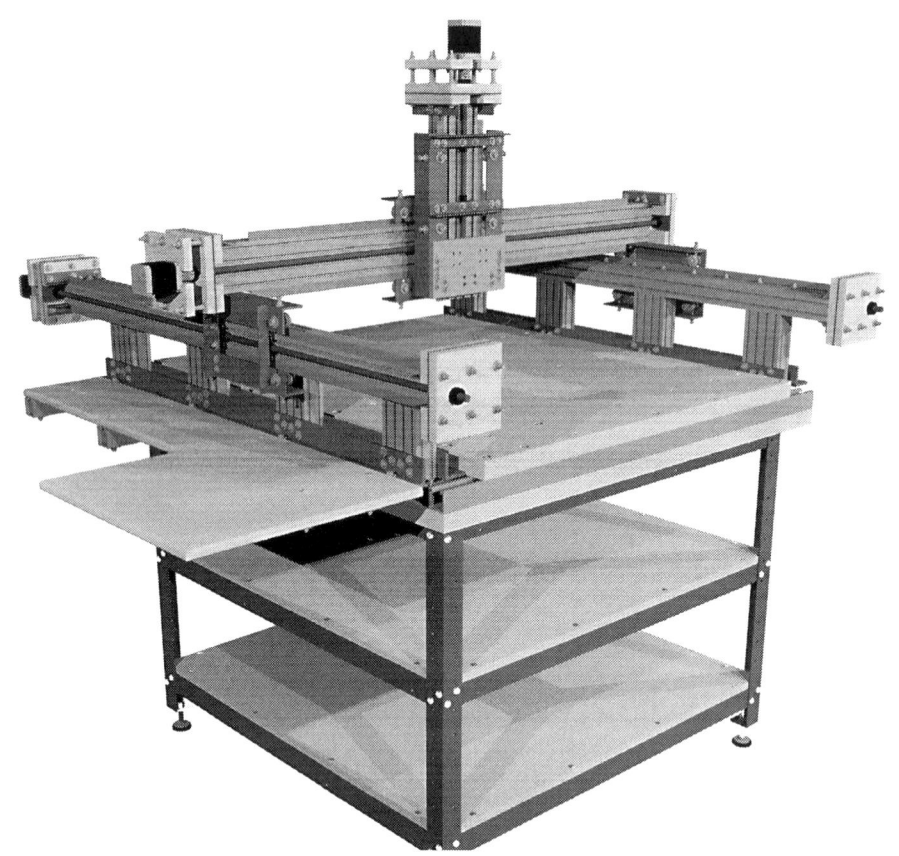

Figure 15.17

Chapter 16

Router Hookup

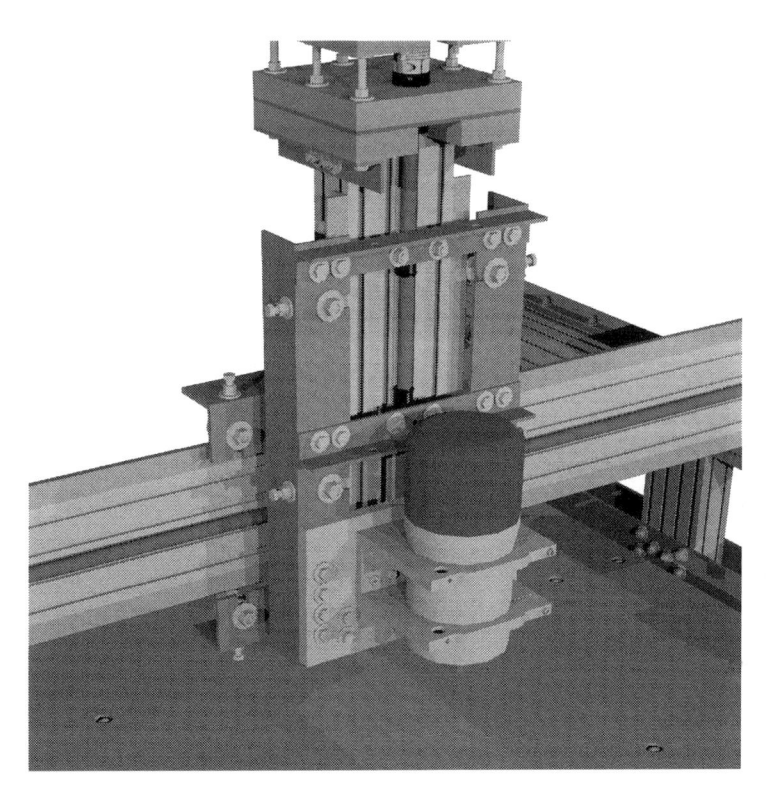

True CNC spindles are very high end components that can cost thousands. Many do-it-yourself CNC machines and some commercial machines utilize woodworking routers. There are many types and sizes of woodworking routers available. The KRMx01 utilizes a K2CNC router mount. These router mounts support many size and types of routers.

Tools Needed For This Chapter

- Phillips screwdriver
- 3/16" Allen wrench

Components Needed For This Chapter

- K2CNC Router Mount
- Router
- 8, #10-24 Hex nuts
- 8, #10 Lock washers
- 8, #10 Washers
- 8, #10-24 x 1-1/4" Machine screws
- 15' Extension cord

This chapter shows the use of a Hitachi router and router mount. The costs reflect these. You are free to use the router of your choice. Of all the routers that K2CNC supports, the three following are recommended.

Bosch 1617EVS

Hitachi M12VC

Makita RF1101

Chapter Estimates

Cost: $180

Time: One day

The the cost estimate includes the cost of the K2CNC mount and the Hitachi router.

Prerequisites

You should have made your choice of routers and have both your K2CNC mount and router in hand before starting this chapter.

Please note that the three routers mentioned previously are recommended because Kronos Robotics sells a kit called the AirExchanger. It is used to mount various dust shrouds to your CNC. Kronos Robotics has an AirExchanger kit for the Bosch, Makita, and Hitachi routers. Please note that by the time this book is printed others may also be available. Check the Kronos Robotics web site for more information on the AirExchanger.

The Kronos Robotics web site can be found at: www.kronosrobotics.com.

The K2CNC mount can be found at www.k2cnc.com.

Step 1 - Attach the K2CNC Mount

Attach the K2CNC mount to the KRMx02 Z-plate as shown in Figure 16.1.

Insert the eight #10 machine screws into the eight holes on the mount, then slip them through the eight holes on the Z-plate. Add a washer, lock washer and hex nut and tighten.

Note, the illustrations shows the Z-plate is detached from the CNC. You may leave the Z-plate in place, but you may need to lower the Z-carriage to gain access to the holes.

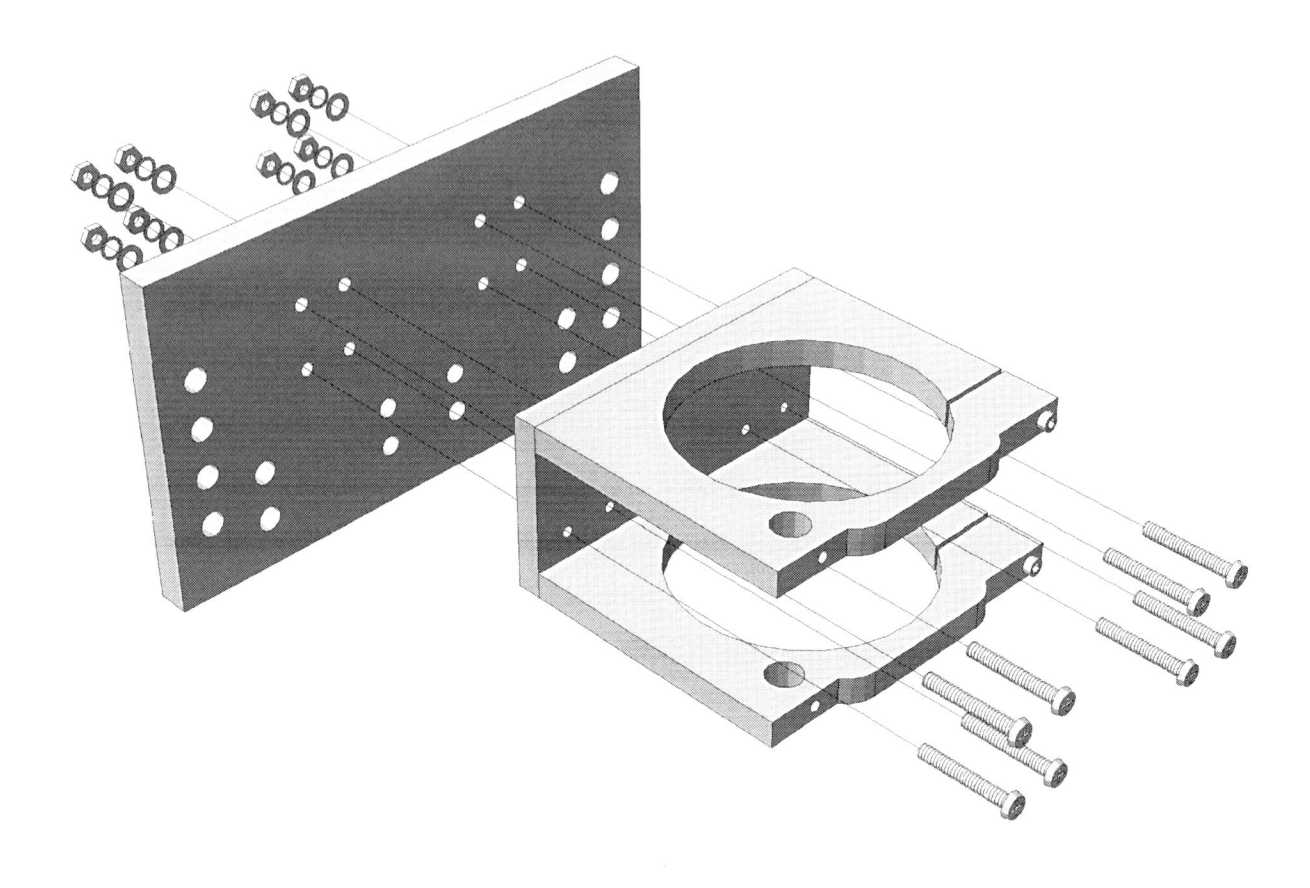

Figure 16.1

Step 2 - Install Router

Install the router into the K2CNC mount as shown in Figure 16.2. Tighten the two screws using the 3/16" Allen wrench. Rout the router power cable up and along the side of the Z-axis motor cable. Be sure to leave enough slack in the cable for the router to descend fully.

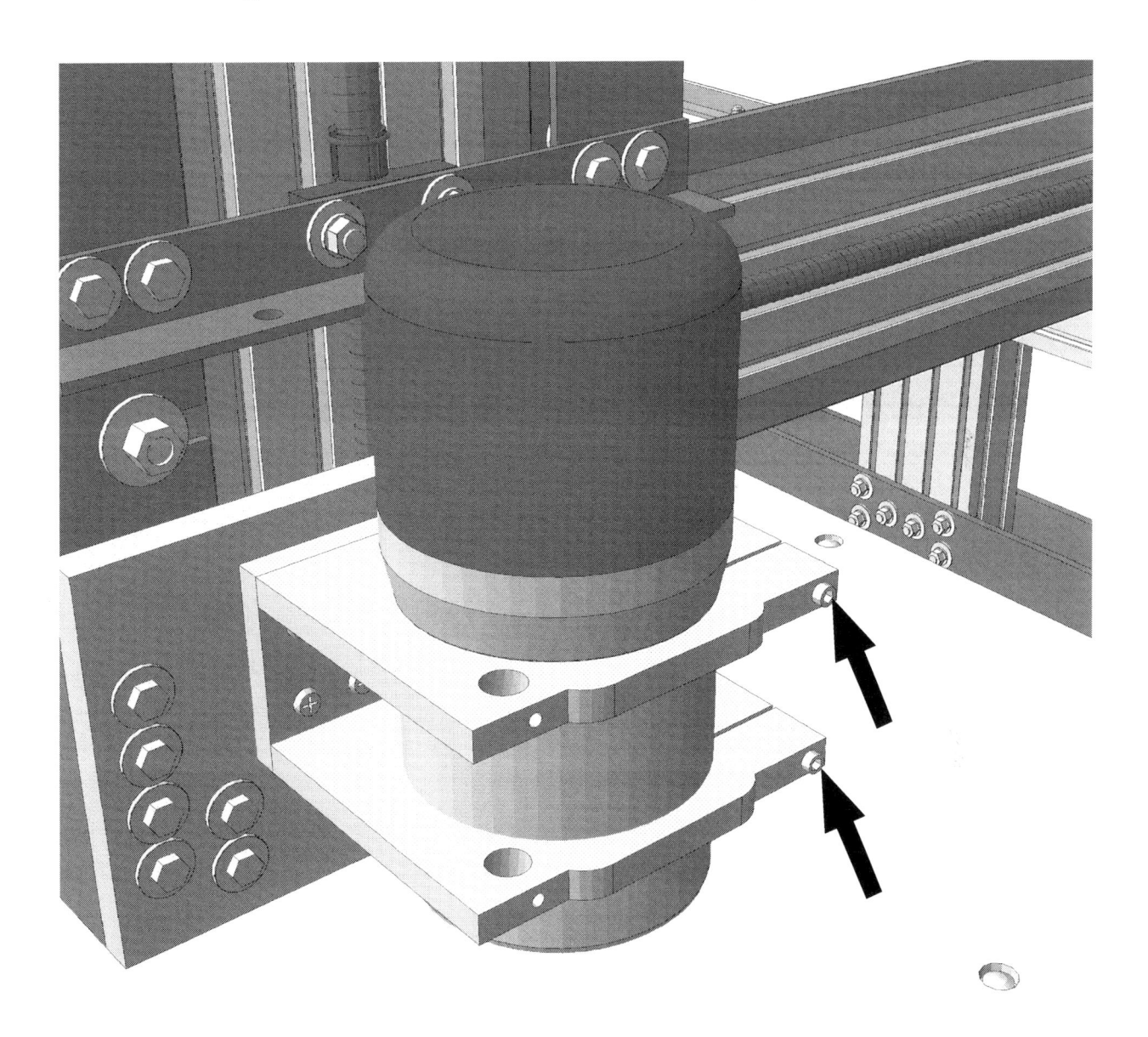

Figure 16.2

Adjustments

It is important that the router bit be perpendicular to the table. The eight mounting bolts on the router mount can allow you to slightly adjust the router tilt right and left. For larger adjustments, loosen the Z-plate.

Place a straight bit in the router and use a small square to test the router placement.

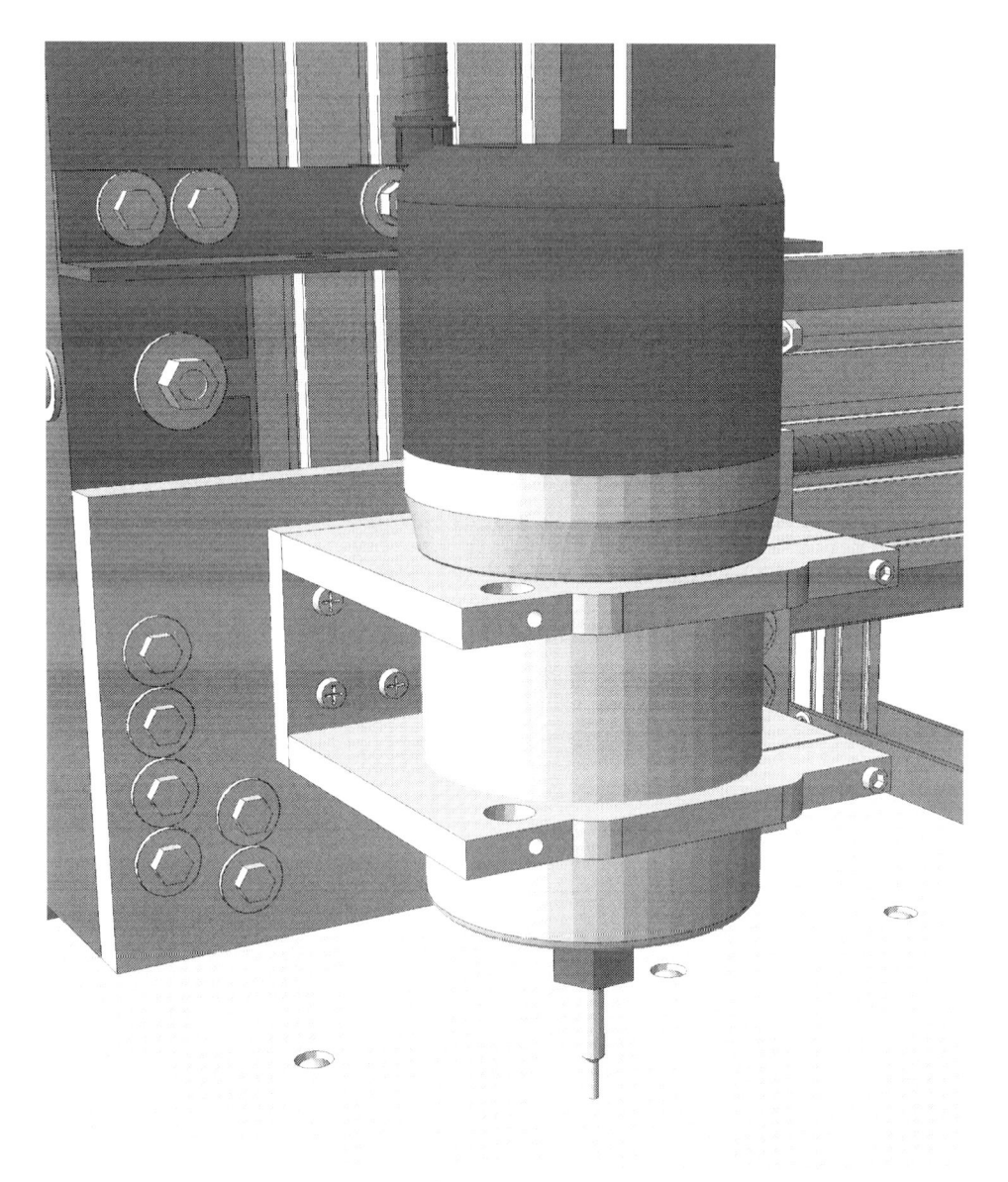

Figure 16.3

Chapter 17

Conclusion

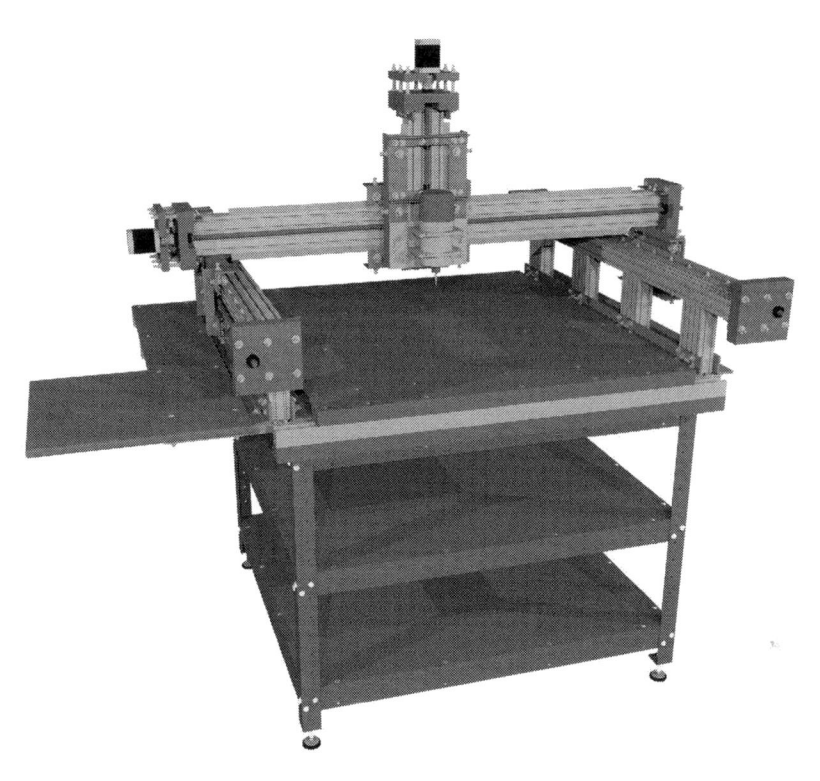

Congratulations! You have finished the basic constriction of the KRMx01. While it is fully operational at this point, there are a great many upgrades you can perform to make it even better.

Many of these upgrades can actually be built with your KRMx01 CNC. For example, the "Dragon Cable" is one of the first upgrades you should add to your CNC. Parts for this system are actually cut on your CNC, which gives you more practice making parts while also making your CNC more efficient.

In Book 2 of the KRMx01 series you will be presented with the Dragon Cable and other crucial upgrades, as well as instructions on how to operate the CNC.

KRMx01 Series

The KRMx01 series consists of the following three books:
- Building the KRMx01 CNC
- Upgrading and Operating the KRMx01 CNC
- More Upgrades for the KRMx01 CNC

For more information on the KRMx01 Series and other enhancements to your KRMx01 CNC, visit the Kronos Robotics web site at:

http://www.kronosrobotics.com/krmx01/dz19781_9386_87105/

In addition to the KRMx01 design, Kronos Robotics also has a KRMx02 design. You can find more information on the KRMx02 here:

http://www.kronosrobotics.com/krmx02/

Printed in Great Britain
by Amazon